Sport in Manchster

Manchester Region History Review

Volume 20
2009

ISSN 0952–4320

ISBN 978–1–85936–202–0

Typeset by Carnegie Book Production, Lancaster.
Printed and bound by Short Run Press, Exeter.

Contents

The editors would like to thank the Manchester European Research Institute for its support in the preparation of this volume.

Illustrations

We are grateful to the following for their help and permission in reproducing illustrations: Manchester Archives and Local Studies, Central Library, Manchester; National Football Museum, Preston; The Priory Collection; Manchester United Museum; Peter Holme. Every effort has been made to contact the copyright holders but if any have been inadvertently overlooked, the editors will be pleased to make the necessary arrangements at the first opportunity.

Notes for contributors

If you would like to contribute to this journal, please contact the editors before submitting copy. Authors should consult: http://www.mcrh.mmu.ac.uk/pubs/guidelines.doc. Conventional articles should not exceed 8,000 words including footnotes, although they can be much shorter. We encourage a variety of contributions and are willing to discuss ideas and draft articles at an early stage. Intending contributors to the Libraries, Museums and Societies sections should consult the editors in the first instance. Book reviews should be sent to the Book Reviews editor. All submitted work should be in Word format.

Advertisements

For details of advertising rates, please contact the editors.

Indexing

Articles appearing in this journal are abstracted and indexed in: HISTORICAL ABSTRACTS and AMERICA: HISTORY AND LIFE.

Contributors' Notes

Richard Cox was the founder of the British Society of Sports History in 1982 and has written and edited a large number of works on British sports history and bibliography including *Sport in Britain* (1991), *Encyclopedia of British sport* (2000) and the three-volume *British sport: a bibliography to 2000* (2003). He is currently a Visiting Fellow in the History of Science and Technology at the University of Manchester.

Hugh Hornby is a freelance writer and sports historian. His *Uppies and Downies: the extraordinary football games of Britain* was published by English Heritage in its 'Played in Britain' series in 2008. He is currently working on a second book for the series, *Bowled over: the bowling greens of Britain*. He is also an accomplished crown green bowler, having represented his county, North Lancs and Fylde, since 1995.

Mike Huggins is Professor of Cultural History at the University of Cumbria. He has written extensively about the place of sport and leisure in British society in the past two centuries. His most recent books include *Horseracing and British society 1919–1939* (2003), *Sport and the Victorians* (2004) and, with Jack Williams, *Sport and the English 1918–1939* (2006). In 2008, he edited a special edition of *Sport in History*, on sport and the British upper classes.

Alexander Jackson is an AHRC Collaborative Doctoral Award student working with the Institute of Northern Studies at Leeds Metropolitan University and the National Football Museum, Preston. He is researching football's consumer culture and the construction of fan identities from 1880 to 1960. He curated the 'Jumpers for Goalposts' exhibition at the National Football Museum in 2008.

Kevin Moore is Director of the National Football Museum, Preston. His personal research interests are in the field of football's heritage and material culture, and the representation of football in museums. His book *Museums and popular culture* was published in 1997 and he has written extensively on museum management and audience attraction.

Dave Russell is Professor of History and Northern Studies at the Institute of Northern Studies, Leeds Metropolitan University. He is the author of *Football and the English* (1997), was an editor of the *Encyclopedia* *of British football* (2002) and has published extensively on the history of English popular culture.

Steve Tate is a journalist who has worked on the provincial daily press in the North of England for thirty years. He received his PhD in History from the University of Central Lancashire in 2007, and his research interests include the history of sports journalism, Victorian newspapers and news-gathering, and the penny-a-liner.

Joyce Woolridge completed her PhD, '"From local hero to national star?" The changing cultural representation of the professional footballer in England, 1945–1985', at the University of Central Lancashire in 2007. A Mancunian football writer, she has published several academic articles on the cultural history of football.

Introduction

As a southerner, albeit one long domiciled in the north of England, I have perhaps been somewhat slow (possibly even unwilling) to appreciate the remarkable richness of the sporting culture of Manchester and its region; living in Yorkshire may have been a further barrier. I am, therefore, intensely grateful to the editorial board of the *Manchester Region History Review*, and especially Craig Horner and Melanie Tebbutt, not only for the unfailingly good-humoured and expert support that they have given to this particular edition of the journal, but for suggesting in the first place that sport would be a suitable topic for it and that I might serve as editor. It has been an enjoyable and educative experience.

Sports history has grown apace in Britain in the last twenty-five years as part of the wider explosion of interest in social and cultural history. Within both the academic and the wider communities, eyebrows are no longer raised (or, at least, not so high) when one admits to studying play for a living, while journalists are now more likely to ask for serious stories and opinions rather than ridicule 'bonkers boffins' for wasting time and effort on such a 'trivial' pursuit as that of sport. However, for all this catching up with the Americans and Australians who came far earlier to appreciate the centrality of sport to so many lives (especially, although not exclusively, male ones), much remains to be done. One of the most pressing tasks is to increase the provision of the detailed local and regional studies that will test out, refine and expand the many national studies of sport that now exist. That work has certainly been underway for a long time but great opportunities, both in regard to subject matter and sources, still remain. It is indeed interesting that this collection of studies is one of the very few dedicated specifically to sport within a specific geographical area. Its production, and certainly that of my own introductory essay to it, was made a great deal easier by the appearance in 2004 of Simon Inglis's *Played in Manchester*, the first in English Heritage's excellent 'Played in Britain' series. Ultimately concerned with the important task of recording and celebrating the city of Manchester's sporting architectural heritage, the book also contains much general information on local sport and is strongly recommended to any readers of this volume who have not previously encountered it.

The contributors to this volume have found a fascinating body of subject matter in their own right. Mike Huggins's study of local betting culture in the nineteenth century serves as an important reminder that, for all the moral virtue that might have been invested in sport, for many across all sections of society it could possess a decidedly financial and pleasure-orientated function. Steve Tate helps build on the 2006 edition of *Manchester Region History Review* that dealt with the literary culture of nineteenth-century Manchester by looking at the pre-1914 Hulton sports-press empire and demonstrating both the critical role of Manchester as a regional and national print media centre, and the remarkable scope and depth of the city's sporting press. In a study that in some ways forms a companion piece to Tate's article, Alexander Jackson looks at the work of sports cartoonists working within the region's Edwardian sporting and wider press, giving particular attention to the talented if extremely elusive figure of Amos Ramsbottom. Hugh Hornby, in his turn, provides an insight into the rarely considered world of professional crown green bowling through the eyes of one candid observer, the bowler Glen Howarth. The Munich air disaster of 1958 is so deeply etched into the national historical memory that it sadly needs little introduction. However, Joyce Woolridge makes us look anew by considering the ways in which the commemoration of the event, both immediately and much later, illuminates contemporary attitudes to grief and remembrance. In our Museums section, Kevin Moore, the Director of the National Football Museum at Preston, identifies some of the many opportunities and resources that can be utilized there; the fact that some of the cartoons discussed by Alexander Jackson come from the Museum is a practical demonstration of what awaits the keen researcher. Finally, Richard Cox offers a rich guide to the primary and secondary sources that are to be found across the region's libraries, museums, archives and record offices. An extended version of this will be posted on the *Review*'s website, a wonderful resource and, surely, a stimulus for researchers old and new alike.

While most of the above writers have experience of various sorts within the world of higher education, many of them have also worked, or still do, in non-academic environments. This is a crucial point. Academic sports historians have no monopoly over the field and it should be acknowledged that some of the most informative work on sport in Manchester has come from sporting enthusiasts or those seeking to honour a particular club or institution. Brian Hughes's many works on boxing, Bob Phillips's work on athletics and M. W. Peers's excellent history of Manchester Golf Club, are amongst the many examples of work of this type which has done so much to open up the subject. Hopefully others will be encouraged to find the innumerable gaps that remain to be filled. They will have an enjoyable as well as a worthwhile time.

Dave Russell
December 2008

Ruth Frow

We are saddened to report the death of Ruth Frow. Ruth, a member of our editorial board, had been the guiding light at the Working Class Movement Library and will be sorely missed. Her obituary appeared too late for publication and will appear in volume 21.

OBITUARIES
Douglas A. Farnie (1926–2008)

The death of Douglas Farnie in June 2008 marks the loss of one of economic history's most distinguished contributors. Most of those who either knew him or read his superbly researched and written work would recognize Douglas as the doyen of cotton-industry historians and an expert on the north-west business community, not to mention having an encyclopaedic knowledge of a wide range of subjects.

Born in 1926 into a Salford tailoring family, Douglas attended Salford Grammar School. Inevitably, his academic studies were interrupted by the Second World War, and in 1944 he joined the Intelligence Corps, with which he served in India and Egypt up to 1948. Having completed his military service, he immediately registered as an undergraduate at Manchester University, achieving a First in History, then an MA which examined the records of over 1,000 Lancashire cotton companies. Between 1953 and 1960, Douglas spent a highly productive period at the University of Natal in Durban. Apart from meeting his wife, Eve Eato, in South Africa, he also started work on the history of the Suez Canal, resulting in a definitive study *East and west of Suez: the Suez Canal in history, 1854 to 1956* (1969).

By 1960, he had returned to England, having been offered a lectureship in economic history at Manchester University, reviving his interest in the Lancashire cotton industry and prompting a series of publications, the most famous of which was the 1979 book *The English cotton industry and the world market, 1815 to 1896*. Given the international reputation Douglas achieved with this work, it is remarkable that although the University made him a reader in 1980, he was never accorded a professorial title. It was only after he retired in 1991 that Manchester Metropolitan University recognized his achievements by making him a Visiting Professor, once he had joined that institution's dynamic Centre for Business History to work with David Jeremy and Geoff Tweedale. Retirement from the full-time post in 1991, of course, was merely regarded by Douglas as an opportunity to focus his considerable energies and abilities on further research and writing, resulting in major contributions to economic history that will stand the test of time. Sadly, Douglas's wife also died in 1991. Among his most distinguished work at that time was *Region and strategy in Britain and Japan: business in Lancashire and Kansai, 1890–1990* (2000), representing nine years of collaborative work with a team of Japanese and British scholars which he ably led to publication. Even in the last years, when he was seriously debilitated by heart disease, he was working with Geoff Tweedale on the comprehensive *A bio-bibliography of economic and social history*, a book to be published in 2009.

Douglas Farnie was truly an international scholar. His contributions to economic history will be memorialized in a forthcoming collection of essays by his admirers, *King Cotton: a tribute to Douglas A. Farnie* (Carnegie Publishing; edited by John F. Wilson). To focus merely on his academic achievements, however, is only to capture a small fraction of Douglas's character, because those who were lucky to come into contact with this generous, self-effacing and committed gentleman will know full well the benefits of this relationship. How many scholars will have received a hand-written file card containing the exact answer to any query they might have run past him? How many people were entertained by spending an hour or so in his company, perhaps at one of the many conferences he attended? Who else was mesmerized by the depth of his knowledge of Hollywood in the 1930s and 1940s? One should also stress that Douglas was a religious person, regularly attending church, even when on trips abroad. He was equally committed to the many societies, national and regional, of which he was a member.

Douglas will be badly missed by both those who had the pleasure of working with him and anybody who either read his exemplary scholarship or listened to one of his thoroughly engrossing lectures.

John F. Wilson
University of Liverpool

John Marshall (1919–2008) and the history of the Manchester region

John Marshall, who died in Grange-over-Sands in the spring of 2008 at the age of 89, was an innovative, combative and creative presence for over half a century. He was a prolific author of articles that advocated a creative and questioning approach to local and regional history, and above all he was a pioneer in Britain of the study of the history of regions as complex entities located firmly within wider historical and geographical contexts. Most of his published research dealt with the Lake District, Furness and industrial west Cumbria (as it became in 1974), from Barrow-in-Furness (the geographical core of his doctoral thesis, *Furness and the industrial revolution*, which was published by Barrow Corporation in 1958 and reprinted by Michael Moon of Beckermet in 1981) to Cleator Moor; and he was a pioneer of the serious study of industrial archaeology. But he also has considerable relevance to the roots and history of this journal.

Perhaps the most important of John Marshall's books was *The tyranny of the discrete* (Scolar Press, 1997), which was effectively a manifesto for an enhanced and outward-looking model of local and regional history, and deserves to be more widely known. It was the core text of his sustained campaign to liberate local history from the particular and the antiquarian, and to promote a new kind of articulated and critically informed regional history which connected with big debates on national and international stages. He was an important figure in the Conference of Regional and Local Historians (CORAL), and helped to create the climate in which a journal like the *Manchester Region History Review* could be created and sustained. He worked in Lancashire for a couple of decades, first in Bolton, then as Reader in the regional history of north-west England at Lancaster University, where he made a vital contribution to the highly influential MA in Modern Social History. His publications included a brief survey of the history of Lancashire, which appeared in 1974, and an excellent edited history of Lancashire County Council, which appeared three years later. He was also a prolific supervisor of theses and promoter of publications. His sole substantial contribution to this journal was a characteristically combative piece on 'The *Manchester Region History Review*: the shape of the next decade' (10, 1996, pp. 70–6). This was one of his last published works, and featured strong advocacy of the promotion of recent history, challenging history as leisure learning, the development of family history as a serious and potentially valuable branch of the discipline, the importance of 'community' history and the nature of history teaching in schools, and the danger of devaluing local historical studies through an over-enthusiastic embrace of 'heritage', putting a good story before the painstaking pursuit of grounded understanding through sustained research. This was a characteristically broad, indeed ecumenical, scholarly and prescient agenda, and it should remind us of the debt that regional history owes to this persevering pioneer.

John K. Walton

Institute of Northern Studies, Leeds Metropolitan University

ARTICLES
Sporting Manchester, from *c*1800 to the present: an introduction

Dave Russell

While advocates for London, Birmingham and Liverpool might disagree, Manchester and its hinterland can lay convincing claim to the richest sporting history of any English city-region.[1] In any such argument, at least Manchester would surely not resort to expropriating a rival's territory in the fashion of the Liverpool newspaper which, in its 1966 World Cup coverage, mischievously listed Old Trafford as a 'Merseyside' location.[2] The topic is vast and this essay simply offers a general overview providing context for the more detailed studies that follow and (hopefully) the encouragement of future work on a subject hitherto scantly studied.

The context for Manchester sport

While the region's sporting history closely resembles that of other major British urban centres, it has undoubtedly been influenced by local circumstance. As well as possessing a population large enough to sustain both a market for sport and a substantial body of participants, it contains an unusually rich mixture of settlement types ranging from Manchester itself to significantly sized towns such as Bolton, Oldham and Stockport and on to smaller towns and villages. This distinct urban network, knitted together by a highly developed transport system, and characterized by the many rivalries between well-matched communities within it, has been ideal for the generation of vibrant sporting activity. In the late-Victorian and Edwardian period so crucial to the emergence of 'modern' sporting culture, this was also a population benefiting from increases in both clearly defined periods of leisure time and disposable income. The emerging Saturday half-holiday and the rise in real wages in the second half of the nineteenth century, especially the 1890s, are staples of any account of the growth of working-class leisure, but these factors had particular significance in industrial, and especially, *textile* Lancashire. Here, the early arrival of Saturday half-holidays from 1850 to 1875 and the favourable impact of relatively high female employment upon family incomes were critical to the county's leadership within the national commercial leisure economy. These benefits were not spread evenly, with inequalities stemming from occupation, age, health and family size impacting significantly upon individual leisure experiences. Nevertheless, the richness of local sporting life undoubtedly owed much to the sheer number of people within the vicinity blessed with sufficient disposable money and spare time.[3]

This favourable context has nurtured a plethora of major sporting institutions and facilities. In association football alone, six of the forty clubs comprising the English Football League in 1914 (Bolton Wanderers, Bury, Glossop North End, Manchester City, Manchester United and Oldham Athletic) were located within twelve miles of Manchester city centre. The region has long been home to a number of major sports stadiums and thus the location for prestigious national and international events. Manchester Athletic Club's Fallowfield Stadium, although inadequate for the purpose, was the venue for the 1893 FA Cup Final, the first provincial stadium thus chosen; it was also to host the Amateur Athletics Association championships in 1897 and 1907 and the British Empire Games cycling events in 1934.[4] Lancashire County Cricket Club's headquarters at Old Trafford has hosted test cricket since 1884, while, more recently, Manchester United's Old Trafford was used during both the 1966 World Cup and the 1996 European Championships and as the location for the 2003 UEFA Champions League Final. Perhaps most strikingly, Manchester City Council's succession of Olympic and other bids from the 1980s has brought a wealth of new sporting infrastructure, as will be discussed below.

As a true regional capital, Manchester has also been a natural location for key meetings – the Royal Hotel held the founding conference of the Football League in April 1888 – and as the headquarters for a variety of bodies. In the early twentieth-first century it houses the national associations for cycling, lacrosse, squash and wrestling, and the offices of the Professional Footballers' Association.[5] As the articles by Mike Huggins on betting, and Steve Tate on the sporting press, demonstrate, it has also generated a flourishing sports service industry, as indeed have a number of the region's larger towns. In 1912, there were twenty sports outfitters and equipment dealers in Manchester, with the Dale Street firm of E. R. Buck proudly terming itself the 'largest athletic clothing company in the world'.[6] A number of manufacturing companies have developed highly specialized lines, often linked to the specific structures of local sport. The still extant Eccles-based firm of T. S. Hattersley and Son, originally cricket bat and racket manufacturers, turned to the making of lacrosse sticks in the 1900s in order to meet the demand for a game which had a particular following in the North West.

What of the specific chronology of sporting development? Its history in the 'pre-industrial' period has been little studied and, unfortunately, this volume does little more than plead for future rectification. There are many avenues to pursue. Hunting dates back to the fourteenth century; street football was played frequently enough to be banned by Manchester's Court Leet in 1608, 1656 and 1657; race meetings began on Kersal Moor in 1681; later eighteenth-century Manchester was a major centre of competitive archery and a variety of animal baiting sports were a long-established feature of local life.[7] This account, however, begins in the nineteenth century when the majority of the population increasingly came to see 'sport' as an integral, almost daily part of industrial and urban life, rather than something episodic and rooted in the calendar of fairs, feasts and rituals; when team games became more significant than blood or field sports and when new forms of organization and bureaucracy became the order of the day.

Between 1801 and 1851, Manchester's population rose from 75,000 to 303,000 and the surrounding towns also experienced often dramatic growth under the impact of commercial and industrial change. In the light of these developments and the intellectual, political, and moral transformations engendered, it is hardly surprising that existing patterns of popular sport and leisure might be disrupted. But how extensive was that disruption? Until relatively recently, Robert Malcolmson's argument that, especially in the period between 1825 and 1850, the impact of 'the rise of a market economy, and the accompanying development of new normative standards and material conditions for the conduct of social relations' led to a 'vacuum' in the recreational life of the lower orders, was widely accepted.[8] However, detailed empirical research has increasingly challenged this position, with Neil Tranter arguing, for example, that 'the weight of such evidence we have suggests growth, or, at the worst, stability rather than persistent, pronounced decline'.[9]

Our admittedly limited knowledge of the local setting would tend to support Tranter's position. The traditional sporting landscape was certainly altered significantly. Bricks and mortar claimed many recreational spaces while new industrial work disciplines, fused with Protestant religious fervour (and, sometimes, political radicalism), challenged important aspects of popular leisure. National legislation in 1835 and 1849, for example, outlawed bull-baiting and cock-fighting respectively, both deemed morally unacceptable diversions. It was not only the poor who felt the impact of such changes; the Earl of Derby had regularly stayed at the Albion Hotel in Salford during Whit week, travelling daily to the cockpit near Greengate by carriage and four.[10]

A number of the smaller wakes and feasts which were the focus for sporting events also fell victim, with Horwich Races, Cross Keys Fair and Tonge Fair all disappearing in the 1840s at the 'promptings of "moralists" and "influential gentlemen"'.[11]

However, evidence of resilience and resistance to change is plentiful. While legislation might bite in large urban centres, it was not always enforceable elsewhere and 'in the mining areas round Manchester and in more rural areas [bloodsports] outlived their legal prohibition by many years'.[12] Even more important, the period saw substantial growth of both new commercial and voluntary activity. Publicans were arguably the key figures in the former category. They were certainly central to the development of athletic track events or 'pedestrianism' in mid century, building on the pre-existing popularity of road racing by opening cinder tracks adjacent to their premises. The Snipe Inn track at Audenshaw, opened by landlady Betty Berry about 1840, was probably the first but others soon followed in pubs or pleasure gardens, including those at Vauxhall Gardens in Collyhurst, Salford's Borough Gardens, the Copenhagen Grounds at the Shears Inn, Newton Heath, the Wellington Grounds at Bury, and the Ash Inn at Heaton Norris near Stockport.[13] With their regular meetings and organized championships, these venues attracted competitors of the highest calibre; at various times between 1840 and 1870 what were claimed as the world's fastest times at 220, 440 and 880 yards and at one and two miles were all recorded on Manchester and district tracks.[14] Berry's Snipe Inn was also home to a bowling green and gymnasium and held wrestling and shooting tournaments, while the Ash Inn was a centre for rabbit coursing.[15] Similarly, recent research has shown that football was encouraged by publicans who acted as both organizers and as stakeholders for the numerous bets placed.[16]

There is plentiful evidence of the growth of voluntary sports clubs. Manchester Cricket Club, founded as Aurora C.C. between 1818 and 1823, was the city's first formally constituted cricketing body. Although cricket grew at a slower rate in Lancashire than in southern England, clubs also emerged at Broughton, Denton and Rochdale between 1823 and 1824.[17] After enjoying several different locations, the Manchester club eventually moved to the current Old Trafford ground in 1857. Until at least the 1850s and probably beyond, formal sports clubs were essentially middle and upper-middle class in social composition. Manchester Golf Club, for example, only the second such organization in the country, was formed between 1814 and 1818. Originally located on a five-hole course on Kersal Moor, it was founded by a Scottish merchant William Mitchell and long maintained both a decidedly Scottish flavour and a deliberately narrow social base. As late as 1870, it had, of choice, only twelve members who met not only to play golf but to dine. (In 1858, a member who found himself the sole participant at a club dinner not only continued with the event but proposed and seconded several toasts and resolutions.)[18] Nevertheless, while most clubs retained a fairly superior social tone until the late nineteenth century, they at least provided a model for later imitation by working-class participants and were themselves sometimes able to take on a more democratic flavour.

1870–1914

It was the late nineteenth and early twentieth centuries that witnessed the full emergence of the modern sporting culture that, for all recent changes, is still recognizable today. By 1914, the Manchester region had a range of major sporting venues which would have been inconceivable to even the most astute mid-Victorian leisure entrepreneur. Manchester and Salford could lay claim to Manchester United's Old Trafford (1910) and Manchester City's Hyde Road (1887) (although the latter, despite much redevelopment in the Edwardian period, was described by one visitor as 'a small, cramped, clammy affair'), the Old Trafford cricket ground, Broughton Rangers' rugby stadium at Wheater's Field (1892), athletics and/or cycling tracks at Belle Vue (1887), Fallowfield (1892) and White City (1907), and the Manchester racecourse at Castle Irwell (1902). Municipal swimming bath provision began in the 1880s with the New Islington Baths in Ancoats and five major baths were built in Manchester between 1906 and 1913.[19] Sporting infrastructure in the wider region was not generally on such a scale but its association football and northern union sides occupied relatively well developed grounds. Bolton Wanderers' Burnden Park (1895) was initially a multi-purpose venue, housing a cycling track for its first ten years, while Oldham Athletic's Boundary Park (1896) featured a stand with a flat roof along which one of the club's managers reputedly ran in order to follow play.[20] Crucially, within these grounds the habit of regular large-scale spectatorship was born. Manchester City and Manchester United saw their average gates rise from 3,000 and 7,000 in 1892–3 (the season of their entry into the Football League as Ardwick and Newton Heath) to 27,000 and 25,500 respectively in 1913–14.

While popular demand for sport was largely fuelled by the changes in lifestyles noted earlier, on the supply side lay the codification and bureaucratization that was such a feature of the second half of the nineteenth century, effectively bringing a whole range of new or vastly altered sports into being. These twin processes stemmed largely from the desire of public and grammar schoolboys exposed to the emergent 'cult of games' to find ways of continuing with sport on entering into

A high-diving
competition
at White
City in 1910
(Manchester
Archives and
Local Studies,
Central Library,
M09144)

adult life, and anxious to find common rules and common organization through which it could be pursued. The Football Association
in 1863 and the Rugby Football Union in 1871 are the best known of
the new governing bodies but others proliferated at national, regional
and local level. Although many within the middle and upper classes
had always accepted that certain categories of professional sportsmen
were a necessity – jockeys to ride, boxers to fight, cricketers to do the
'ungentlemanly' tasks of fielding and bowling – the world envisaged
by the founding fathers of codified sport was undoubtedly an amateur
one. At least in theory, the game was to be played for its own sake and
not to satisfy local partisanship or to enrich participants or organizers.

Some, too, like the founders of Christ Church F.C., Bolton or St Marks Parish Church F.C., Gorton, believed sport to be an ideal vehicle for the civilization and Christianization of young men, an engrossing and rational pastime but no more.

The cultural clash that ensued in the 1880s and 1890s when the proponents of amateurism met a working class (in alliance with a significant section of the industrial and commercial *middle* class) perfectly happy to pay to watch professionals uphold local and regional honour, was inevitable, intense, and often inimical to the amateur cause. Christ Church F.C., for example, eventually became Bolton Wanderers, and St Marks, Manchester City. While a breakaway from the ruling Football Association by proto-professional clubs, including several in the Manchester area, was averted by the introduction of a policed professionalism in July 1885, within the Rugby Football Union a compromise over the issue of 'broken-time' payments to players missing work due to playing engagements could not be reached. Consequently, on 29 August 1895, representatives of twenty-one clubs (soon to be twenty-two) broke away to form the Northern Rugby Football Union (it took the name Rugby League in 1922). When its season began weeks later, the competition included six clubs (Broughton Rangers, Leigh, Oldham, Rochdale Hornets, Stockport and Tyldesley) from the Manchester region.[21]

Yet, while it is this new professional (and semi-professional) sporting culture that tends to capture our attention, it must not be forgotten that underlying and feeding it was an extraordinarily rich voluntary tradition. For all the attention that professionals receive, the 'typical' sportsman – and sportswomen almost exclusively – has always been an amateur. Some may have been adroit at bending or avoiding rules governing payment and prizes and those policing the regulations were endlessly searching for miscreants, 'those gentry with strong muscles and close-cropped hair' as they were described by a member of the fiercely amateur Manchester Athletic Club.[22] However, the vast majority of those who played or ran or cycled did so for love rather than money and most worked within often rigid regulations with, if not always good grace, then a dogged acceptance. By 1900, the region was criss-crossed by leagues and networks that pulled thousands of individuals into this sporting sphere. By 1910, there were at least seventy-three golf clubs, then still socially exclusive institutions, within twenty miles of Manchester, catering for perhaps 20,000 golfers. In the spring of 1906, the *Manchester Evening News* carried details of local teams playing in six football and seven cricket leagues. The area became (and remains) a major centre of lacrosse, for reasons which are not fully apparent, and of water polo, with clubs from the Manchester League dominating English competition from the 1890s until the 1920s; Hyde Seal S.C. won nine national titles between 1903 and 1924.[23] Individuals of every level of ability and aspiration were involved, from incompetent tennis players to multiple Olympic Gold Medal winners such as Bolton collier and cyclist Ben Jones.[24] All had their place in this vibrant new sporting world.

1919–1939

With sport in much reduced supply between 1914 and 1918, the immediate post-war years witnessed a boom in attendance and interest that set the tone for another important period of growth and consolidation. The negative impact of unemployment and short-time working in the inter-war period must certainly not be underestimated.

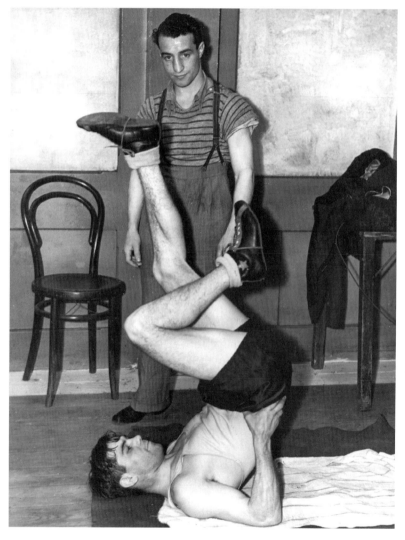

Johnny King, both British and Empire Bantamweight title-holder in the early 1930s (Manchester Archives and Local Studies, Central Library, M06804)

Although the correlation between unemployment rates and levels of attendance at, and participation in, sporting events was never a neat one, the place for sport was often much reduced. Andrew Davies has commented that, in the 1930s, unemployment could undermine even deep-rooted activities, noting 'a serious decline in sports such as pigeon fancying, which required a consistent commitment of resources' in both Bolton and Salford.[25] Nevertheless, it is undeniable that further increases in real wages, especially from the early 1930s, and reductions in working hours continued to expand the scale of the sporting world. As Steve Jones noted in a pioneering study, spending power in the Manchester area in the 1930s came 'only just behind London and [was] far in excess of the depressed areas in south Wales, the north east and Scotland', and sport was an undoubted beneficiary.[26]

Many existing sports experienced rising patronage, not least the professional boxing that had begun to emerge in the Edwardian period. About 200 paid fighters were based in Manchester and Salford in the 1930s, with three, flyweight Jackie Brown, bantamweight Johnny King and middle- and light-heavyweight, Jock McAvoy, gaining the highest national and international recognition and honours.[27] The region was rich in boxing venues, with Manchester promoter Harry Furness utilizing some thirty separate locations within fifteen miles of Manchester in the early 1940s. The Free Trade Hall and Belle Vue's King's Hall were the city's major sites, with the latter, used for the sport from 1929, regarded by some as Europe's leading boxing location. At the other extreme lay a network of small halls including the often unlicensed 'blood tubs' and the fairground booths where all-comers attempted to earn perhaps ten shillings by surviving three rounds with a professional.[28]

Maybe the most striking feature within the professional sporting environment, however, was the emergence of new forms of spectator sport, most notably greyhound racing and speedway, consciously modern and attempting to attract new sporting audiences through an emphasis on improved facilities, excitement and spectacle. Although as Mike Huggins points out elsewhere in the journal, greyhound racing had roots in local betting culture – hare and rabbit coursing, from which greyhound racing ultimately derived, was an extremely popular activity, as was whippet racing, or 'flapping' – in its modern form it was, like speedway, a foreign import.[29] The racing of dogs around a circular track in pursuit of an electric hare had begun in the US in 1912, gaining huge popularity once betting became commonplace in the 1920s. Belle Vue was the site of Britain's first-ever American-style track and while only 1,700 people turned up for the opening meeting on 24 July 1926, attendances reached 25,000 by spring 1927. Tracks were opened in 1928 at the Albion Ground, Salford, and at the newly revamped White City, and others were established throughout the region including those at Bolton, Rochdale, and Stockport. By 1931, annual attendances at the three Manchester and Salford venues reached 1.7 million.[30]

Speedway derived from the grass and dirt-track racing developed in the US and Australia.[31] A dirt track event at the Moorside Trotting Stadium, Droylsden, in June 1927 is regarded by some as Manchester's first exposure to the sport, but, as in the rest of the country, it emerged properly in 1928, with tracks established at Belle Vue (Kirkmanshulme Lane), Salford Albion Greyhound Stadium, Audenshaw Racecourse (actually a trotting track) and White City. All were extremely short-lived and the only track to survive the inter-war period was that at Belle Vue Pleasure Gardens, opened in March 1929 after the failure of the Kirkmanshulme Lane venture. With a capacity of 34,000, it was home to the Belle Vue Aces, Britain's most successful speedway team of the inter-war period. Some of the smaller tracks were poorly run, with the governing body refusing to sanction meetings at Audenshaw due to unsuitable track conditions. Nevertheless, many riders, working under pseudonyms, were prepared to appear there, with fatal consequences for at least one. In August 1931 'Jack Smith' (actually Salford-born James Kenny) was badly injured in a crash partly resulting from poor track maintenance. The promoter, James Wolfenden, then dropped the injured rider on a solid floor while carrying him to the medical room and neglected to call an ambulance. Even Wolfenden, severely criticized at Smith/Kenny's inquest, the outcome of which he had attempted to pervert, felt the need to abandon meetings a few weeks later.[32]

While professional sport captured most of the headlines, once again it must not be allowed to disguise the growth of less dramatic but still highly important sporting activity. Municipal sporting provision increased – Manchester gained seven new swimming baths between 1920 and 1939 – although exact levels of provision varied from town to town and according to the economic and political climate.[33] Similarly, an increasing number of large employers followed contemporary trends within industrial welfare policy by providing extensive sporting facilities. One of the most impressive was the Co-operative Wholesale Society's sports ground at Victoria Avenue, Moston, opened in 1928 and only sold by the CWS in 1998.[34] Perhaps the most notable feature, however, was the sheer scale of amateur participatory sport. One of the most significant features was the huge expansion of interest in rambling. The 1932 Kinder Trespass in which some 4,000 ramblers, many from Manchester, tried to gain access to private land in the Derbyshire Peak District, is perhaps the single event most closely associated with the outdoor movement at this time. However, while

this initiative, led by communists and others on the left, points up an important political strand within rambling culture, it was not typical of most of the rambling activity that took place or necessarily, some have argued, particularly significant in the process that led to subsequent 'freedom to roam' legislation.[35]

1945–1985

With a few minor exceptions, the inter-war period saw the completion of Manchester's sporting provision, at least in terms of the establishment of new sporting activities. The immediate post-war period saw professional sport in the city, as in the rest of the nation, reach its zenith in terms of popularity with a public too long starved of regular, high-level public entertainment between 1939 and 1945. Given the poor maintenance of so many grounds over the war years, and an often cavalier attitude to fan safety, it was luck rather than judgement that meant that the Burnden Park disaster of 1946 in which thirty-three people died and over 400 were injured when crush barriers collapsed during an FA Cup tie between Bolton and Stoke, was the region's (and nation's) only major sporting disaster.

From the early 1950s, attendances at all forms of live sport began to fall as the post-war novelty abated and increased levels of personal spending power made other forms of leisure expenditure more easily available. Rising real wages, traditionally a key engine of sporting growth, now rendered many forms of sporting activity an 'inferior good' as television, the motor car, foreign holidays and a variety of other activities emerged into the new leisure ecology. With football again the exemplar here, most clubs in the region saw crowds fall over the period from about 1950 and with ever greater pace from the 1970s. Only Manchester United, a regional club with a national fan base from the 1960s, maintained its support, suffering just a one per cent attendance loss between 1964 and 1986 and standing as the country's best-supported club for nineteen out of these twenty-two seasons. By the 1970s and 1980s, declining revenues and the concomitant lack of reinvestment in infrastructure led to a spiral of decline in which often poorly attended stadiums fell into ever greater disrepair. New safety regulations following the Bradford City football ground fire in 1985 added a new dimension by effectively outlawing the wooden grandstands so common in many longer-established venues. As a result of these various factors, the late twentieth century saw the disappearance of many local historic sporting sites. Although it was not finally closed until 1994, Fallowfield Stadium was effectively finished as a senior venue from 1976. White City closed in 1981, Belle Vue's King's Hall in 1982 and its speedway stadium, a victim of the new safety regulations, followed suit five years later. The same regulations claimed Rochdale Hornets RLFC's Athletic Grounds stadium in 1989 (as well as individual stands at a number of grounds) and played a major part in the closure of Swinton RLFC's Station Road in 1992. This list is by no means exhaustive. Many municipal facilities, now often viewed as burdens on the rates rather than sources of civic amenity and pride, declined, were closed or demolished. Swimming baths were particular victims.[36]

Sport since 1985

Manchester's recent sporting environment has undoubtedly carried strong continuities from previous periods. Although the hard-worked secretaries of numerous local and regional voluntary bodies must now be computer-literate, expert at bidding for new funding opportunities and alert to new 'partnerships', in most fundamental senses the way in which they and their organizations operate would be broadly recognizable to their late-Victorian counterparts. Again, sport still carries much of the same significance and many of the same cultural and social meanings that it has always generated and often takes place in arenas not dissimilar from those that might be found earlier in the twentieth century; not all professional sports grounds are models of modern engineering ingenuity, amenity and comfort. Nevertheless, it is undeniable that a new set of influences has come to shape the sporting landscape, almost all to some degree the product of, or a response to, the forces of globalization that have both disrupted older patterns of economic and social life and shaped new ones.

Since the early 1990s the role of sport, especially professional sport, within contemporary British public life has taken on a far greater significance for a far wider body of people than has ever before been the case; its hugely increased place within both the printed and electronic media is more than adequate testimony to this.[37] Partly reflecting, partly driving, this process of 'sportification' has been a complex array of overlapping commercial interests embracing the media, sports goods manufacturers, publishers and a raft of international and national business interests. What is particularly striking at elite professional level is that the ensuing flows of capital, goods and labour are truly global. While there had always been a global dimension to professional sport – the Manchester Rapids ice hockey team of the late 1930s was comprised entirely of French Canadians, and American and Australian riders featured in local speedway – the scale is now of a totally different magnitude.[38] Thus on 19 August 2007, when Manchester City, a club then owned by an ex-prime minister of Thailand and managed by a Swede, played Manchester United, a club owned by an American businessman, only fourteen of the thirty-two players on the pitch or substitute benches were British or Irish.[39]

Manchester and its immediate environs also demonstrate another feature of the modern sporting environment to an unusually well-developed degree. While new or radically modernized sporting venues exist throughout the country, the strength of Manchester's embrace of sport as a major element within the process of economic regeneration in the 1980s has led to the city enjoying an unusually rich crop of new facilities. Although bids in 1985 and 1989 to host future Olympic Games were unsuccessful, in 1995 the city was finally successful in attracting the 2002 Commonwealth Games. Undoubtedly the most dramatic product of this process was the building of the 146-hectare Sportcity, a complex of six sports arenas and facilities combined with commercial outlets and housing on an industrial wasteland in the east Manchester district of Bradford.[40] The key issue at the so-called 'Eastlands' site was to ensure that the City of Manchester Stadium, build as the athletic stadium for the Commonwealth Games, became a viable feature of the region's long-term sporting infrastructure and not an expensive monument to a specific event in civic history. The pivotal moment was Manchester City Football Club's agreement in 1999 to leave its Maine Road ground and move into the Stadium in August 2003 as the Council's tenants on a 250-year lease, a municipal-club partnership highly unusual within the context of British football.

The Nynex (now the *Manchester Evening News*) Arena – opened in 1995 and briefly home to the short-lived Manchester Storm ice hockey and Manchester Giants basketball teams in the 1990s – and the Manchester Aquatics Centre (2000) are further products of the 'Games effect'.[41] Outside of the city, Bolton Wanderers' Reebok Stadium, opened in 1997, originated in plans for an Olympic hockey stadium into which the club would eventually move. After the failure of the bid, the local council and the club pursued the decision to leave Burnden Park.[42] Effectively a 'tradium', the Reebok sits at the centre of a large retail park with much of the ground doubling as a hotel and conference centre, highly visible evidence of both sport's new role within the urban economy and the new economy of sport.

Sport and society

As has long been recognized, sport is invariably heavily charged with social and cultural meaning. While not down-playing the many intrinsic pleasures that it engenders, sport inevitably makes manifest the social and cultural practices of the society that created it while also possessing the power to shape that society in its turn. This final section explores some of the ways in which personal and social identities have been both articulated and inscribed by the region's sporting world. Once again, while Manchester's contribution to these processes often mirrors those evident in other British settings, local peculiarity and nuance can have a distinctive impact.

Perhaps the clearest feature is that sport has ultimately been essentially a male preserve; playing, watching and talking about sport have long been crucial to the 'making' of men, with the exclusion of women (consciously or unconsciously) an integral part of that process.[43] Women have certainly played a role, often quite a significant one, in sporting life. Betty Berry of the Snipe Inn found twentieth-century equivalents in Belle Vue wrestling promoters Kathleen Look and Jessie Rodgers (along with husband Dick) in the 1930s and 1940s respectively.[44] In terms of participation, the middle classes were the main beneficiaries from a growth in organized women's sport from the middle of the nineteenth century, with a number of activities including croquet, archery – women outnumbered men in some tournaments – tennis, and golf attracting increasing numbers of adherents; the inaugural Manchester Golf Club Ladies Challenge Competition in 1902 saw seventy-four entries from seventeen separate clubs.[45] Working-class girls gained greater access in the inter-war period through such organizations as the Lancashire Women's Cricket Federation, the four rounders leagues that existed in Bolton by 1930, and the Manchester Sunday School Union's women's hockey league, which had over sixty clubs in the late 1930s.[46] A handful of local women, including Fay Taylour and Babs Nield, daughter of a Broughton coal-merchant, even rode professionally in speedway before a ban on women competitors in 1930 (following a case when an injured woman rider had to be publicly undressed by medical attendants) ended such involvement.[47] Since the 1950s the region has produced a number of highly successful sportswomen from a number of different social and sporting backgrounds including high jumper and Salford Harrier Dorothy Shirley, an Olympic silver medallist in 1960, and Stretford Athletic Club's Shirley Strong, who won similar honours in the 1982 100-metres hurdles.[48]

Women have also always enjoyed some presence at most sporting events as spectators and have at times been positively encouraged to attend by promoters and entrepreneurs anxious to gain the cachet of respectability often associated with female attendance. Edwardian boxing promoter Harry Schofield was certainly aware of this particular stratagem, advertising a show at the Free Trade Hall under the heading 'Ladies Specially Invited', while speedway and greyhound tracks made serious attempts to attract women (and family groups) as part of their bids for acceptability; the Salford Albion greyhound track offered women both reduced entry prices and a pram park.[49] Indeed, attempts by contemporary professional football clubs to create an environment less threatening to women can be seen as part continuation, part variant, of this age-old approach.

For all the importance of this still somewhat hidden history of women's sporting involvement and the fact that women's role within sporting culture is undoubtedly increasing in the twenty-first century, women have generally held only a decidedly marginal place within the male republic that is sport. Male spectating and participation rates have always comfortably outweighed women's and their performances taken more seriously both within the sporting world and the media. Moreover, women have often been second-class sporting citizens, allowed membership to institutions at reduced rates but without voting rights and with restricted rights of access. Women, for example, were only granted full membership at Lancashire County Cricket

Club from 1989. This secondary place could result from a simple lack of interest in sport (shared, admittedly, by many men) or a conscious desire to find clear leisure space; male absence at a sporting event created a welcome opportunity for other social activity. However, it is undeniable that the whole range of social, cultural and economic conventions that more generally restricted women's access to public life long affected the nature of women's sporting experience.[50]

If the significance of gender is soon apparent, so, too, is that of class. Historians have long debated sport through the lens of class, analysing the social structure of particular sports and then attempting to discern whether they reflect, reinforce or structure patterns of class allegiance and subsequent political culture. While such discussion simply cannot be undertaken in any depth in a study of this length, general observations can be offered. The most obvious is that class position has always strongly influenced the level and nature of sporting activity that individuals and social groups can pursue. Unsurprisingly, income level is the critical factor here; quite simply, the greater the degree of individual wealth, the greater the opportunity for the fullest participation across the sporting world. Obviously, divisions within classes also come into play here. Andrew Davies' research into earlier twentieth-century leisure patterns in Manchester and Salford, for example, demonstrates that attendance at professional football was beyond many within the working-class community throughout the period to 1939 and that local games, often pub-based, sometimes played without proper kit on areas of waste ground, were a common and popular alternative.[51]

Sport, then, clearly has the capacity to reflect and reinforce differentials of class and status, creating a degree of social zoning – the football grandstand was long in Tony Mason's memorable phrase 'a bourgeois island in a sea of working-class faces' – and often a clear sense of social tone.[52] This was not necessarily fixed. While Lancashire County Cricket Club generally attracted restrained crowds comprised of individuals whose occupation (or lack of it) allowed attendance at a game commencing when most manual workers were contemplating a midday break, Saturdays and bank holidays could bring a very different clientele and atmosphere. In 1908, for example, although one local newspaper report of the Old Trafford August Bank Holiday 'Roses' match claimed that 'the rough horseplay, prehistoric humour, overflowing animal spirits, were less in evidence than on any previous occasion we can remember', another could still note that 'songs and jokes were rife all round the packed enclosure, and bursts of laughter were mingled with the strains of such melodies as "Swanee River" and "Cock Robin"'.[53] In certain contexts, social zoning became effectively a form of social apartheid. Many institutions were extremely anxious to defend the status of existing members through varying mechanisms of exclusion. An entry fee in 1912 of five guineas and an annual subscription of a further three for the significantly termed 'gentlemen' members of Manchester Golf Club (one and two guineas respectively for 'ladies') maintained a fairly elevated atmosphere at their new Hopwood Park course, and the club was not amongst those who introduced artisan sections to widen the social mix.[54] Most of our knowledge of status consciousness and its defence concerns middle-class sport but it would be interesting to see the extent to which it was significant in sporting bodies lower down the social scale. The differentiation between 'rough' and 'respectable', although never rigid and often drawn according to different criteria within different social groups, was nevertheless a demarcation frequently drawn within working-class communities and it would be useful for future research to probe its sporting ramifications more fully.

It was in the collisions between 'amateurs' and 'professionals' that conflicts over social status were at their most obvious. The late-Victorian battles within association football and rugby have already been noted, but rowing, athletics and a number of other sports were also affected at this time and, indeed, until much later, by problems often centring on the strictest imaginable definitions of 'amateurism'. As late as the 1950s local distance runner John Tarrant was earning national celebrity as the 'ghost runner' by turning up uninvited to run in a variety of amateur events in protest at losing his amateur status for once receiving four pounds as a boxer; his re-instatement finally came in 1958.[55] Certainly, these conflicts were multi-faceted and the motives of those on the middle-class amateur side cannot always be reduced to a fear of losing social status. There were genuine fears that the middle classes might abandon sports if they found themselves constantly pitted against 'men who give up their whole time and abilities to it'.[56] Nevertheless, the desire for exclusivity and the defence of social space and status lay behind much middle-class opposition to the penetration of sport by professionals.

Access to sporting opportunity was yet further influenced by issues of race, ethnicity and religion. Members of the Jewish, Irish, Afro-Caribbean and Asian communities have frequently formed their own sporting organizations, sometimes as a proud act of racial or ethnic celebration, but sometimes as a defensive mechanism against the significant discriminatory practices they suffered and, in some instances, still suffer from. Anti-semitism was clearly a potent force within many British golf clubs in the Victorian and Edwardian periods and, indeed, beyond, and it is significant that the country's second-ever Jewish club opened at Whitefields in 1921 (non-Jews could and did join, however). A second club, Dunham Forest, opened near Altrincham in 1960–1 as Jews from south Manchester sought a course closer to home.[57] Discrimination on grounds of colour was also prevalent in many areas of sport. It was institutionalized in some – Manchester boxer Len Johnson, regarded by many as the finest middleweight in the country in the mid 1920s, was prevented from fighting for the national title by the colour bar that existed in the sport until 1948 – but more informal in others. When it was rumoured in the 1930s that West Indian cricketer Learie Constantine might be signed by Lancashire County Cricket Club, there was strong opposition amongst the players. As one later recalled, 'the thought of a black man taking the place of a white man in our side was an anathema. It was as simple as that'.[58]

However, there is also plentiful evidence of integration and mutual tolerance. Many Jewish males were happy to support existing sporting bodies – Broughton Rangers RLFC had a significant Jewish following from the 1890s – and Tony Collins has suggested that in the post-1945 period, many more Jews have been happy to join non-Jewish golf and tennis clubs in acknowledgement of either an increased feeling of acceptance or a reduced sense of their Jewishness. Constantine was a hero amongst the people of Nelson where he played league cricket, and Len Johnson found many, including the *Manchester Evening Chronicle*, who had sympathy with his plight.[59] In modern times, Bolton-born boxer Amir Khan has become a local and national hero despite the sometimes intense hostility young Muslim men have faced from within sections of British society. The patterns of racial and ethnic sporting culture are complex and worthy of much closer scrutiny in a local and regional context than has thus far been the case.

The same can also be said for issue of the relationship between sport and local and regional (and indeed national) identities. Once again, complex and sometimes apparently contradictory patterns emerge here. Sport undoubtedly has great power to bind communities, or substantial sections of them, across boundaries of class, gender and race. Although as Joyce Woolridge's study demonstrates, this was perhaps most graphically illustrated in the response to tragedy, in the form of the Munich air disaster, it thankfully stemmed more commonly from team or individual triumph. This sense of sport as a common community bond could lead to exaggerated, almost utopian statements. In 1932, for example, the *Ashton-under-Lyne Reporter* – speaking generally, it must be assumed, for it had no obvious centre of local footballing excellence to trumpet – argued that 'it is generally acknowledged that football provides one of the finest antidotes to unrest in this country … In such an atmosphere the possibilities of a settlement of Lancashire's cotton problems are considerably strengthened. Employers and operatives meet on common ground as lovers of the winter pastime, and, win, lose or draw, ill will and prejudice

disappear when both sides "play the game"'.[60] This was clearly a rather dramatic version of the 'idealized vision of community' that Jeff Hill sees as central to local-press reporting of civic celebration upon cup-final success in the north of England, a vision which he compellingly argues 'reveals an all-too-keen awareness of the actual disharmonies present in the everyday life of Northern towns'.[61] Nevertheless, sport was undoubtedly a common topic of conversation and interest across potentially antagonistic social classes and groupings, and may have formed one of the thin but critical bonds that have helped to hold society together.

One of the most crucial roles of sport in this context has been a site in which 'myths', in the anthropological sense of stories which we tell in order to make sense of the world, can be created and sharpened. Such stories celebrate and define local and regional communities both by identifying indigenous virtues and external vices. In terms of the former, Manchester's strong inter-war boxing tradition, both at the time and subsequently, has become a signifier for the toughness and resilience of the city's working class, especially in Collyhurst on whose 'tough streets' Jackie Brown and Johnny King were raised, and where Jock McAvoy trained alongside them at Harry Fleming's gym. An external 'other' was often provided by London with its supposed superiority complex and capacity for discrimination against the north. In 1960, for example, David Meek in the *Manchester Evening News* hinted that Londoners Johnny Haynes and Jimmy Greaves had shown an uncanny sense of geography during the previous night's England *versus* Young England game, effectively starving local hero Bobby Charlton of possession:

> Although he had an overall fine game [Haynes] hardly gave outside left Charlton a pass. Little of the ball came from Jimmy Greaves either. Perhaps it's just coincidence that right winger Peter Brabrook, of Chelsea, got all the service.[62]

Both Haynes and his Fulham club colleague Jimmy Hill saw what the latter referred to as 'the great tendency in the north of England to belittle Haynes' as a product of press manipulation (fuelled, Hill argued, by Manchester United manager Matt Busby) rather than genuine popular sentiment.[63] Whatever the case, the journalists responsible clearly sensed a deep resentment toward the capital which they could tap into and reinforce.

Sport can also, however, divide localities and regions. Territorial rivalries have never been static, either in their nature or expression. In the period from 1945 to about the mid sixties, for example, football rivalries between or within towns or cities were fierce but often underpinned by good humour and a degree of regional unity. Gavin

Mellor has shown that while supporters of the two Manchester clubs obviously wished for their own side to dominate, rivalry was essentially friendly and often respectful. Further afield, even the Liverpool press was happy to congratulate Manchester United on victory in the 1968 European Cup Final.[64] By the early 1970s, a more aggressive terrace culture rooted in both a fundamental shift in the public behaviour of the working class and a diminution of certain shared aspects of regional identity and culture – the decline of shared traditional industries was probably key here – made such sporting ecumenism virtually an impossibility.

Perhaps the closest to a 'conclusion' on this issue that can be drawn here would be an acknowledgement that, while the multiple personal and collective identities held by all individuals are in constant flux and inter-play, perhaps those rooted in territorial allegiance are especially prone to swift changes of emphasis and weighting. The 'passions' aroused by the contests between rival Salford-pub football teams and their equivalents that Davies describes could, for example, be set aside as some-time enemies subsumed street-level loyalties in the mutual support for Manchester United or Manchester City, or for a Lancashire boxer against a Yorkshire rival in the 'Roses' encounters with which Royton boxing promoter Tom Chapman enlivened his shows in the 1930s.[65] More widely still, a team or individual from another town or city might be temporarily adopted as a 'northern' champion,

Nobby Stiles (on ground) and his Manchester United team-mates suffer as his last-minute own goal gives Manchester City a point in the January 1967 derby match (Manchester Archives and Local Studies, Central Library, M06993)

particularly when a representative of London provided the opposition, or be seen to represent the nation against foreign opposition. These wider bonds could, of course, in their turn be as easily broken or challenged when more parochial concerns reasserted themselves.

These constant shifts and fluctuations offer much to the historian who wants to witness identify formation and reinforcement at close quarters. Indeed, as the following articles demonstrate, the history of sport has much to tell us about so many aspects of the way we live and used to live. How we play matters a great deal.

Notes

1. Unless otherwise stated, the 'Manchester region' refers here to the area within a twelve-mile radius of the city centre.
2. *Liverpool Daily Post*, supplement, 4 July 1966.
3. J. K. Walton, 'The demand for working-class seaside holidays in Victorian England', *Economic History Review*, 34 (1981), pp. 249–65.
4. Simon Inglis, *Played in Manchester: the architectural heritage of a city at play* (London, 2004), p. 62.
5. Simon Inglis, *The Football League and the men who made it* (London, 1988), p. 8; Inglis, *Manchester* (London, 2004), p. 14.
6. *Slater's Directory*, 1912; *The Sports Trader*, Oct. 1912.
7. Inglis, *Manchester*, pp. 15–17; W. J. Smith, 'Sir Ashton Lever of Alkrington and his museum, 1729–1788', *Transactions of the Lancashire and Cheshire Antiquarian Society*, 72 (1962), pp. 79–80.
8. Robert W. Malcolmson, *Popular recreations in English society, 1700–1850* (Cambridge, 1973), p. 170.
9. Neil Tranter, *Sport, economy and society in Britain, 1750–1914* (Cambridge, 1998), p. 5.
10. J. T. Slugg, *Reminiscences of Manchester fifty years ago* (Manchester, 1881), p. 310.
11. Peter Bailey, *Leisure and class in Victorian England* (London, 1978), p. 26.
12. Robert Poole, *The Lancashire wakes holiday* (Preston, 1994), p. 18.
13. Bob Phillips, *Iron in his soul* (Manchester, 2002), pp. 30–41.
14. Ibid., p. 41.
15. Ibid., pp. 31, 35.
16. Peter Swain, 'New directions in football's history: some notes from the north-west of England', *LSA Newsletter*, 77 (July 2007), pp. 26–31. More generally, see Adrian Harvey, *The beginnings of a commercial sporting culture in Britain, 1793–1850* (Aldershot, 2004).
17. Brian Bearshaw, *From the Stretford End: the official history of Lancashire County Cricket Club* (London, 1990), pp. 1–3.
18. M. W. Peers, *A history of the Manchester Golf Club Limited, 1882–1982* (Manchester, 1982), pp. 2, 4.

19. Inglis, *Manchester*, pp. 120–7.

20. Simon Inglis, *Football grounds of Britain* (London, 1996), pp. 59, 282.

21. Tony Mason, *Association football and English society, 1863–1915* (Brighton, 1981), p. 81; Tony Collins, *Rugby's great split: class, culture and the origins of rugby league football* (London, 1998), pp. 112–53.

22. *Manchester Athletic Club Magazine*, Mar. 1894, p. 25.

23. John W. Bancroft, *Olympic champions in Manchester* (Eccles, 1993), pp. 7–8.

24. Ibid., pp. 8, 12.

25. D. Russell, 'Football and society in the North West, 1919–1939', *North West Labour History*, 24 (1999–2000), pp. 3–11; Andrew Davies, *Leisure, gender and poverty: working-class culture in Salford and Manchester, 1900–1939* (Buckingham, 1992), p. 44.

26. S. G. Jones, 'Working-class sport in Manchester between the wars', in R. Holt, ed., *Sport and the working class in modern Britain* (Manchester, 1990), p. 67.

27. Brian Hughes, *Jackie Brown: the man, the myth, the legend* (Manchester, 1996); and idem., *For king and country* (Manchester, 1999).

28. Denis Fleming, *The Manchester fighters* (Swinton, 1986), pp. 15, 49, 51–3, 58–63.

29. Mark Clapson, *A bit of a flutter* (Manchester, 1992), pp. 138–44.

30. Ibid., p. 146.

31. Jack Williams, '"A wild orgy of speed". Responses to speedway in Britain before the Second World War', *The Sports Historian*, 19 (1999), pp. 1–15; Trevor Jones and Barry Stephenson, *Speedway in Manchester, 1927–1945* (Stroud, 2003).

32. Jones and Stephenson, *Speedway*, pp. 159–60.

33. Jones, 'Working-class sport', pp. 77–8; D. Bowker, 'Parks and baths: sport, recreation and municipal government in Ashton-under-Lyne between the wars', in Holt, ed., *Sport and the working class*, pp. 84–100; Alan J. Kidd, *Manchester* (Keele, 1996), p. 231.

34. Inglis, *Manchester*, p. 73.

35. John H. Smith, 'Ramblers in the High Peak', paper delivered to Lancashire and Cheshire Antiquarian Society day school on popular leisure, Manchester, 24 Mar. 2007.

36. Inglis, *Manchester*, pp. 28, 49, 62, 58–9, 119–23.

37. David Rowe, *Sport, culture and the media* (Maidenhead, 2nd ed., 2004).

38. Inglis, *Manchester*, p. 100; Hughes, *Jackie Brown*, pp. 233–6.

39. Only four Manchester City players fell into the latter category.

40. Inglis, *Manchester*, pp. 52–7.

41. Ibid., pp. 100–1, 127.

42. Inglis, *Grounds*, p. 62.

43. Jennifer Hargreaves, *Sporting females: critical issues in the history and sociology of women's sport* (London, 1994).

44. [Anon.,] *Belle Vue: Manchester's playground* (Altrincham, 2005), pp. 89–95.

45. Peers, *Golf*, p. 17.

46. Ibid., pp. 17–18, 78; Sarah Cowell, 'Working-class women and rounders in inter-war Bolton', *North West Labour History*, 24 (1999–2000), pp. 15–29; Jones, 'Working-class sport', p. 76.

47. James and Stephenson, *Speedway*, pp. 166, 172; Williams, '"Orgy of speed"', p. 10.

48. Duncan Scott with Chris Bent, *Borrowed time: a social history of running. Salford Harriers, 1894–1984* (Salford, 1984), p. 40.

49. Fleming, *Fighters*, p. 8; Jones, 'Working-class sport', p. 73.

50. For a study with rich Manchester material, Clare Langhamer, *Women's leisure in England, 1920–1960* (Manchester, 2000).

51. Davies, *Leisure*, pp. 38–9.

52. Mason, *Association football*, p. 153.

53. Bearshaw, *Stretford End*, pp. 183–4. See also pp. 239–44.

54. Peers, *Manchester Golf Club*, pp. 41, 72.

55. Scott with Bent, *Borrowed time*, pp. 38–9.

56. Arthur Budd of the RFU in 1886, quoted in Collins, *Great Split*, p. 57.

57. Tony Collins, 'Jews, anti-semitism and sport in Britain, 1900–1939', in Michael Brenner and Gideon Reuveni, eds., *Emancipation through muscles: Jews in inter-war European sport* (Lincoln, NB; 2006), pp. 142–55; Graham Turner, *The north country* (London, 1967), p. 44.

58. Michael Herbert, *Never counted out* (Manchester, 1992); Bearshaw, *Stretford End*, p. 271.

59. Jeffrey Hill, 'Reading the stars: a post-modernist approach to sports history', *The Sports Historian*, 14 (1994), pp. 49–55; Herbert, *Never counted out*, pp. 32–3.

60. Quoted in Jones, 'Working-class sport', pp. 179–80.

61. Jeff Hill, 'Rite of spring: cup finals and community in the North of England', in Jeff Hill and Jack Williams, eds., *Sport and identity in the north of England* (Keele, 1996), p. 108.

62. 7 May 1960.

63. Johnny Haynes, *It's all in the game* (London, 1962), pp. 136–9; Jimmy Hill, *Striking for soccer* (London, 1961), pp. 207–9.

64. Gavin Mellor, 'Professional football and its supporters in Lancashire, c1946–1985' (PhD thesis, University of Central Lancashire, 2003), pp. 209–27.

65. Davies, *Leisure*, p. 38; Fleming, *Fighters*, p. 31.

Betting capital of the provinces: Manchester, 1800–1900

Mike Huggins

Many of Manchester's nineteenth-century representations are well known to any student of history. The flashing blades of the yeomanry that cut down men, women and children at the reform rally in St Peter's Fields in August 1819 are still powerful symbols of oppression.[1] To Engels, in 1844, the slums of old Manchester were 'Hell on Earth', part of the squalor and ill health associated with great wealth. For his contemporary Leon Faucher, Manchester was the cradle of universal industrialism.[2] It was the 'shock city' of the world, a 'symbol of a new age' in the 1840s, mixing great wealth and great poverty in equal proportions, a centre for the organization of the middle-class radicalism of the Anti-Corn Law League and also for Chartism.[3] The Anti-Corn Law campaign helped create the 'Manchester School', the philosophy of political economy trusting in the virtues and mission of the new industrial middle class, and its emerging consciousness. Manchester was 'Cottonopolis', the centre of an industry employing nearly half a million by the beginning of the twentieth century, a city of power and wealth, with its own Cotton Exchange. It was the headquarters of that leading prohibition temperance organization, the United Kingdom Alliance, financially supported by some Manchester manufacturers.[4]

But such work has largely overlooked the ways in which Manchester in the past two centuries also played a key national and regional role in betting history, though this has been noted in a growing specialist literature.[5] Betting's substantial turnover and the numbers employed in the racing and betting industries on at least a part-time basis made betting a significant contributor to the regional as well as the national economy. In the nineteenth century it was racing, *not* soccer or cricket, that had the greatest claim to be Britain's 'national sport', while during the twentieth century gambling has ranged between 1.3 and 7.5 per cent of British consumer expenditure.[6] The National Anti-Gambling League was set up to fight gambling in 1889, and Manchester, along with London and York, became the main centre of its operation for the next four decades. In 1923 the Select Committee on Betting Duty was told by two witnesses that betting was 'more rife' there than elsewhere.

It was no accident that Manchester, not London, was where the 'modern' form of greyhound racing with the artificial hare was first introduced in 1926. The organizers, Brigadier-General Critchley, Charles Munn and Major Lyne Dixon, chose it because, as Critchley pointed out, gambling on whippet racing was particularly popular there. In the summer of 1927 they tried and failed to induce the Belle Vue management to let them use its football field, but leased twelve acres nearby, and the sport took off almost immediately. The initial company, the Greyhound Racing Association (Manchester) Ltd, changed its name to the conglomerate Greyhound Racing Association Trust Ltd as it expanded into new sites. Within a year, the shilling shares in the company were changing hands at £10, and later stabilized at £7.50.[7] By 1933 the Manchester area had three leading stadiums, Salford, Belle Vue and White City. Manchester's name also appeared on the first horse-race sweep tickets of the Irish Hospitals Trust sweepstakes, introduced in 1930 with the approval of the Irish government. The sweep tickets offered a first prize of £100,000 – a huge sum at the time – for the person drawing the winner of Manchester's November Handicap. This was then one of Britain's leading betting races and was broadcast by the BBC in 1935. High demand thereafter, especially in northern England, led to an Act making the sweeps illegal in 1934, but they continued to be widely sold in Britain until after World War II.[8] In 1951 Manchester was the first racecourse in Britain to have evening meetings to encourage attendance.

Manchester's middle-class cultural life, institutions and cultural production have been of increasing interest to scholars such as Alan Kidd and Martin Hewitt in recent years.[9] Despite this, Manchester's betting culture and betting industry – for industry it was – rarely, if ever, surfaces. Asa Briggs, for example, in his seminal *Victorian cities*, made no mention of betting's popularity in the city. Instead he chose to stereotype Australian gambling, pointing up the popularity of the Melbourne Cup, first run in 1861, and its high prize money, which reached over £10,000 in 1890. Had he looked more closely at Manchester, he might have noted that between 1888 and 1893 Manchester's race meeting was the most highly capitalized and modern in Britain, and that its Lancashire Plate, a seven-furlong weight-for-age race for two-year-olds and upwards, with over £10,000 added prize money (slightly more than Melbourne's), was the most valuable horse-race in the world, worth more than twice that of the Derby or the St Leger.[10]

Manchester's business life was rooted in risk. Gambling on stocks and shares was an activity that made some of its most respectable leading figures rich. By 1838 the Manchester Cotton Exchange was 'the largest exchange room in Europe', a powerful symbol of its role in trade and business. Managing risk, along with temporary escape from the pressures of work and domesticity, a cathartic letting off of steam, were also major appeals of gambling amongst the middle classes, as studies of Victorian Liverpool and the inter-war years have revealed.[11]

Up to the end of the 1860s metropolitan London and provincial Manchester were rival centres of the national betting market, providing competing guides to ante-post betting prices for major races. Tattersall's Subscription Rooms first opened in 1815 at London's Hyde Park Corner and moved to new Albert Gate premises in 1865. They became a centre of organized metropolitan large-scale credit betting. Their quotations of odds on horses running at forthcoming major races were to racing men 'what those of Mark Lane are to the farmer, Lloyd's are to the insurer, the Stock Exchange to the broker, or Greenwich time to the horologist'.[12] Manchester prices provided an equivalent guide to northern book-makers and punters.

At first glance there might seem little reason for Manchester to have had such a betting focus. Manchester could not claim to be a centre for thoroughbred breeding or training. Nor was it a town attractive to members of the aristocratic Jockey Club. Manchester, with its business, industry and pollution, had little appeal to the majority of wealthy upper-class racing men. Few of them attended Manchester's popular Whitsuntide races, preferring instead to spend their racing time each year mainly at Newmarket and other elite courses. Mentions of Manchester racing rarely surfaced in books about 'the turf' written by and for a more select audience, although Nimrod's *The chase, the turf and the road*, written in 1837, described Manchester, along with Liverpool, as 'amongst the principal country race meetings', and George Chetwynd, writing in the late 1880s, called it 'admirably conducted'.[13] The Duke of Bedford's book *Racing and steeplechasing* (1886) was more typical of elite coverage, confining its discussions of flat racing to Newmarket, home of the Jockey Club, and 'provincial racing' at Epsom (for the Derby), Doncaster (for the St Leger), Ascot, York and Goodwood.

But it appears that the culture of risk in Manchester's trade environment generated more public interest in betting than in thoroughbred stock. Henry Hall Dixon (alias 'The Druid'), a racing writer for the monthly *Sporting Magazine* around mid-century, accepted that Manchester's Whitsuntide meeting attracted large crowds, but commented disdainfully that unlike Yorkshiremen, 'they seem to go much more because it is the conventional way of passing the Whitsuntide week than from any constitutional interest in race horses'.[14] Off-course betting was already popular amongst many Mancunians when Dixon was writing. Some respectable, reformist sections of Manchester society looked down upon gambling, but other, equally respectable middle-class men ran Manchester racing, or betted using credit with Manchester betting commissioners. In the nineteenth century there were more Manchester credit book-makers than in any other city but London, though by the 1920s Birmingham had overtaken it, and Liverpool had similar numbers.[15] Manchester betting interest was further fostered because it was a major centre for the betting press, much to the annoyance of anti-gamblers. In 1904 the Oxford Christian Union remarked bitterly that in Lancashire the only widely read daily papers were sporting ones, concentrating on horse-racing.[16]

So this paper attempts to recover a long-lost dimension to Manchester's nineteenth-century cultural history. It provides a succinct overview of the race meetings and their changing sites, credit betting and Manchester's betting 'exchange', working-class cash-betting on horses and other sporting events, and the Manchester betting journalism which emerged to cover them.

Race meetings at Manchester

Manchester races date from c1681, and were first reported in the *London Gazette* in May 1687. There were occasional breaks, and there was no racing at all from 1746 to 1759 because of opposition from local churches, but renewed financial support provided by Sir Ashton Lever of Alkrington then set them off again on a firm footing. By the beginning of the nineteenth century Manchester was already well known for the large crowds attending its annual three-day meeting. Manchester's racing attendance was firmly cross-class in character, and the area, like London, seems to have attracted entries and thus on-course betting, firstly because its wealth allowed it to raise sufficient prize money through subscriptions, and secondly because of local betting interest. As *Sporting Magazine* recognized, the meeting attracted 'a large subscription of public money'.[17] Manchester's Kersal Moor is famous (at least amongst labour-movement historians) for its Chartist rally in September 1838, when the *Manchester Guardian* claimed 30,000 attended whilst the Chartist press claimed half a million, an illustration of the difficulties of estimating attendance numbers. But Kersal Moor was then more generally famous for its racecourse. It had a new grandstand (built in 1819), rows of booths, a Turf Tavern and a saddling enclosure (built in 1840). Even during the worst years of social unrest, there was never any attempt to stop the races. Indeed, Lord Strafford, in his evidence to the 1844 Select Committee on Betting, argued that at the races the conduct of the people was 'quiet, good humoured, and orderly', and that given their enjoyment, it would have been more dangerous to have banned them.[18] Uncorroborated estimates of attendances to see the Manchester Cup, first run in 1816, were between 100,000 and 150,000 even in the 1820s.[19] In 1846, when the racing moved from the Moor, it had been a racing centre for over 160 years.

There was also a three-day September Manchester meeting for 'gentlemen' riders organized by the Earl of Wilton at his Heaton Park estate from 1827 to 1838, although he was reputed to use his hospitality to induce handicappers to treat his horses favourably.[20] Although the races were put on a week after the Doncaster St Leger meeting for the benefit of his house-party guests, there was a substantial working-class presence despite admission being only with a ticket, for those on horseback or in a wheeled vehicle.[21] There were other race meetings around this time too, at Eccles (1839), Stretford (1841 and 1852–4), Gorton Hall (1844–6), Harpurhey (1845), and Blakeley (1847). H. H. Dixon, a sound judge on sporting matters, believed that at this time, 'Lancashire had better racing on the whole than Yorkshire'.[22]

The Kersal Moor course was abandoned when the Clowes family refused to extend the £30 annual lease because they wanted to develop the land. The race committee sought new premises[23] and a new Manchester Racecourse Company was formed. This took a new, innovative direction, being amongst the very first in Britain to put a race meeting on a more commercial basis. In 1847 it took a lease on land at Castle Irwell, within two miles of the city centre but occasionally prone to flooding, from a Salford colliery proprietor, Mr Fitzgerald. The new meeting started as a single two-day event, but expanded to two meetings totalling four days from 1862. With only three entrances and the river on one side, the leaseholder took the opportunity to charge a toll to all crossing the suspension bridge or taking the road to the races, so it became one of the early race meetings to charge an entrance fee, although of only a penny. This was an early indication to other race meetings that enclosure might raise more revenue than collecting subscriptions, since the decision caused controversy but did not deter the crowd.[24] The race committee made charges for grandstand and paddock, and carriage and horse entry, but most income at this time was collected by subscription, as it was at most race meetings. The Manchester Whitsuntide races in the 1860s now lasted for three days and caused the closure of almost all the factories, such that the *Free Lance* claimed 'the city was quite deserted, the air is clear', and 'the people have gone to the races; the cabs have gone to the races ... and there is nothing and nobody left in town'. It conceded that 'the course is not an aristocratic meeting', but stressed that the grand stand 'is graced ... by a great many who regard themselves as the aristocracy from a monetary and cottonian point of view'. Attendance lists show that many amongst the respectable middle class and merchant urban elite attended, a support that was vital. Drinking accompanied the betting. The course was described as 'a complete canvas city of public houses', one where 'the publican was ubiquitous' and, 'it seems, indeed, to be taken for granted that all visitors to the races require a lot of something to drink and a little of something to eat'.[25]

When the lease came up for renewal Fitzgerald's son, an eccentric with strong evangelical leanings, refused to extend it. Racing was 'an evil'. His letters complained that the proprietors made 'large profits' of about 9.5 per cent per annum from their investment, and while he accepted that they were 'gentlemen' of 'respectability', he argued that racing was 'a great system of immorality'. He bitterly remarked in an 1868 letter to the committee that the moral and Christian view was that racing was an immoral act, while 'the greater mass of working people gather, not to see a race which lasts but two minutes of time, but to gamble according to their power, and to drink, not for refreshment, but for drinking's sake'.[26] But his refusal was irrelevant, as the entrepreneurial Manchester Race Course Company had decided to put the meeting on an even more commercial footing. They built a new, fully enclosed course at New Barns (now the site of the Lowry Centre), acquiring a hundred acres of land at the end

The newly opened Castle Irwell racecourse in 1847 (Manchester Archives and Local Studies, Central Library, M07811)

of December 1867.[27] The owners, the Clowes family, had initially demanded £350 per acre but sold for £200. The company made modifications to course facilities: an improved grandstand, business offices, and retiring and dressing rooms, though it was unable to get vitally important electric telegraph facilities for betting men to utilize, despite approaching the United and Electric Telegraph companies.[28] The enterprise had a nominal capital of £40,000, and according to Board of Trade records, the majority of shares was initially held by five self-ascribed 'gentlemen'. E. Miller and W. Phillips held the most part of these, while James Bake, a former innkeeper, key member of the previous committee and now the chairman, called himself a 'gentleman' too.[29] Two merchants, a gun manufacturer, a licensed victualler, a commercial traveller, a cattle salesman and farmer, and J. and A. H. Holmes, importers and salesmen of fancy goods, held the other shares. By 1869 there were three meetings a year, a total only exceeded by three London courses and Newmarket. Crowds were less than before the enclosure, with fewer children and women, because an entry fee was now demanded. Even so, in 1875 the *Salford Weekly News* estimated that on the Whit Tuesday there were 'not less than 50,000 people on the course'.

The company expanded when Mark Price took over as secretary. Price was active politically, a councillor and advocate of household suffrage, but very entrepreneurial. There were five days of flat-race meetings in 1881 and 1882, and increased prize money. Large prizes attracted larger paying crowds. The enclosed course was now a trend copied elsewhere, thanks to Manchester's success. The Jockey Club noted that 'the racing public have a very strong partiality for these gate money events like Manchester'.[30] The use of the course expanded to include more steeplechases too. By 1892 there were nearly 900 shares, as the Company drew on capital to invest in improved facilities. There were even 200 stables so that trainers paid for stabling on the course rather than in stables elsewhere.

It was nationally recognized as very profitable for the shareholders. Even Louis Henry Curzon – a critic of many of racing's practices, calling them a business of a 'most sordid kind', with horses run as instruments of gambling, and practices that would 'not bear the light of day' – saw Manchester as occupying 'the premier position' in terms of gate-money meetings, paying 'enormous dividends to its shareholders'. It attracted 'hundreds of thousands' of workers to its Whitsuntide meetings, all paying a shilling or sixpence just for admission to the course, while the 'plethora of gambling' associated with it represented hundreds of thousands of pounds.[31] Behaviour was unproblematic. Manchester's town clerk, writing to Chester Race Committee in 1891, told them that Manchester's enclosed course was 'decidedly preferable [with] rarely any complaints. Disreputable of racing fraternity do not frequent Manchester racecourse'.[32]

It was clear by the end of the century that with increased industrial expansion, the course's days were numbered and with the Castle Irwell site again available following the death of Fitzgerald, it was bought by the Company in 1898 preparatory to a move. At this time the profits of the racecourse were reportedly at least £10,000 a year, and £100 shares were worth £700 or more.[33] By this time four of the five directors of the company were self-described as gentlemen, while the other, J. Whittaker, was a Salford publican. The chairman was J. E. Davies, a magistrate, town councillor and secretary of the Salford Liberal Association. In 1902 the Manchester Ship Canal project finally bought part of the course to extend their waterway. Racing then resumed at Castle Irwell until World War I intervened.

Manchester credit betting

Even in the early nineteenth century the 'ring' of gamblers congregating round the betting post at leading race meetings were no longer just composed of the upper and middle classes. There were increasing numbers of more plebeian gamblers, exploiting their insider knowledge of horseflesh, training, mathematical probability, and their growing wealth to gain a betting edge. The ideal was to back good but unknown horses at long odds many months before a race, and then lay (bet against the same horse) at much shorter odds later, as the public learnt of their good form. This allowed the more knowledgeable to lose nothing if the horse lost, but make a profit if the horse won. The term 'book-makers' came from the practice of recording such bets in small hand-sized betting books. By taking enough bets on sufficient horses it was occasionally possible to make a profit no matter which horse won. So high levels of mathematical skill were necessary. Looked down on by the aristocracy as 'provincial blacklegs', working-class betters with cash were nevertheless accepted as a necessary evil, making it far easier to create a betting market and so place bets. Writers regularly described this social mixing, with mounted and pedestrian betters forming an on-course 'ring' to make bets. Later references make clear that several of this group were Lancastrians, many originally from Manchester. 'Sylvanus', looking back in 1850, for example, remembered Lord Chesterfield or Lord Wilton rubbing shoulders with 'a round shouldered knave from Manchester'.[34] In the 1830s and 1840s Harry Hill, who had originally been a Manchester book-maker, was the betting commissioner of Lord George Bentinck, then the dominating figure on the English turf. Hargreaves, active in the 1840s, and who became one of the wealthiest and most influential members of the betting ring, had originally been a Manchester warehouseman. These peripatetic 'legs' would travel to London's Tattersall's and to the various betting rooms across the country associated with major races. They made book-making their career.[35] In the 1840s and 1850s there were enough travelling Manchester book-makers to be described as the 'Manchester division'.

Many racing towns converted particular public house premises into subscription betting rooms for the duration of the races. Quite often these pubs were betting centres for the rest of the year too. In nearby Liverpool, for example, the Adelphi, the Talbot, and Lucas's repository functioned as betting centres by the 1840s. But other than Tattersall's, only Manchester's 'prices' or 'odds' were nationally recognized. The origins of Manchester's betting rooms are unclear but they were already well established by the 1830s. The key figure here, as with the later racecourse developments, was James Bake (1800–79). He was keen on racing from his youth, when he was an apprentice saddler. From 1824 he had his own saddlery business, and in 1833 he became the proprietor of the Bull's Head, a 'betting' public house where Bake's subscription betting rooms were located. Bake also organized the bringing of the St Leger results to Manchester by fast horse, and large crowds would await his arrival. In 1836 the St Leger result came the fifty-eight miles from Doncaster to Manchester in the short space of two hours and twenty minutes.[36]

By around 1840 several London daily papers, including *The Times* which provided ante-post odds on forthcoming leading national races, sometimes provided 'the latest betting in Manchester' as well as London odds. So did *Bell's Life in London*, London's leading sporting paper. Northern regional papers such as the *Nottingham Gazette* or the *York Herald* did so on an *ad hoc* basis through the 1840s, as did the Sunday paper, the *News of the World*. This confirmed that Manchester was becoming regarded as the only serious betting rival to London. It was clear, however, that many of the leading figures were absent from the Rooms quite regularly, travelling to race meetings to make their betting books there. In 1844, for example, there were few book-makers at the Whitsuntide Manchester race meeting because they had to be in London for the Derby settlements at Tattersall's.[37] Again, in June 1847, as the *Manchester Courier* pointed out, there were few bets placed in the betting rooms: 'with all the members absent at the great coal meeting [Newcastle] it would be useless attempting to give a price current'.[38]

In the early 1840s Bake both managed the rooms and played a regionally prominent role in betting, acting as a cash book-maker, offering lists of odds on major races, and organizing racing sweeps on the leading races. These were essentially a lottery and so technically illegal, but were rarely prosecuted. Indeed many publicans had Derby or St Leger sweeps. Most purchasers would, in the phrase of the day, 'draw a blank', but a lucky few would draw a horse entered in the race, and the holder of the winning horse took the majority of prize money. Bake was one of a number of entrepreneurs who advertised his sweeps in the regional press and in *Bell's Life in London*, attracting sufficient entries to offer quite substantial prizes. This was sufficiently profitable to allow him to retire from the hotel in 1849 as a very wealthy man, although he continued to be heavily involved in racing as clerk of the course, at Manchester from 1847 and later also at Newton, jobs which required good relationships with both owners and trainers. From 1843 he represented the Oxford Ward as a municipal councillor. When he moved to Cheetham he became a councillor there from 1856 to 1865, when he was elected an alderman. This reflected the extent to which he had already become a wealthy, respected and respectable figure in Manchester society.[39]

The Manchester betting rooms attracted a cross-class clientele of both layers and backers, creating a betting market where the 'prices' against horses could be established, and 'speculation' could take place. Essentially it functioned in much the same way as a stock exchange. Owners and trainers who wished to back favoured horses without letting the public know their chances might get commissioners to place the bets on their behalf. Those secretly aware of a horse's poor form or ill health would be trying to lay the odds against it. The upper classes attended rarely, most usually only to get ante-post bets on before and during Manchester race meetings. The famous Yorkshire sportsman, Squire George Osbaldeston, for example, attended the rooms in 1835 when riding at Heaton Park with other 'gentlemen jocks'.[40] One leading turf writer believed in 1840 that Manchester, Liverpool and Birmingham each had 'almost as much and as heavy betting … on the leading events of the turf as in London itself'.[41] Initially, betting information was brought to and fro via the coaching service, pigeons or rapid riders, but after the introduction of the electric telegraph, results of races were brought much more rapidly from the telegraph offices.

The betting rooms played a major role over the 1840s, 1850s and 1860s, increasingly extending into heavy handicap betting races such as the City and Suburban and the Metropolitan Handicap Stakes.[42] The anonymous writer of a history of horse-racing, writing in 1863, told his readers that

> like their Yorkshire brethren, the lads of Lancashire are greatly given to the pleasures and excitements of horse racing. Their meetings

are always well attended, and they are so keen with respect to the Prices Current of the turf that they have an 'Exchange' of their own which regulates betting transactions, just like Tattersall's.[43]

In 1867 the *Free Lance* printed a detailed description of Manchester betting in the week before the running of the Derby, a major betting race, making the links between betting, business, exchange quotations and economics quite explicit:

> As in every other kind of business, Manchester does a good stroke in betting. Its betting lists are perused throughout the kingdom, with an interest only second to that which appertains to the quotations from Tattersall's, or those that come direct from the course. In fact, the amount of business that is transacted in Manchester throughout the year must have no small effect in keeping what is called 'the truly British sport' still on its legs.[44]

It cited the Post Office Hotel as the principal resort of such gambling, a place where proceedings were carried on 'with open and unblushing candour in spite of all legal enactments', though conceding that in other inns 'a good deal of money' also changed hands. Its description of the rooms indicates that they were decorated with mirrors and pictures of racehorses. It had a 'varied' attendance, again implying this cross-class element. They were 'well fed' and 'prosperous' in appearance. Any shabby clothes were 'probably more from choice than necessity'. A few could be 'prosperous merchants or professional men'. Few occupations were mentioned, though the writer mentions 'small beershop keepers', 'successors of Caxton', 'clerks and warehousemen' and their 'employers'.

Some members would have been heavy betters, looking for the best odds. Others were leading credit book-makers and turf-commission agents, receiving guidance from owners, jockeys, trainers and country betters, and putting their money on for a fee. But Manchester's days as a betting 'Exchange' were numbered. The national betting market was changing. The Post Office Hotel was still a place for posting betting lists, and 'the principal resort of the betting men' according to Fitzgerald in 1868, but in the 1870s Manchester's 'Exchange' faded from the historical record. The reasons lay outside Manchester's control. Such markets provided odds well before the race, so odds changed regularly as views fluctuated about a horse's chances. Any bet was made at the odds available that day, usually on credit, not cash. But even if the horse was injured or was later withdrawn before the race, if the horse failed to win then the better was still expected to pay up. The better could refuse to pay, but to become a defaulter meant that further bets would not be taken.

This type of betting (called ante-post betting) was becoming unpopular. It was open to exploitation by owners and book-makers. Many owners and breeders were becoming more reluctant to bet in large amounts. The sporting press provided daily information about how horses were going in training, and the electric telegraph made news available with great immediacy. Moreover, betting was changing from smaller numbers of very substantial bets (perhaps several thousand pounds) laid by the wealthier, to much larger numbers of smaller bets placed before the race in cash by the middle and working classes and taken by leading cash book-makers, even though cash betting, unlike credit betting, was illegal. Such book-makers could then use the money they took well before the race to help manipulate odds to their advantage in this formal betting market.

So from the late 1860s cash betting nationally was moving towards starting price betting, when the punters put down their money beforehand, but got the odds at the start, assessed by the newspaper correspondents of the *Sporting Life* or the *Sportsman*. Starting prices facilitated much more betting.

Manchester's credit book-makers, however, did not disappear. Some became part of the travelling band of on-course book-makers following the wealthy from meeting to meeting. Others, calling themselves turf agents, or commission agents, expanded their credit offices, rendering accounts daily or weekly. Thomas Bradbury, describing himself as a member of Manchester and London Subscription Rooms, already claimed to have been 'established twenty years' in 1869.[45] Manchester book-makers such as Arthur Magnus, Tom Gibbins and William Vincent were first established in the 1870s and 1880s, and were still advertising in the 1920s. Credit profits could be considerable, although so were bad debts. In 1902 Manchester's Chief Constable described one commission agent, living on the outskirts of Manchester, as having made a profit of £5,846 in five months.[46]

Cash betting in Manchester

We know little of early off-course betting, but by the beginning of the 1840s Manchester already had a limited working-class cash ante-post betting market, focusing almost entirely on the major races. The annual *General and miscellaneous statistical returns of the Manchester police* show that in 1840 160, and in 1843 190 people, mainly working class, were arrested for betting and gaming, although this was not then a public-order problem. In 1849 sixty-nine men and three women were arrested. The 1853 Betting Houses Act, which was supposed to prevent cash betting, had little effect in Manchester, where 'list houses' continued to be common, despite a brief flurry of police raids in the late 1850s. In general, as the police were distracted by other concerns, they were more reluctant to make arrests, and betting rarely figured in the statistics. But this did not mean betting was in decline. As elsewhere in Britain, arrests usually only followed complaining letters in the press, a brief outbreak of moral panic or the arrival of an officer keen to make his mark.

By the later 1860s lists were sometimes displayed in pubs and beer houses, but specialist shops were also emerging. Some were just private houses but others had shop fronts, suggesting that they were tobacco or cigar shops, butchers, hairdressers, or food suppliers, although no such trade was carried out. This provided an apparent explanation for the numbers of callers. Generally lists of forthcoming races were displayed on the outside of a counter, along with the current odds. Because betting had to be in cash, the odds offered were not as good as in the betting rooms.

The press details about forthcoming races and the rapidity with which results now came in, thanks to the electric telegraph, meant that by the 1860s such cash betting was no longer just on forthcoming major races, but on *any* race on *any* day. According to the Manchester *Free Lance*, in 1867, 'swarms of clerks, operatives, stable-men, soldiers and even women pass in and out in an unceasing stream'. Book-makers sat behind a desk or counter, surrounded by betting lists and cards, entered 'investment' in a book and gave out numbered tickets with the book-maker's name and address. The *Free Lance* reported that two shillings was 'the minimum sum that the "respectable" list keepers will take the trouble to enter in their ledgers'. For those unable to afford the expense of list betting, further facilities, and even poorer odds, were available in an open yard near St Paul's church, which was surrounded by what the paper described as 'little hutches', timber structures where large crowds of 'mechanics', 'operatives' and 'more women' could bet a shilling with book-makers who were less reliable, since they lacked a clear address, and so were more likely to abscond. Crowds would hang around until 'the result of the last race' was known.[47]

Advertisements from turf tipsters also increasingly figured in the local press. The *Free Lance* saw that these were 'pushing themselves into greater prominence', and appealed particularly to clerks and assistants.[48] Despite complaints from reformers and the liberal press about 'the betting nuisance' or the 'betting pest', betting was evidently becoming increasingly popular, yet the Manchester police appeared uninterested in prosecutions. Even the appearance of a lengthy editorial in the *Free Lance* in February 1868, complaining that the failure to address betting was 'a grave dereliction of duty', filling the streets with 'idle people' and with 'hundreds' ruined every year, had little initial effect. The editorial claimed that 'clerks, packers, salesmen, footmen, and omnibus guards, drivers &c, nay, even miserable looking women' all thronged the list house environs when a major race was being run, while policemen simply walked 'pompously' up and down, ignoring what was going on.[49]

But in 1869, following the example of London raids on list houses, the Manchester police finally carried out a major raid. Most contemporary references to betting focused on an urban zoning centred on two streets, Thomas Street and Turner Street, and the raids here singled out a private house off Turner Street; the Vine in Thomas Street; Moulder's Arms in John Street; the Red Lion; and some properties on Back Turner Street as list house addresses. They found some book-makers had already 'taken flight'. They may well have been tipped off. Fifteen men were, however, arrested. Police evidence described how punters enquired after odds on named horses, put down money and got a card recording their bet, which was entered in a betting ledger. One book-maker, Aaron Worsley, had been arrested previously in 1858, but the subsequent lack of police action had brought him back into the occupation. He thought the 1853 Act was 'a dead letter' and that betting was 'winked at' by the authorities, so he reopened his business 'office' (other book-makers also used such commercial discursive language). His mistake cost him dear. The fines imposed were heavy, between £75 and £100 plus costs, but were met in all but one case. The magistrates told the prisoners that they were 'determined to put down the nuisance from betting' and stop the 'ruin to so many clerks and servants'.[50]

In general, however, the police were reluctant to act against a popular cultural activity, and some magistrates appear to have been reluctant to convict. As successful prosecutions proved difficult, in 1875 a by-law was passed to enable a charge of obstruction to be made against any three or more people assembled together in any street for the purpose of betting, with the intention of targeting book-makers.[51]

Police made renewed attempts to raid betting houses and clubs in Manchester in the 1880s. In 1885 there was a major raid on clubs involving over 170 policemen, led by strongly anti-gambling detective Jerome Caminada, netting publicans, book-makers and bar staff in hopes of reducing betting provision.[52] Some 200 were arrested. But this simply had the effect, as elsewhere, of putting increased numbers of book-makers onto the street, and more prosecutions for obstruction. Police activity then tailed off and in the later 1880s and early 1890s there were never more than sixteen proceeded against annually under the Betting Houses Act, and some years with no prosecutions. Edward Hulton junior, the newspaper proprietor, when questioned in 1902, believed that there were increasing numbers of

prosecutions in the 1890s.[53] The crime figures bear this out, though here again, the conviction rate was not high: fourteen out of forty-five in 1984, twenty-one out of forty-two in 1897.

In 1902 the Manchester Chief Constable R. Peacock provided evidence on Manchester betting to the Select Committee on Betting. Manchester, he said, had its betting clubs, and he believed that horse-race betting had 'grown considerably' in the last few years 'chiefly' amongst artisans and the working class. Book-makers could be found in the street and waiting outside large works to meet their agents inside. He claimed there were 'thousands' of known book-makers throughout the county, but accepted that the profession was generally honest. Peacock avoided any suggestion that collusion between book-makers and policemen at local level was an open secret in Manchester itself. Another Manchester witness, Charles Russell, a London and North West Railway representative who ran a lads' club in Manchester, reported that some of his mechanics and warehouse lads bet with small-scale book-makers in stationers' shops or beer-houses, and bought the early editions of the evening papers. The ubiquitous presence of book-makers was borne out by other contemporary sources. Most were men, but there were women too. In 1900 Teresa Butcher, a respectably dressed, 'elderly white-haired lady', who ran a greengrocer's shop, was fined £10 for taking bets.[54]

Huge crowds at the replacement Castle Irwell course in 1902 (Manchester Archives and Local Studies, Central Library, M07812)

The betting press

As indicated earlier, Manchester working-class betting was given much of its momentum by the sporting press, its reports from touts on horses in training, its tips for forthcoming races, its details of horses, jockeys and trainers, and accounts of running. Although Steve Tate provides an extended discussion of the topic elsewhere in this journal, it is worthy of brief mention at this juncture. By the late nineteenth century Manchester was a leading centre for the publication of racing and betting sheets. The most successful and long-lived was the *Sporting Chronicle*, first brought out by Edward Hulton from his Withy Grove printing business in 1871. He had recognized a business opportunity when the three morning papers in Manchester tried to curb betting by refusing to print betting tips. The *Chronicle* went on to be the leading racing paper in northern England. By 1882 it claimed 30,000 readers an issue. In 1885 Hulton purchased the *Sporting Life*, the leading London sporting paper, making Manchester 'the provincial capital of the sporting press'.[55] Other less successful Manchester papers included the *Turf Telegraphic News* (earliest copy, 1881), *Locket's Indicator and Sporting News* (1885–9), *Sporting Echo* (1887), *Chilton's Special Guide* (1893–1914), *Sporting Echo* (1887–9), *The Sporting Journal* (1893), *The Racing Mail* (1894–9) and *Manchester Sportsman's Special* (1897–1901). By 1900 most high-circulation Manchester papers, including Hulton's *Daily Despatch*, *Evening Chronicle* and the *Sunday Chronicle*, provided racing tips for punters. Even the *Manchester Guardian* and the *Manchester Evening News*, both opposed to gambling, now reluctantly included results and starting prices. Russell Allen, one of the owners of the latter, in evidence to the 1902 House of Lords Select Committee, felt that the increase in betting was largely due to the sporting press, and that the early editions of evening papers contained little but betting news. His paper did not publish tips and had 'suffered considerably … by that attitude'.[56]

As well as the newspaper tipsters, there were still commercial tipsters too, 'turf prophets' pretending to have insider information at a price. A. T. Bottomley, of Jackson Street, was offering 'selections' in the *Courier* as early as the 1860s. A *Baily's Magazine* article in the 1880s claimed that tipsters were especially prominent in large commercial cities like Manchester and Liverpool, and were mostly 'barefaced trickery', but that at a time when Manchester and Salford had 'over 200 bookmakers', the 'Manchester school' of tipsters earned a more honest living.[57]

Betting and other Manchester sports

Manchester was also amongst the earliest to produce those forerunners of the football pools, the newspaper football coupons, which were given away with editions of newspapers. According to soccer historian Tony Mason these began in north-west England in the 1880s, and Manchester, as the largest urban conurbation, soon became a major centre.[58] Manchester's *Athletic News*, Britain's leading professional football-reporting paper, began offering fixed weekly prizes of £5 for the most accurate coupon forecast in the 1880s. Another Manchester paper, *Football Programme and Weekly Calendar*, offered £3 each week between 1889 and 1891 for the highest number of correct predictions of win-or-draw from twelve matches.[59] In March 1890 the Manchester printing family, the Stoddards, brought out *Sporting Luck*, at a penny a week, containing racing tips, winter football coupons and summer horse-race coupons. Punters had to guess the first three horses in a race at a penny per prediction. The success of *Sporting Luck* led to it transferring to London in August, and by 1899 it was paying out nearly £49,000 a year, largely on its racing competitions. The Manchester police tried to discourage coupon betting in 1891 by prosecuting one paper but unavailingly. Other Manchester papers soon got involved in offering soccer competitions. The *Manchester Evening Chronicle* offered a prize of £40 in 1899 for twelve correct entries. Manchester police finally achieved a conviction when in November 1901 Hulton and Co Ltd were convicted of a betting coupon competition offence, and the practice stopped for a time.

Manchester, like other northern 'sporting' towns, had much betting on rowing, pedestrianism, dog racing, rabbit coursing, pigeon shooting, wresting and bowling. Such competitions were particularly popular when large stake money was involved, usually put up partly by the competitors and their patrons, and, quite often, further 'added money' put up by the organizers, who acted as stakeholders and referees. The competitions usually took place in enclosed grounds, often attached to public houses. Publicans profited by combining the sale of alcohol with the charging of an admission fee to spectators, who were often keen to bet on the result. Cultural historians have overlooked Manchester's enclosed sporting grounds, partly because most left little or no evidence of their existence. Even Simon Inglis's excellent *Played in Manchester* fails to mention them.[60] In the 1860s, the Salford Borough grounds, the City grounds and Copenhagen grounds in Manchester, and the Park Inn grounds, Prestwich, were popular venues. Leading entrepreneurs, sometimes leasing these as occasion demanded, included innkeepers such as A. Attenbury of the Borough Inn, Salford; J. Holden of the White Lion Manchester; or G. Hardy of the Rising Sun, Manchester. The use of such grounds came and went, thanks to housing development, changes of landlord, and occasional police prosecutions. By the 1890s there was a move to supposedly more permanent venues such as Ardwick athletic grounds, Belle Vue, or the Broughton Rangers football ground, especially for pedestrianism and dog races. Chief Constable Peacock believed in 1902 that at most pedestrian meetings 'betting was very largely indulged in' and was a 'principal feature'. Late in the nineteenth century trotting races, first popular in the US, spread to England and became especially popular in London and the Manchester region, run under the rules of the Trotting Union of Great Britain and Ireland.

Conclusion

A study of Manchester betting takes us back, full circle, to the various representations of the city with which this paper began. In many ways Manchester's betting world offered a parallel universe or mirror image to Manchester's Cotton Exchange. Both forms of gambling involved risk and reputation. Betting's references to 'offices', 'ledgers', 'books', 'commission agents', 'speculation' and 'prices', effectively caught the language of Manchester capitalist enterprise. Increasingly too, as the century wore on, it took up the language of class, pointing out that working-class cash betting and book-makers of 'low degree' were illegal, whilst upper- and middle-class betting was unrestrained. Lawyers defending book-makers would argue that it was tolerated in Tattersall's and accepted in the Stock Markets.[61] As one regional paper pointed out:

> As for gambling, where is the man or woman who would or could get up an agitation against the buying or selling of cotton on 'Change, deals in stocks and shares on the Stock exchange, the dealing in cereals in the Corn Market, or the acquiring of cargoes of ham or bacon in the provision market?[62]

For some of Manchester's large working-class population, many living in shocking poverty, betting, like drink, provided a way of temporary escape – the quickest way out of Manchester.[63] Betting made sense as a way of making scarce money do two jobs. At the very least it provided a cheap form of leisure and excitement. A big win acted as a potential savings mechanism, especially when the availability of work could be unreliable. Even at the very height of the Chartist disturbances, when any large meeting was looked upon suspiciously by the authorities, there was never any suggestion that the local races would be abandoned. It would have been a far more powerful incitement to riot. And the police never attempted to do much more than carry out ritual prosecutions of street betting.

At the same time, betting and the opposition to it shared the 'liberal' attitudes to the rights and duties of the individual that characterized other aspects of Manchester culture at this time. Both respected the freedom of the individual. The same section of Manchester nonconformist thought that supported the UK Alliance campaign against drink developed a social, moral and religious critique of betting. But most press coverage tended to be far more ambiguous.

Betting was rooted in capitalist thinking, and offered other social, economic and cultural opportunities. In Manchester, as in Liverpool and many other major centres, it offered significant full time employment, as well as part-time employment prospects at the racecourse or as a bookie's runner. For urban publicans, taking bets, accommodating book-makers and supplying punters with drink offered a useful addition to their income stream. For the middle-class businessmen who owned racecourse shares, the business offered another route to commercial profitability. For Manchester's gamblers, betting could provide opportunities for developing literacy, the study of form and the growing expertise to demonstrate cultural capital in the pub or workplace. Betting money was 'an investment'. For some, their gambling simply made their poverty worse. But for others, betting offered, like a lottery win today, a lump sum almost impossible to save for in any other way.

Although Liverpool and Manchester were major British betting centres in the Victorian age, it was Manchester that then led the way. By 1921, as census occupational tables reveal, there were more book-makers in the North West than any other region than Greater London. But between the wars Manchester, though still a major betting centre, found itself challenged by Liverpool as a major regional competitor. Aintree's Grand National had become one of Britain's leading races, while the two cities headed the table of betting prosecutions in the north of England. Manchester and Salford had the most prosecutions per capita, but also had a particularly vociferous anti-gambling lobby. Surveys such as the Liverpool Council of Voluntary Aid's *Report on betting in Liverpool* (Liverpool, 1936) revealed the cultural importance of betting in Liverpool, which also became a leading football pools centre. Even though the famous Littlewood pools organization first began in Manchester, it, along with Vernon's pools, found more success in Liverpool. But the later history of Manchester's gambling industry is another story.

Notes

1. For a recent analysis see Robert Poole, 'Peterloo Revisited', *History*, 91 (2006), pp. 254–76.
2. Friedrich Engels, *The condition of the working class in England* (London, 1844); Leon Faucher, *Etudes sur l'Angleterre* (1845), both quoted in Asa Briggs, *Victorian cities* (Harmondsworth, 1988), pp. 94, 117.
3. Briggs, *Victorian cities*, ch. 3.
4. Brian Harrison, *Drink and the Victorians* (1968; Keele, 1994), pp. 203–6.
5. Mark Clapson, *A bit of a flutter: popular gambling and English society, c1823–1961* (Manchester, 1992); Mike Huggins, *Flat racing and British*

society, 1790–1914 (London, 2000); Ross McKibbin, *The ideologies of class* (Oxford,1990).

6. Roger Munting, *An economic and social history of gambling in Britain and the USA* (Manchester, 1996), p. 231.

7. A. C. Critchley, *Critch: the memoirs of Brigadier A. C. Critchley* (London, 1961), pp. 132–6.

8. Marie Coleman, '"A terrible danger to the morals of the country": the Irish hospitals' sweepstake in Great Britain, 1930–87', *Proceedings of the Irish Academy* (Dublin, 2005), pp. 197–220.

9. Alan Kidd and K. W. Roberts, eds., *City, class and cultural production in Victorian Manchester* (Manchester, 1985); Alan Kidd, *Manchester* (Keele, 1993); Alan Kidd, *Manchester: a history* (Lancaster, 2006); Martin Hewitt, *The emergence of stability in the industrial city: Manchester 1832–67* (Aldershot, 1996).

10. Caroline Ramsden, *Farewell Manchester* (London, 1965), p. 20.

11. John Pinfold, 'Dandy rats at play: the Liverpudlian middle classes and horse-racing in the nineteenth century', in Mike Huggins and J. A. Mangan, eds., *Disreputable pleasures* (London, 2004), pp. 57–82; Mike Huggins, *Horseracing and the British, 1919–1939* (Manchester, 2003), pp. 83–94.

12. The Druid [Henry Hall Dixon], *The post and paddock* (London, 1862), p. 114.

13. Nimrod [Charles James Apperley], *The chase, the turf and the road* (London, 1850), p. 109.

14. Druid, *Post and paddock*, p. 4.

15. Based on figures in Turf Guardian Society, *Directory of turf accountants and commission agents* (London, 1921).

16. A. Lee, *The origins of the popular press in England 1855–1914* (London, 1976), p. 40.

17. *Sporting Magazine*, Feb. 1844, p. 144.

18. House of Lords Select Committee on betting, 1844, Strafford evidence, 26 Apr. 1844.

19. 'An Octogenarian', *Reminiscences of old Manchester and Salford* (Manchester, 1887), p. 26.

20. George Osbaldeston, *Squire Osbaldeston: his autobiography* (London, 1926), p. 182.

21. The Druid [Henry Hall Dixon], *Saddle and sirloin* (London, 1895), p. 359.

22. Druid, *Saddle and sirloin*, p. 360.

23. R. W. Proctor, *Our turf, our stage, our ring* (Manchester, 1862), provides details.

24. *Manchester Courier*, 15, 22, and 29 May 1847. See also *Manchester and Salford Advertiser*, 17 June 1848.

25. *The Free Lance*, 15 June 1867.

26. Ramsden, *Farewell Manchester*, p. 16.

27. Detailed description in *Salford Weekly News*, 10 June 1876.

28. *Newcastle Daily Journal*, 20 May 1869.

29. Board of Trade [BT] file 31, The National Archives; see also Manchester Racecourse Association Minutes, 1867–80, in Salford Public Library.

30. 'Turf Legislation', *Baily's magazine*, Dec. 1887, p. 307.

31. Louis Curzon, *A mirror of the turf* (London, 1892), pp. vi, 35–8.

32. R. M. Bevan, *The Roodee: 450 years of racing in Chester* (Northwich, 1989), p. 77.

33. Arbitration: Manchester Race Course Company *versus* Lancashire and Yorkshire Railway Company, 2 Feb. 1898, Salford Public Library.

34. Sylvanus [Robert Colton], *The byeways and downs of England* (London, 1850), pp. 305–7.

35. J. C. Whyte, *History of the British turf* (London, 1840), II, p. 625.

36. *Yorkshire Gazette*, 17 Sep. 1836.

37. *The Yorkshireman*, 1 June 1844.

38. *Manchester Courier*, 23 June 1847.

39. T. Swindells, *Manchester streets and Manchester men* (Manchester, 2nd. ser., 1907), pp. 174–5.

40. *Squire Osbaldeston*, p. 184.

41. Whyte, *History of the British turf*, p. 261.

42. *Bell's Life*, 6 Apr. 1862.

43. [Anon.], *Horse racing: its history and early records of the principal and other race meetings* (London, 1863) p. 248.

44. *Free Lance*, 26 May 1867.

45. *Manchester Courier*, 18 May 1869.

46. House of Lords Select Committee on Betting 1902, Minutes of Evidence, Peacock, QQ. 202–3.

47. *Free Lance*, 26 May 1867.

48. *Free Lance*, 25 May 1867, 20 May 1871.

49. *Free Lance*, 22 Feb. 1868.

50. *Manchester Courier*, 18 and 19 May 1869. The events were widely reported. See, for example, *Newcastle Daily Chronicle*, 10 June 1869.

51. 1902 Select Committee of the House of Lords on Betting (389) v. 445, Evidence of Manchester Chief Constable R. Peacock, Qs 152, 300.

52. *Manchester Evening News*, 20 and 21 May 1885. See J. Caminada, *25 years of detective life* (London, 1985), ii, pp. 7–17.

53. Select Committee on Betting 1902, Hulton, Q. 2608

54. Clapson, *Bit of a flutter*, p. 58.

55. Clapson, *Bit of a flutter*, p. 29.

56. Select Committee on Betting, 1902, Allen, QQ 1598–1613.

57. 'About the profitable prophets', *Baily's Magazine*, Nov. 1887, pp. 219–26.

58. Tony Mason, *Association football and English society, 1863–1915* (London, 1981), p. 175.

59. Clapson, *Bit of a flutter*, p. 163.
60. Simon Inglis, *Played in Manchester: the architectural heritage of a city at play* (London, 2004).
61. *Manchester Courier*, 22 May 1869.
62. *Liverpool Review*, 5 Sep. 1896.
63. Huggins, *Flat racing*, pp. 88–116.

Edward Hulton and sports journalism in late-Victorian Manchester

Steve Tate

Edward Hulton helped create one of the most dynamic newspaper publishing houses in Victorian Britain, a Manchester-based print centre that by 1900 was reckoned to produce almost five million newspapers a week for both national and regional markets.[1] It was a business empire founded in the early 1870s on racing results and betting tips, and one that grew to meet the demand for news and gossip surrounding the late-Victorian and Edwardian craze for organized sports. Hulton was a self-made man who rose from humble beginnings, a hard-headed entrepreneur with an eye for a business opportunity. At the time of his death in 1904, contemporaries appeared sure of the enduring reputation Hulton had earned for himself in the development of Britain's popular press. Lauded by industry commentators as 'the most original and potent figure in Provincial Journalism in the last quarter of the nineteenth century',[2] his newspaper chain stood as a lasting memorial; 'it may almost be described as his autobiography', wrote an employee.[3] Flagship titles, the *Sporting Chronicle* and *Athletic News* became leaders in the field of sports journalism. However, the newspaper group was later sold out of family hands. That, combined with subsequent amalgamations, the remorseless drift to, and dominance of, a national press, and the ultimate demise of all the titles, has relegated Edward Hulton to the margins of press history. What follows is an examination of the circumstances surrounding Hulton's business success.[4]

It is intended that this article will go a little way towards addressing the need, highlighted by Michael Powell and Terry Wyke in this journal in 2006, for a greater understanding of Manchester's role in the development of the sporting press.[5] However, a detailed history of the growth of Britain's Victorian sporting press, and the adoption of sport by the popular press as an aid to newspaper sales, has yet to be written. Consequently, this paper's examination of Edward Hulton's initiative in establishing popular Manchester-based sports titles with national appeal awaits similar studies of any one of a number of London sporting titles, together with sports newspapers in other provincial cities. Further research of that nature will help put Hulton's enterprise, and this paper's findings, in a more detailed national and regional context.[6]

Sport and the press

The British newspaper industry was experiencing rapid change in the second half of the nineteenth century. A host of new titles, priced at a penny and halfpenny, were gradually established to cater for an expanding readership and a heightened demand for news. No daily papers had been published outside London before 1855, but in a period described as the threshold of post-repeal journalism,[7] as the taxes on the press were removed, newspaper ownership, whether weekly or daily, became a viable, if commercially risky, proposition for men of relatively limited means.[8] As Alan Lee notes in his study of the development of the *Manchester City News*, 'Proprietors all over the country were beginning to recognize that profitable small journals could be run, with a sizeable local readership attracting valuable and consistent advertising, all at a modest cost'.[9] Part-time racing writer, poet and barber Richard Wright Procter provides a colourful contemporary account of the Manchester newspaper market in the years spanning the end of the newspaper taxes. He provides a flavour of the novel realization among the city's artisan classes that a regular newspaper was within their means, and of the rush to meet the new demand:

> The luxury of a daily paper is becoming commonplace, and news grows old in a few hours. Editions chase each other through the day like Indian runners, each one bearing a telegram ... There is a charming variety of fresh ventures, plain, pictorial, and even coloured, starting forth from every direction.[10]

Manchester and Salford were home to a number of weekly titles, two of the country's first provincial daily papers – both the *Manchester Guardian* and *Manchester Examiner and Times* opting for daily production in 1855, followed by the *Manchester Courier* (1864) – and one of the country's first evening papers, the *Manchester Evening News* (1868).[11]

Sports news was a relatively minor consideration for the general press of the mid-Victorian period, although with racing a key element of that coverage. The make-up of the press reflected the limited extent of the sporting calendar and the unregulated nature of several of the slowly developing popular pastimes, such as the various football codes. A handful of specialist sporting titles had developed in the first half of the nineteenth century to cover a disjointed and at times unpredictable sporting programme.[12] Monthly journals such as the

Old Sporting Magazine, *New Sporting Magazine*, *Sporting Review* and *Sportsman* had catered for an audience drawn from the middle and upper classes prepared to pay from 1s 6d to 2s 6d to satisfy their interest in horse-racing, country pursuits and the prize ring. Even the cheaper early weeklies, such as *Bell's Life in London* 'were clearly aimed above the heads of even the literate lower-class punter'.[13] But as the century progressed, a more vibrant, organized and competitive sporting calendar developed. The adoption of regular fixtures and, eventually, league competitions, prompted the press to devote additional resources to a more detailed coverage. Two immensely important cultural phenomena, the newspaper industry and organized sport, became fused and melded in the sports columns as the century matured. As Tony Mason suggests, 'Modern sport and the modern press grew up together. The intricacies of the relationship perhaps remain to be unravelled. But it's a commonplace that newspapers contributed to the growth of sport in many ways'.[14]

Possibly the most famous sporting title of the period was *Bell's Life*. Chief rivals after mid-century appear to have been the London-based penny titles, *Sporting Life* (1859), and the *Sportsman* (1865), with Hulton's *Sporting Chronicle* joining the market in the early 1870s.

A humble start in life

Edward Hulton was born in Manchester in 1838, son of James Hulton, a tinplate worker, seemingly self-employed, and textile worker, Dublin-born, Mary Hulton. He grew up in the working-class streets around Long Millgate where Victoria railway station was to develop, north of the city centre. The 1841 census found three-year-old Edward and his parents living in Beswick Row, with neighbours who included a porter, tailor, joiner, mechanic, blacksmith and printer, suggesting a solidly 'respectable' home environment among the city's aspiring artisan classes. By 1851, the census reveals a growing family living in Irk Street, with five children, the youngest aged two. Mary, classed as a silk winder, is described as head of household, still listed as married, but with no sign of her husband James.[15] Edward Hulton's grandson (also Edward) was to later claim that James abandoned his family and emigrated to the United States following a fire that destroyed his workshop. His recollection of family lore included the fanciful suggestion that, 'Rescuing a gold bar from the blazing building, he threw it into the lap of his astonished wife ... never to be seen again'. James was credited by his great-grandson with inventing 'several signalling devices for the first railways in England'.[16] Between the bare record of a working-class family glimpsed through the census, and an at times whimsical autobiography written a century after the event by an immensely wealthy descendant, a picture emerges of a serious dislocation to family life in about 1850, when Edward Hulton was twelve. In later life, secure in his position as a newspaper magnate, Hulton made no effort to disguise his rise from straitened circumstances. Hulton's *Manchester Evening Chronicle* stated at the time of his death, 'There was no concealment of the fact that at an early age he had to rely on his own resources'.[17] A biographical sketch written in 1901 mentioned his 'humble' start in life.[18] Whatever the truth surrounding James Hulton's disappearance from the records, his wife was describing herself as a widow by the time of the 1861 census. Edward had married in 1859, aged twenty, with his wife, nineteen, a cotton weaver.[19] The couple shared his mother's home with their two infant daughters and a further son and daughter of Mary and James, the son described as a cotton weaver. One of Edward's younger sisters, and possibly two, had left home to work as general servants.[20] Edward is listed as a joiner in the census, and a letterpress printer on his marriage certificate, and at some stage it would appear he was working in the joiner's shop at a print works.[21]

The picture that emerges from an aggregate of census information suggests a family 'getting by' in mid-century, with Mary Hulton successfully overcoming the hardships associated with being a single mother with five young children. Edward Hulton was later described as having served a 'print apprenticeship' in 'a small jobbing office', emerging as a 'journeyman printer'.[22] To have gained a foothold in the industry as a boy, Hulton would have needed to prove a degree of literacy and numeracy suggestive of exposure to learning of some sort. It was claimed he had been 'an omnivorous reader' as a youth.[23] Clearly, at least prior to his father's departure, Edward's education had not been ignored.

Patrick Duffy has described a printing industry in the third quarter of the nineteenth century that was prey to fluctuations in trade, with seasonal unemployment always a threat, especially for the compositor. An overstocked labour market added to the problem. Out-of-work relief was a means of helping men take to the road to seek work elsewhere, with a 'ticket' or 'tramp card' proof of their right to cash doled out by typographical societies across Britain:

> On arrival in a town the tramp needed to present his 'card' to the secretary of the local society who then gave him an allowance to cover the cost of a bed for the night. If work was available locally, the man was expected to take it and reimburse the society; otherwise he had to move on the next morning to reach another town by nightfall ...[24]

It would seem Edward Hulton experienced the indignities of life on the tramp as a young man in search of employment. At the height of his success the newspaper magnate regaled a senior employee as to how 'he had tramped through Ireland with an older man in search of casual jobbing work'.[25]

On his return to Lancashire, Hulton eventually found employment with the *Manchester Guardian* as a compositor in the 'general printing department'.[26] Duffy writes of newspaper compositors earning higher rates of pay than those in jobbing offices, 'allowing something of an elite to develop within the trade'. The compositor enjoyed an enviable position within the ranks of the Victorian artisan classes, with relatively high pay and reasonable working conditions, together with 'some prestige through the image that people had of his education and the literary associations of his work'.[27] Hulton, it would seem, had made a promising start to his working life, securing a position and prospects at the higher end of the working-class economy.

Hulton, Bleackley and 'Kettledrum'

Hulton's fortunes in the late 1860s and early 1870s were to be transformed through a combination of circumstances, with a passion for horse-racing, a keen business sense, and an unlikely partnership with Manchester cotton broker Edward Overall Bleackley central to that change. The rise from hired hand to print entrepreneur was driven by the city's appetite for betting, and a commercial blunder by the city's established daily press over its treatment of the betting habit.[28]

Contemporaries were in agreement over Hulton's fascination for, and intimate knowledge of, the turf:

> Mr Hulton devoted his leisure ... to an intelligent study of horse racing ... He studied the form and pedigree of horses; he knew pretty well what most of them had done, what was expected of them, and what in all probability they were capable of doing.[29]

His understanding of the sport of kings was said to be 'profound', with an early appreciation of the 'horses for courses' dictum.[30] Seen as 'shrewd, hard-headed' by the time he reached manhood, it seems Hulton, 'pitted his judgement against those of older men and – invariably won'.[31] Or, in more prosaic terms, Hulton 'made a book on the side',[32] standing the bets of his workmates in a potentially lucrative sideline requiring strong nerves, a thick skin, and sound turf intelligence. Hulton's judgement and luck held, and he capitalized on his reputation as a noted workshop tipster by breaking into print.

The exact circumstances surrounding the move have appeared a little unclear, with sources at times contradictory.[33] Nevertheless,

when those sources are used alongside the city's trade directories, the census, and the tipsters' advertisements in the *Manchester Guardian*, a more detailed, and more colourful, account of Hulton's journey into print takes shape.

Hulton made his press debut as a racing tipster in the mid 1860s in a turf news business run by letterpress printer George Read Clegg. Judging by the 1861 census, Blackburn-born Clegg, then aged 52, was getting by in a small family-run business with three men on the payroll.[34] In the autumn of 1865, at the latest, Clegg had branched out into turf-tipping with the *Daily Sporting Bell*. The paper, undoubtedly a sideline to Clegg's general jobbing work, advertised its racing-tips service and 'inside information' in the *Manchester Guardian*, alongside those of a number of other self-proclaimed turf experts.[35] The *Daily Sporting Bell*, 'published every race morning', priced 1d, was complemented by up to three afternoon and evening 'tissues', one-page additions updating that day's news and results from the racecourses.[36] By spring 1866 the advertisements include mention of the tipping prowess of 'Kettledrum',[37] a pen-name adopted by Hulton at the outset of his print career.[38] The sales focus of the *Daily Sporting Bell* was on the customers served by Manchester's 'Publicans and Beerhouse Keepers', with daily delivery promised[39] and the full package of morning paper and tissues offered at one shilling for subscribers.[40] A copy of the paper would appear to have been a welcome addition to the comforts provided by the city's licensed premises. The exact format of Clegg's title is unclear, although he advertised it as 'the most successful paper published',[41] alone among the tipping experts to describe his product as a 'paper', with several rivals offering 'circulars' and advice through the post.[42] By 1871, Clegg's business had grown to employ four men and six boys, and had relocated from Nicholas Croft, High Street, to premises in nearby Thomas Street, Shudehill.[43] Throughout the late 1860s, Clegg's advertisements sought to make considerable capital out of 'Kettledrum's' successful predictions. For example, in early 1869 race enthusiasts seeking inspiration as to which 'certainty' to back next could not fail to have been impressed by the tipster's publicized record. 'Kettledrum' was claiming 'nine absolute winners' in one entry in mid April, with eleven in the Manchester meeting in late May. Readers were encouraged to purchase the paper for the latest predictions, or to subscribe to a 'Private Circular' for a more exclusive service. Hulton's success was such that by spring 1870, although still connected with Clegg's paper, the 'Kettledrum' sobriquet alone was deemed sufficient to attract reader attention in the *Manchester Guardian* small advertisements, without recourse to identifying the host publication.[44] Judging from the accompanying advertisements, there was intense competition to provide all classes of Manchester turf enthusiast with information.

It would have been only natural for Hulton to be a little circumspect when considering the next step in his career as a tipster. Just turned thirty in 1869, he, his wife and six young children were living in Fir Street, Hulme, once again in an upper-working class street, but at one remove from the noise and grime of the inner city.[45] The *Manchester Guardian* was a daily newspaper offering relatively secure work prospects, judging by the profits made from the 1860s onwards.[46] At this distance in time it would seem to have been financial folly for the father of a young family to contemplate quitting his regular employment as a compositor to devote himself full-time to a speculative press venture before first testing the market.

Frederick Leary, in his history of the Manchester press written in the late nineteenth century, mentions the 'short existence' of a *Prophetic Bell*, first published by Thomas Northcote at 16 Spear Street in 1870.[47] In fact, the *Prophetic Bell* made its debut on 14 February 1871, its imminent arrival announced by advertisement in the *Manchester Guardian* four days earlier:

> The *"Prophetic Bell"* will appear on Tuesday morning, and give the probable winner of the Waterloo at a long shot. "Kettledrum" writes for this paper alone. 1s weekly, including morning paper, evening returns and weekly circular.

Available 'everywhere' each race day, priced 1d, the paper proclaimed an 'immense reception', an 'immense success', and 'wonderful success', with 'every paper sold' in the days and weeks following its first number. Edited by 'Kettledrum', successful predictions were highlighted in the advertisements.[48] Hulton had obviously split from Clegg, and the *Prophetic Bell* was keen to make capital of his pen name and his reputation, built up over several years, for picking winners. Just how amicable the parting was, is unknowable. Hulton kept hold of his print signature, an obviously marketable commodity, although the fact the new title felt obliged to advertise the exclusive services of 'Kettledrum' may suggest an element of acrimony on Clegg's part. The day after the first edition of the new paper, the rival *Daily Sporting Bell* took out an unprecedented two advertisements in the *Manchester Guardian*, proclaiming its services.

By late May 1871, number 61 of the *Prophetic Bell*, a 'Journal of Turf Prophecy', was claiming publication 'every race morning' at 6am. It offered the latest betting, details of previous running, 'latest arrivals', 'Quickest Intelligence', and the 'Tips of all the Prophets'. Promising 'a good readable paper', the editor 'Kettledrum' boasted coverage of theatre and entertainment news, and articles on 'Pedestrianism' and training. Readers seeking a more detailed and exclusive tipping service were advised to send one shilling a week to 'Tips, Northcote, Spear Street' to secure telegrams containing 'private intelligence'.[49] The evidence suggests Northcote, listed as a 'printer publisher' in the 1871 census, and as publisher of the *Prophetic Bell* in an 1871 trade directory, was in some form of partnership with the tipster/compositor. For a short time, Hulton may well have still combined his tipster work with a job on the *Manchester Guardian*, probably risking instant dismissal if discovered. If that was the case, then at some point in 1871, perhaps emboldened by the success of the venture, or made unemployed, Hulton enlisted the help of Bleackley to launch himself full-time into the sporting press, with Northcote out of the picture. Bleackley's initial investment has been put at between £100 and £500.[50] The pair enlarged and renamed the paper the *Manchester Sporting Chronicle and Prophetic Bell*. Northcote's brief involvement in the enterprise is suggestive of an ebb and flow of men drawn to the industry by the twin dynamics of change and opportunity. A Cornishman, Northcote was working as an accountant in west London in 1861, and he appears to have returned to that profession soon after relinquishing his interests in the *Prophetic Bell*.[51]

When writing of Hulton's success in later years, contemporaries appear agreed on his astute assessment of the market for sporting news in the city at the start of the 1870s, 'and the inadequate manner in which the public were catered for by the existing press in matters of sport'.[52] The city's established daily press, the *Manchester Guardian*, *Examiner and Times* and *Courier* appear to have opened the door to rival publications when, in 1870, they 'agreed between them not to publish betting news', although only the *Manchester Guardian* 'abided by the agreement for any length of time, and at some financial loss'.[53] The author of a Hulton pen portrait suggested 'This did not meet the requirements of the sporting public. Mr Hulton, with that quickness and shrewdness of judgment so characteristic of him in moments of emergency, saw his chance here and took hold of it with both hands.'[54]

Historians of the newspaper industry and of sport have noted the complex balance between a popular press seeking to maximize profits by widening its appeal to all classes – with betting news a selling point – and the subsequent charge levied against it of aiding and abetting the temptation to gamble, particularly among the working classes.[55] The shunning of betting news, however temporary, by Manchester's established newspapers in order to appease the powerful anti-gambling lobby, and to prove their standing as suitable reading matter for 'respectable' families, created an opening for Hulton and Bleackley. The opportunity was further heightened by developments in press telegraphy charges. The private telegraph companies were transferred to the Post Office in 1870, with relatively low rates introduced for press telegrams. 'For the small provincial paper the supply of news was revolutionized, and cheaply'.[56] The cost of supplying the latest betting information, results, and tips from the courses and training gallops via telegrams to the newspaper office were at 'rock bottom'.

Hulton and Bleackley were said to share a passion for horse-racing and, no doubt, the turf was instrumental in two such disparate characters meeting.[57] At the time of the shared venture, Bleackley, seven years Hulton's senior, had been a partner in the business of Mayson and Bleackley, yarn and cloth agents, since 1862. Married with no children, the Bleackleys employed a servant in their home in the suburb of Chorlton upon Medlock, their street a middle-class enclave on a main thoroughfare. Born in Prestwich and apprenticed in the 'Manchester trade' as a sixteen-year-old, Bleackley had originally been destined for the bar before family fortunes – his grandfather had established a bleach works – took a turn for the worse. His father, a large shareholder in an unlimited bank, lost heavily when the bank foundered. Bleackley appears to have prospered as a cotton agent, with the ambition and resources to take over his employer's business, in partnership, when the owner sold up. The sources portray him as something of a man about town. He seems to have dabbled in journalism from an early age. In his spare time he was a correspondent of the *Volunteer Service Gazette*, a leader writer and dramatic critic on the *Volunteer Journal*, even acting as trade editor and dramatic critic on the *Manchester Evening News* for a year, where his 'graphic and unique market reports ... converted the dry details of commerce into absolutely enjoyable reading'. He had campaigned successfully for the election of a Conservative MP in the city in 1865 (Hulton was a Liberal), and was one of the founders of the Manchester Conservative Club. He was a member of several social organizations, including the city's arts and literary clubs. Bleackley was portrayed as 'somewhat brusque', 'a trifle too "loud" and self-assertive for the tastes of some people'. An amateur actor and 'speaker of prologues', he had written a play, 'Real Life', staged at a city entertainments hall in 1872. The production ran a week, roundly condemned by the critics. Bleackley's response confirms the suggestion of a somewhat direct manner. On the closing night he took to the stage to harangue his critics with 'trenchant' and 'forcible' language.

Bleackley remained a partner in the newspaper business until his death in 1898. In a short obituary in the *Sporting Chronicle*, the paper he helped found, it was claimed, 'Although never taking an active part in the business of these newspapers, Mr Bleackley's connection with the firm remained until the end'. It was a claim repeated in Hulton's obituary in the *Manchester City News* six years later. A senior employee with the business in the late 1880s described Bleackley as 'the social ornament and orator of the firm'.

Edward Hulton in 1885, an emerging press entrepreneur (Manchester Archives and Local Studies, Central Library, M73541)

The somewhat disparaging and peripheral portrait sits a little uneasily with evidence of a more constructive role. Together with financial help, Bleackley, it seems, in the early days, wrote sporting articles for the *Prophetic Bell*, a natural step for a man with journalistic aspirations and turf knowledge. When a decision was made to expand in London in the mid 1880s, Bleackley went to the capital to oversee day-to-day operations.[58] Tellingly, his partnership in a city firm of cloth and yarn agents was dissolved in 1871.[59] The timing might have been coincidental. But equally, perhaps the money to finance the sporting title was generated by a release of assets tied up in the business. Maybe Bleackley had cleared the way to devote time and energy to the new project, rather than act as a mere cash backer. Although he went on to set himself up as a broker, he was stated to have 'ultimately drifted away from commerce altogether' to further his interest in 'sporting papers'.[60] Bleackley was described by a trade journal as 'the senior partner' in 1878.[61] Hulton appears to have been too shrewd a man and, in the early 1870s, too risky a financial position not to have made the most of his partner's potential. Described as one of the most popular and well known characters in the city,[62] no doubt with the concomitant ability to attract support and goodwill to the venture, Bleackley appears to have been an ideal complement to Hulton's print expertise. His financial acumen, too, drawn from his cotton trade experience, can only have been a boon to the new enterprise.

Expansion

The penny *Prophetic Bell*, printed in a cellar in Spear Street, central Manchester, developed into the *Manchester Sporting Chronicle and Prophetic Bell*, and then the *Sporting Chronicle*, all within a matter of two or three years, with each new masthead change a pointer to Hulton and Bleackley's progress as sports-paper proprietors. The rival tipping sheet, the *Daily Sporting Bell*, ceased its independent existence in about 1875.[63] The title became a subsidiary line in the *Chronicle* masthead – the *Sporting Chronicle and Prophetic Bell with which is incorporated the Daily Sporting Bell* – a loser in what must have been a fiercely conducted tipping and circulation battle, now all but lost to the historical record. Hulton and Bleackley had pitched their product to appeal to the same readership as the *Daily Sporting Bell*. 'No publican,' wrote a later employee, 'could afford to be without it'.[64] In 1875, Hulton and Co were also producing the *Athletic News*, a weekly sports paper eschewing racing and gambling to present news, results and gossip surrounding the various football codes, cricket, cycling, and other spectator and participation sports fast gaining adherents among the Victorian working and middle classes. At first on sale for 2d, it soon adopted a 1d price. In 1885, the partners bought out their ailing London-based rival, *Bell's Life*, and also established the Manchester-based *Sunday Chronicle*, which, with a constant eye on the racing market, featured a Saturday sports edition. The *Manchester Evening Chronicle* followed in 1897, and the morning *Daily Dispatch* in 1899. It was a thirty-year publishing record of unprecedented success, with sales of the *Sporting Chronicle* claimed to have reached 30,000 a day by 1883, and 60,000 in 1889. Sales were advertised at 150,000 daily in 1898, with the *Sunday Chronicle* 400,000, *Evening Chronicle* 150,000, and *Athletic News* 250,000.[65] The papers were accompanied by a variety of annuals, weekly and monthly betting titles, and specialist sports productions.

The business required room to grow, and by 1874 both 14 and 16 Spear Street were being used, before a move to 2 Mark Lane, Withy Grove, which was to develop into one of the most modern printing works in Britain. Hulton is credited by a former colleague with establishing a print and distribution network in cities across the North, including Newcastle, to augment Manchester's prime location as a transport hub. It lay at the centre of an 'intricate pattern of rail routes which linked it to the surrounding mill towns'.[66] Hulton is

News-boys and delivery carts pour forth from Hulton's Withy Grove press in 1905 (Manchester Archives and Local Studies, Central Library, M56208)

quoted as saying, 'I knew that there was a bigger population within a fifty-mile radius and I'd mapped it out that the railway service could deliver papers anywhere north of the Midlands, hours earlier than London'.[67]

The early decision to drop Manchester from the *Sporting Chronicle* title shows the ambition harboured by Hulton and Bleackley to attract a regional, and eventually, a national, audience. The business employed 123 hands in 1881, with a staff of 200 based at Withy Grove ten years later.[68] By 1901, the plant and building were valued at £250,000[69] and there were 'upwards' of 600 on the payroll, with a weekly wages bill approaching £2,000.[70]

Printed each Tuesday, Wednesday, Thursday and Friday, the four-page *Sporting Chronicle* had added a Saturday edition by 1877 and moved to daily production in 1880. The main paper was supplemented throughout the racing season by afternoon sheets carrying the latest betting and results. It appears the business was not exclusively a newspaper concern, with outside contracts taken on.[71] Pedestrianism, coursing, cricket, and the football codes were among an array of sports covered by the *Sporting Chronicle*, but with racing always a priority. Along with its national rivals, *Bell's*, the *Sporting Life*, and the *Sportsman*, the paper played an active role in the promotion of sport, offering prize competitions, providing judges and referees for important sports events, and acting as honest broker, holding stake money put up by opposing camps in important sporting wagers.[72]

In 1883 Hulton had won the important contract to supply the national news agency, the Press Association, with a racing service to be distributed to evening and morning papers across the country.[73] The deal stands testament to the *Sporting Chronicle*'s extensive and, no doubt, expensive network of touts and racing journalists, part-time and full-time, who were on the payroll, keeping an eye on racing stables and courses across the country, and to its organizational and administrative expertise established over the previous decade.[74] The business also made money through associated publications, such as the penny weekly *Sporting Chronicle Handicap Book*, launched in 1887, and containing details of forthcoming races with an attached free coupon for readers to identify a run of likely winners. For example, the edition for one week in August 1890 sold 36,000 out of a 48,000 print run. More than 27,000 coupons were filled in and returned. The top prize of £80 was unclaimed.[75] The penny 'stakes' on the *Handicap Book* were just one symptom of the growing appeal of a wager to the working man as the century progressed. In tandem with the development of organized sport in the last quarter of the nineteenth century, historians have pinpointed a marked take-off in mass betting in the 1880s when 'a large enough part of the working classes had sufficient disposable income to bet even on the small scale that they did'.[76] In fact, 'Working-class betting, generated by local interest … had become a mass leisure activity by the 1880s after a slow but steady build up from the 1840s'.[77] It is clear that Hulton and Bleackley were in an enviable position to make profit from both the new games craze and the appetite for gambling.

Once the partners had successfully seen off Clegg's title, the *Daily Sporting Bell*, in 1875, they were involved in another circulation contest. The *Athletic News*, launched that year to meet a demand for sports news other than racing, found itself in competition with the new Manchester penny weekly, *The Athlete*, published with a similar readership in mind. *The Athlete* was to run for six years, changing hands twice before, seemingly, giving up an unequal struggle with the *Athletic News*. The struggle was uneven on economic grounds alone. Profits from the *Sporting Chronicle* appear to have underpinned

Hulton's press expansion over the following decades, a financial prop unavailable to rival publications new to the market. The 1880s were to see an unprecedented scramble for readers among a colourful raft of speculative publishing ventures. But by then, the *Sporting Chronicle* and *Athletic News* had enjoyed several years in which to understand their market, to fine-tune the supply of news, hone distribution skills, and build up readership loyalty and editorial expertise. Tempered by competition with earlier rivals, the two sports papers proved formidable opponents to a rush of new titles.

An idea of the competition the two men faced is hinted at in Leary's research into the Manchester press. A culture of enterprise among a body of now largely anonymous print entrepreneurs is sketched through the brief mention of a variety of sporting periodicals. Modest turf-tipping sheets took their place alongside often more substantial journals covering a wider sporting panorama. Prices ranged from 1d to 1s. Between 1880 and 1889, some sixteen rival daily and weekly titles were launched, most short-lived, along with a number of annuals and sporting season reviews. Seemingly typical of their number were the *Northern Athlete: A Weekly Journal of Sports and Pastimes* begun in April 1882, only to cease trading the same year; the Saturday evening *Result*, which lasted just two issues in February 1885; and *Latest Sporting News*, published daily in 1887, but with a run of only a few weeks. More successful examples included the *Sporting Telegraphic News*, which published for about four years starting in 1880 with two editions a day. Between 1890 and 1895 a further eleven sporting titles were launched, according to Leary.[78]

Resistance to Hulton's expansion plans occasionally ended in litigation. For example, the introduction of an evening edition of the *Sporting Chronicle* in Newcastle in 1882 provoked a failed attempt to win an injunction against its sale; the legality of the handicap books and prize coupons was tested in the Queen's Bench Division under the Betting Acts in 1891, and in the Manchester City Police Court in 1900; the *Evening Chronicle* launch in 1897 created 'fierce opposition … which led to at least two lawsuits'.[79] Undoubted confrontation outside the courtroom, on the city pavements, in newsagents and on the trains, has left little mark, although the fact Hulton had to buy two sides of an adjoining street to enable the horses and carts used in the Withy Grove distribution network to await the papers unhindered, hints at circulation battles of some intensity.[80] Management at the *Manchester Guardian* viewed the growth of the Hulton business with some concern.[81] For example, the launch of the *Evening Chronicle* saw the city's wholesale newsagents, numbering about forty and who handled bulk deliveries of papers to the shops and newsboys, threatened with the withdrawal of their supplies of both the *Manchester Guardian* and its sister paper, the *Manchester Evening News*, unless they boycotted the new newspaper.[82] The sources are silent on Hulton's own techniques for outsmarting his press rivals. But the often-rapid demise of a string of now all but forgotten sporting titles is suggestive of a shrewd, and possibly ruthless, competitor. Hulton played an active role in all aspects of the business, from the 'mechanical' side to the editorial. An anecdote concerning Thomas Harris, senior journalist on the *Sunday Chronicle*, illustrates the point. Harris, campaigning as a prospective MP in the city, was described in the Manchester press as *Chronicle* editor. 'Next day came a disclaimer. "Mr Hulton," wrote Mr Harris, "is editor of all the newspapers under his control".'[83] It is unclear just how soon after establishing himself as a newspaper publisher that Hulton ended his tipping duties. The first employee to take on the 'Kettledrum' mantle was William Vicars, like Hulton a former compositor, and the pen name continued to the paper's final edition in 1983.[84]

Perhaps one charge that could be levied against Hulton was the failure to expand in London. The move was attempted in 1885 when Hulton and Bleackley opted to take on their London-based rivals, the *Sportsman* and *Sporting Life*, on their doorstep by taking over *Bell's Life*. The paper, published on Wednesdays and Saturdays, was struggling, having changed hands two years earlier, and having reduced its price from 6d to 1d. In the spring of 1885, the new Manchester owners announced to readers that *Bell's Life* would be produced daily, and that new print machinery had been bought to facilitate the change. The move appears to have been accompanied by a change of editor and senior staff at Hulton's behest. But, for once, a Hulton initiative appears to have failed, and by May 1886 the owners of *Sporting Life* were announcing the acquisition of the title and its incorporation into their own journal.[85] The sale included a condition that the northern entrepreneurs rule out any further attempt to print a sports paper in the capital.[86]

Conclusion

Hulton's stable of sporting titles thrived due to a variety of favourable market conditions. In demographic terms alone, Manchester was ideal as a print centre, with a huge population within the city, together with a hinterland made up of expanding industrial towns, all served by a comprehensive rail network.[87] By the time of the 1880s' increase in the betting habit and the expansion of organized, commercial sport, the Hulton titles were well established and capable of meeting a new demand. The North West was no stranger to the development of the late-Victorian and Edwardian working-class consumer society, with 'substantial family incomes' boosting spending in the cotton towns of Lancashire.[88] In his history of Manchester, Alan Kidd notes how, in the second half of the nineteenth century,

> Whilst the casual worker might often languish in poverty, the purchasing power of the factory worker was greater than ever and ... whole industries of leisure and consumerism arose to exploit the commercial possibilities of a working class with money in its pockets.[89]

Business success brought significant material rewards for Hulton and Bleackley. Hulton's estate was valued at £558,436 upon his death, aged 65, in 1904, with Bleackley worth £184,824 at death in 1898 at the age of 67.[90] There is no mention in Bleackley's will of any residual holding in the newspaper group, although he was still being described as part-owner. Perhaps his holding had amounted to an annual dividend on his original investment that ceased upon his death. After the failed venture with *Bell's Life*, Bleackley moved to Brighton where, in the 1891 census, he is described as a retired merchant, a widower, employing four servants. In retirement he had been a regular visitor to the races, and he had further indulged his love of the turf as a racehorse owner, with more than thirty wins to his credit. A severe accident at Chester races in 1878 had left him 'more or less an invalid, being unable to get about without the assistance of crutches and other surgical appliances', and his disability had worsened in the final five years of his life. His Brighton home had become 'a rendezvous' for men in sport and politics, and he mixed with minor aristocracy and the landed set, investing part of his wealth from the *Sporting Chronicle* in a racing stables in Sussex.[91]

As Edward Hulton prospered, the family moved to eight-bedroomed Oakfield House in the suburb of Ashton-on Mersey, and Manchester villadom.[92] His plans to groom his eldest son James as a potential successor were altered in the mid 1880s when James was badly injured in a cycling accident, from which he never fully recovered. James's younger brother, Edward, entered the business in his place, taking day-to-day control in his father's final years, with part-credit for some of the later expansion plans, including the evening paper.[93] Hulton senior, a diabetic in later years, appears to have played little or no part in public life, with one obituary noting 'the severe simplicity of his life. His hobby was his business.' Apart from his love of racing, he had 'occasionally watched a great encounter at football', and was a member of Lancashire County Cricket Club. He was acknowledged as a good judge of men, and astute in his choice of journalists for his payroll, 'a powerful personality', with 'a determined indifference to opposition, and an equally determined confidence in his own resources'. For James Catton, editor of the *Athletic News*, Hulton's chief business feature was his ability to anticipate trends in popular tastes in advance of his rivals, and to react accordingly. For the *Sporting Chronicle* obituary writer, Hulton 'not only catered for readers, he created readers'.[94]

Clearly, Hulton was a keen judge of horses and of journalists. He had an eye for a business opportunity and was in touch with public tastes and sporting trends. He was among the 'front-runners' in appreciating the potential profits to be made in a complex relationship between the popular press and the fast-developing world of commercial sport. Luck, too, must have been a feature in his business success. Above all, though, he appears to have been prepared to back his own judgement when the stakes were at their highest.

Notes

1. *Sunday Chronicle*, 3 Apr. 1904, p. 4.
2. *Sell's dictionary of the world's press* (London, 1905), p. 70.
3. *Daily Dispatch*, Manchester, 30 Mar. 1904, p. 4.
4. The absence of business records, personal papers, or memoirs has further added to the air of marginality surrounding Hulton's posthumous reputation. Interest in the business has centred on the post-1900 career of his son, Sir Edward Hulton, and his position as a Fleet Street press baron. See Dilwyn Porter's entry on 'Hulton, Sir Edward, baronet (1869–1925), newspaper proprietor', in the *Oxford Dictionary of National Biography*.
5. Michael Powell and Terry Wyke, 'Charting the Manchester tributary of the golden stream: Leary's history of the Manchester periodical press', *Manchester Region History Review*, 17 (2006), pp. 43–62. For an insight into the career of one of Manchester's foremost sporting journalists in the decades spanning 1900, see Steve Tate, 'James Catton, "Tityrus" of the *Athletic News* (1860–1936)', *Sport in History*, 25 (2005), pp. 98–115.
6. For an insight into how the role of the sports reporter developed alongside the newly professionalized and codified world of late-Victorian sport, and within an expanding popular newspaper industry, see Stephen Tate, 'The professionalisation of sports journalism, c1850–1939, with particular reference to the career of James Catton' (PhD thesis, University of Central Lancashire, 2007).
7. A. J. Lee, 'The management of a Victorian local newspaper, the *Manchester City News*, 1864–1900', *Business History*, 15 (1973), at p.71, suggests 1870 as 'the threshold of post-repeal journalism, in terms both of quality and quantity'.
8. For a summary of the circumstances surrounding the removal of the taxes on the press, see Virginia Stewart Berridge, 'Popular journalism

and working class attitudes 1854–1886. A study of *Reynold's Newspaper*, *Lloyd's Weekly Newspaper* and the *Weekly Times*' (PhD thesis, University of London, 1976), pp. 12–26.

9. Lee, 'Management', p. 132.

10. Richard Wright Procter, *Literary reminiscences and gleanings* (Manchester, 1860), pp. 33–4.

11. Alan J. Lee, *The origins of the popular press in England, 1855–1914* (London, 1976), pp. 274–5.

12. For an overview of the development of the sporting press of the period see Tony Mason, *Association football and English society, 1863–1915* (Brighton, 1980), pp. 187–203; and Tony Mason, 'Sporting news', in M. Harris and A. Lee, eds., *The press and English society from the seventeenth to nineteenth centuries* (London, 1986), pp. 168–86.

13. Wray Vamplew, *The turf: a social and economic history of horse racing* (London, 1976), p. 220.

14. Tony Mason, 'All the winners and the half-times', *Sports Historian*, 13 (1993), p. 3. For a brief review of what has come to be seen as a sporting revolution, see Neil Tranter, *Sport, economy and society in Britain 1750–1914* (Cambridge, 1998), pp. 13–31.

15. The children are Edward, James, Elizabeth, Mary Ann and Ellen.

16. Edward Hulton, *When I was a child* (London, 1952), pp. 141–2.

17. *Manchester Evening Chronicle*, 29 Mar. 1904, p. 2.

18. *Lancashire faces and places* (vol. 1, new ser., no. 4, Manchester, 1901), p. 52.

19. Hulton marriage certificate (his wife Mary Mosley was from Salford); 1861 census.

20. 1861 census. Mary Ann Hulton, fifteen, is a general servant in a household in nearby Shude Hill, with sister Ellen, eleven, listed as a visitor. An Elizabeth Hulton, seventeen, is a general servant in a widow's household in Bolton. Her details tie in with those of Mary's daughter Elizabeth in the 1851 census.

21. The 1871 census lists Edward Hulton's brother James, formerly a cotton weaver, as a 'printer's joiner'.

22. *The Sporting Mirror*, 2, July–Dec. 1881, p. 201; *Lancashire faces*, p. 52; *Sporting Chronicle*, 30 Mar. 1904, p. 2.

23. *Sunday Chronicle*, 3 Apr. 1904, p. 4.

24. Patrick Duffy, *The skilled compositor, 1850–1914: an aristocrat among working men* (Aldershot, 2000), pp. 80–2, 89–91.

25. Alex M. Thompson, *Here I lie: the memorial of an old journalist* (London, 1937), pp. 40–1.

26. *Lancashire faces*, p. 52.

27. Duffy, *Skilled compositor*, pp. 36–7, 117. Duffy notes that 'operatives who had been trained as craftsmen in jobbing offices' provided a pool of casual labour for newspapers, and it seems probable that Hulton initially

joined that pool of labour before securing full-time employment with the *Manchester Guardian.*

28. For a study of one aspect of the enthusiasm for betting in the city, see Mark Clapson, 'Playing the system: the world of organised street betting in Manchester, Salford and Bolton, c1880 to 1939', in Andrew Davies and Steven Fielding, eds., *Workers' worlds: cultures and communities in Manchester and Salford, 1880–1939* (Manchester, 1992), pp. 156–78. See also Ross McKibbin, 'Working-class gambling in Britain 1880–1939', *Past and Present*, 82 (1979), pp. 147–78.

29. *Lancashire faces*, p. 53.

30. *Sporting Chronicle*, 30 Mar. 1904, p. 2.

31. *Manchester Evening Chronicle*, 29 Mar. 1904, p. 4; *Lancashire faces*, p. 53.

32. *Sporting Chronicle*, centenary supplement, 29 May 1971, p. 15. The edition featured the recollections of racing reporter Edward Dawson, first recorded in the paper on his retirement in 1953. Dawson, who seems to have joined the paper in the early 1890s, was the son of one of the *Sporting Chronicle's* original compositors.

33. F. Leary, *History of the Manchester periodical press*, Manchester Central Reference Library, manuscript (handwritten/bound), 1889/1896, pp. 322, 334, 343; *Lancashire faces*, pp. 52–3; *Manchester Evening Chronicle*, 29 Mar. 1904, p. 4; *Manchester City News*, 2 Apr. 1904, p. 3; *Fifty years of us: a jubilee retrospect of men and newspapers by the Manchester Press Club* (Manchester, 1922), pp. 41–2; *Daily Telegraph*, 25 May 1925, p. 8; Thompson, *Here I lie*, pp. 41–2; *Sporting Chronicle*, 29 May 1971, pp. 10, 15; Mason, *Association football*, p. 200, n. 57. For an assessment of the place of Leary's work in the history of the Manchester press, and an examination of his motives and success, see Powell and Wyke, 'Charting the Manchester tributary', in particular pp. 52–3 for a detailed review of the dating of the work.

34. For an insight into the typical size of print businesses of the period, see Duffy, *Skilled compositor*, p. 31.

35. For example, *Manchester Guardian*, 10 Oct. 1865, p. 8; 11 Sep. 1865, p. 4; 7 Nov. 1865, p. 8.

36. *Manchester Guardian*, 24 Apr. 1866, p. 8.

37. Ibid., 20 Mar. 1866, p. 8; 13 Apr. 1866, p. 4; 18 May 1866, p. 4.

38. *The Sporting Mirror*, 2, July-Dec. 1881, p. 201.

39. *Manchester Guardian*, 14 Mar. 1866, p. 4.

40. Ibid., 24 Apr. 1866, p. 8.

41. Ibid., 18 May 1866, p. 4.

42. Leary, *Periodical Press*, p. 322, states the *Daily Sporting Bell* first appeared in 1868, a mistake or, possibly, a matter of interpretation as to what constituted a sporting newspaper, with the product possibly going through a number of format and content changes as it developed.

43. 1871 census, *Slater's Directory for Manchester and Salford*, 1871–2, p. 130.

44. *Manchester Guardian*, various dates, 1869 and 1870, in particular (for

1869), 7 Apr., p. 8; 15 Apr., p. 8; 22 May, p. 5; (for 1870) 6 Apr., p. 8; 1 June, p. 8; and 16 June, p. 8.

45. *Slater's Directory* 1869, p. 289; 1871 census.

46. David Ayerst, *Guardian: biography of a newspaper* (London, 1971), pp. 151–2; see also Alan Lee, 'The structure, ownership and control of the press, 1855–1914', in George Boyce, James Curran and Pauline Wingate, eds., *Newspaper history from the seventeenth century to the present day* (London, 1978), pp. 120–4.

47. Leary, *Periodical press*, p. 334. *Slater's Directory* (1871–2), p. 479, lists Northcote as publisher of the *Prophetic Bell*.

48. *Manchester Guardian*, various dates in 1871, in particular 11 Feb., p. 8; 16 Feb., p. 8; 13 Apr., p. 8; 13 Mar., p. 4.

49. Any review of Hulton's first steps into print journalism is hampered by the ephemeral nature of much of the material produced. The holdings of the *Sporting Chronicle* at the British Newspaper Library, London, begin with no. 645 for Mar. 1874, with no holdings for the *Prophetic Bell*. Details of the edition quoted above are taken from a photographic image of p. 1, carried in much reduced form in the *Sporting Chronicle centenary*, supplement, 29 May 1971.

50. Thompson, *Here I lie*, p. 57; *Sporting Chronicle centenary*, supplement, 20 May 1971, p. 15.

51. *Slater's Directory* (1874), p. 540, lists him as an accountant.

52. *Manchester Evening Chronicle*, 29 Mar. 1904, p. 2.

53. Lee, *Origins*, p. 127.

54. *Lancashire faces*, p. 53.

55. Lee, *Origins*, pp. 127–8; Mike Huggins, *Flat racing and British society, 1790–1914* (London, 2000), p. 14 and ch. 8.

56. Lucy Brown, *Victorian news and newspapers* (Oxford, 1985), pp. 13–15. For contemporary impressions of the impact of reduced telegraph rates on the newspaper business see 'The special staff', *Chambers's Journal of Popular Literature Science and Art*, 11 Jan. 1873, pp. 17–20; and Wemyss Reid, 'Some reminiscences of English journalism', *The Nineteenth Century*, 42 (1897), pp. 58–9.

57. The following character sketch is based upon: *Slater's Directory*, 1863; 1871 census; *Momus*, iii, 19 June 1879, pp. 3–5; *Manchester Evening News*, 9 May 1898, p. 4; *Manchester Courier and Lancashire General Advertiser*, 10 May 1898, p. 6; *Manchester Guardian*, 10 May 1898, p. 5; *Sporting Chronicle*, 10 May 1898; *Manchester City News*, 14 May 1898, p. 3; *Papers of the Manchester Literary Club*, 25 (1899) pp. 460–1; *Manchester City News*, 2 Apr. 1904, p. 3; Thompson, *Here I lie*, p. 56.

58. Thompson, *Here I lie*, pp. 41, 56–7.

59. *Manchester Guardian*, 10 May 1898, p. 5.

60. *Manchester Evening News*, 9 May 1898, p. 4. The balance he achieved between his press commitments and the textile industry is unknowable.

61. *The Provincial Typographical Association Circular*, May 1878, p. 7.

62. *Momus*, iii, 19 June 1879, pp. 3–5.

63. Leary, *Periodical press*, p. 322.

64. Thompson, *Here I lie*, pp. 41–2.

65. *Waterloo Directory* (London, 1883), x, p. 390; *Sell's dictionary* (London, 1889), pp. 1, 249; *Willing's British and Irish press guide* (London, 1898), p. 316.

66. Alan Kidd, *Manchester* (Keele, 1996), p. 113.

67. Thompson, *Here I lie*, pp. 41–2.

68. 1881 census; *The Times*, 1 May 1891, p. 14.

69. *Lancashire faces*, p. 54.

70. *Manchester Guardian*, 10 Aug. 1900, p. 3, Edward Hulton jr. evidence to police in Betting Acts prosecution.

71. Leary, *Periodical press*, p. 362.

72. In its first year of publication, the *Athletic News*, for example, established what was to become an annual Manchester-based athletics festival attracting 'all the Champions of the North': see *Manchester Guardian* advertisements 30 Oct. 1875, p. 1; 27 Oct. 1877, p. 1. For examples of how the stake money system worked see *Manchester Guardian*, 11 Feb. 1896, p. 3; 16 Apr. 1896, p. 3 (for court cases where the system broke down).

73. George Scott, *Reporter anonymous: the story of the Press Association* (London, 1968), p. 123.

74. For example, *Sporting Chronicle*, 3 Jan. 1895, p. 2.

75. Details emerge in a report on proceedings before the Queen's Bench Division in a test case, won by Hulton, over the coupon's legality under the Betting Acts, *The Times*, 1 May 1891, p. 14.

76. McKibbin, 'Working-class gambling', p. 148.

77. Huggins, *Flat racing*, p. 236. See also Clapson, 'Playing the system', pp. 156–78.

78. This sketch of developments in the Manchester sporting press in the 1870s and 1880s is based on a reading of Leary, *Periodical press*, pp. 343–61, 391, 408–92.

79. *The Times*, 6 May 1882, p. 6; and 11 May 1882, p. 10; *The Times*, 1 May 1891, p. 14; *Manchester Guardian*, 10 Aug. 1900, p. 3; *Sell's dictionary* (London, 1905), pp. 68–70; *Lancashire faces*, p. 53.

80. *Lancashire faces*, p. 53.

81. Ayerst, *Guardian*, pp. 297–302.

82. *Manchester Guardian*, 7 Aug. 1897, p. 4, report of legal action taken by Hulton to secure an injunction to end the boycott.

83. *Manchester City News*, 2 Apr. 1904, p. 3.

84. *Sporting Chronicle*, 13 Sep. 1897, p. 2, brief obituary note; 29 May 1971, p. 15, centenary edition; 23 July 1983, last edition.

85. *Bell's Life*, 28 Feb. 1885, p. 4, announced that the proposed move to daily production had been prompted by the 'great success' of the price cut in

March the previous year; daily production began on March 23: Robert Blatchford, *My eighty years* (London, 1931), pp. 171–4, writes of a period of tension between the new owners and existing editor; *Sporting Life*, 29 May 1886, pp. 2, 4. See also Mason, 'Sporting news', p. 171.

86. *The Times*, 19 Apr. 1899, p. 3, report of High Court hearing over an alleged breach of the agreement.

87. For population figures for both the city's growth and that of Lancashire, see C. B. Phillips and J. H. Smith, *Lancashire and Cheshire from AD 1540* (London, 1994), pp. 136, 229.

88. John Walton, *Lancashire: a social history, 1558–1939* (Manchester, 1994), p. 283.

89. Kidd, *Manchester*, p. 123.

90. Hulton and Bleackley, wills.

91. *Daily Dispatch*, 10 May 1898; *Manchester Courier and Lancashire General Advertiser*, 14 May 1898, p. 9; *The Times*, 9 July 1898, p. 21.

92. An idea of the villa's size is given in a notice of auction for the property in the *Manchester Guardian*, 28 Apr. 1906, p. 16.

93. 1881 and 1891 census; *Typographical Circular*, Feb. 1889, p. 10; Thompson, *Here I lie*, p. 43; *Sunday Chronicle*, 3 Apr. 1904, p. 4; *The Times*, 3 June 1916, p. 3.

94. *Manchester Evening Chronicle*, 29 Mar. 1904, p. 4; *Sporting Chronicle*, 30 Mar. 1904, p. 2; *Athletic News*, 4 Apr. 1904, p. 1.

Sporting cartoons and cartoonists in Edwardian Manchester: Amos Ramsbottom and his imps*

Alexander Jackson

Cartoons have long been a popular source with historians. Traditionally – and, if we are honest, this can still appertain – they tended to be used as 'wallpaper', an attractive distraction from the more serious matters at hand in the academic text. However, a body of work has established the cartoon and cartoonists as valuable topics in their own right and the best of such work, such as L. P. Curtis's *Apes and angels* (1971), a ground-breaking study of depictions of the Irish in Victorian political cartoons, has long taken its place at the highest level of scholarly debate. The establishment of the British Cartoon Archive at the University of Kent has been critical to this process and its catalogued database of over 90,000 cartoons provides an outstanding resource to students of almost any aspect of modern British history.[1] Sports historians have perhaps been a little less interested than some in the genre, although important work by Constanzo on the representation of gender in *Punch* cartoons in the Edwardian period; and Huggins's wide-ranging discussion of cartoons as a source within the sports history arena, have been important in drawing attention to the possibilities on offer.[2]

This paper, which is very much work in progress, attempts to contribute to what Huggins has termed 'a new and exciting field of exploration for the cultural history of sport' by looking at the production and use of sporting cartoons within both locally produced sports papers such as the *Athletic News* (the major source here) and the local press more generally.[3] It features a case study of Amos Ramsbottom, a prolific although somewhat elusive artist active in Manchester in the Edwardian period. It is thus largely concerned with an interesting figure that operated within the rich world of Mancunian sporting print culture opened up by Steve Tate elsewhere in this journal, rather than with that culture itself. After a brief survey of the emergence and spread of the sporting cartoon it discusses the problems encountered in attempting to research Ramsbottom's life and career, assess the major genres of sporting art that he produced and, finally, consider some of the meanings and importance of his work.

Major changes in printing technology in the mid-Victorian period made the illustrated periodical press one of the most prominent elements within nineteenth-century print culture. While many of its titles such as *Punch* (1841) and the *Illustrated London News* (1842) were undoubtedly aimed at a prosperous middle-class audience, many others including the *Penny Magazine* (1832), the *London Journal* (1845) and *Reynold's Miscellany* (1845) were much more widely rooted and found a readership among the working and lower-middle classes.[4] Cartoons and comic illustrations specifically were not a feature of all these publications, but, where they were, they clearly proved popular. *Ally Sloper's Half Holiday* (1884–1916), for example, the leading adult comic paper and the biggest selling of all British illustrated papers, had an estimated peak circulation of 340,000.[5] Moreover, cartoons and other comic illustrations rapidly found their way into the standard non-illustrated publications and added much to them. In the context of the Manchester region, Alan Fowler and Terry Wyke have provided fertile studies of the cartoons of Sam Fitton, whose work adorned the *Cotton Factory Times* (1885–1937) from the early 1900s.[6]

The sporting press was no exception to these processes. While there was undoubtedly a long tradition of caricature and other forms of comic visual material related to sport, the sporting cartoon in a modern sense appears to have become a feature of the sporting and wider press from the 1890s. This seems to accord with the arrival of the political cartoon as an aspect of newspaper production, with Francis Carruthers Gould ('FCG') of the *Pall Mall Gazette* and the *Westminster Gazette* usually regarded as the first modern practitioner.[7] Obviously, not all publications devoted to, or including, sports coverage carried cartoons. In the Edwardian period, weekly local papers such as the *Stockport Advertiser* or the *Manchester City News* and even some of the smaller dailies such as the *Oldham Standard* carried very little illustrative material of any description beyond a small number of advertisements. However, national sporting papers such as the *Athletic News* and the larger dailies such as the *Manchester Evening News* and *Manchester Evening Chronicle* included the rich material that receives its preliminary exploration below.

While the Manchester-based press is the focus here, it was by no means unusual in its adoption of the genre. Brief surveys of late-Victorian and Edwardian newspapers in Liverpool, Newcastle and Sheffield show that by about 1910, sporting cartoons and other graphic illustrations had become standard fare. If we consider artistic material relating to association football alone, Liverpool produced three prominent artists in the later Edwardian period. Lee Bennett produced caricatures of leading footballers for the *Liverpool Weekly Courier*; the Monday edition of the *Liverpool Echo* carried sketches of prominent incidents from either Liverpool or Everton matches by 'W.H.D'; and the *Liverpool Football Echo* featured three or four pieces a week by 'J.L' – the principal visual feature of the front page was '"J.L's" Football Sketch-Book' in which written captions for recent events were given visual depiction. The first such material to appear in the football and cricket edition of the *Newcastle Evening Chronicle* were the head and shoulder portraits of 'Notable Football Players' that began in 1896, while between 1903 and 1905 'T.F' provided cartoons that covered topical events relating to Newcastle United; his trademark characters of 'Magpie' and 'Geordie' represented the club and its fans respectively. Finally, in Sheffield we encounter a rich artistic seam in the pages of the *Sheffield Telegraph and Star Sports Special*, or *Green'Un*, founded in 1907. Three artists in particular produced significant bodies of work. Two of these artists signed themselves with particularly ornate signatures that I have transcribed (possibly inaccurately) as 'D.J' and 'L.H.' From around 1912 their work seems to have been replaced by that of J. Q. Williams who would continue to provide the cover cartoon for the *Green'Un* throughout the 1920s and 1930s, contributing to the visual imagery of Sheffield Wednesday and Sheffield United via his 'Owl' and 'Blade' figures. Overall, in the period before 1914 when sporting photography was in its relative infancy and probably added significantly to costs, the cartoon was a welcome addition to the pages of often extremely dense text that typified the contemporary sports pages.

The term 'cartoon' is used here in a broad sense to refer to drawings and sketches that amuse (or not, according to individual perspective) by portraying people and events in a comic or exaggerated fashion. Before exploring Amos Ramsbottom's work in any detail, it is useful to construct typologies of sporting illustrations available in the press; historians have not yet perhaps fully acknowledged the variety of artistic sporting material to be found there. Sporting illustrations in the Edwardian period generally took one of three formats. First, sporting artists often portrayed individual players. Their subjects were often caricatured with distinctive facial or other physical character-istics much exaggerated. However, as will be noted below, they could capture certain aspects of an individual's movement or style in a surprisingly effective fashion: the distinction between comic caricature and realism is not always a neat one. Another favoured format was what is referred to here as the 'match sketch', a large box comprising anything from six to a dozen sketches of a particular sporting event and covering such issues as playing personalities, the crowd and the weather as well as the nature and outcome of the activity. These visual reports became a particularly popular genre and were still a feature of the sports pages into at least the 1960s. Although other forms of social life were given such treatment, it is perhaps in this guise that the sporting cartoon made one of its most significant contributions to the larger genre. The final aspect was the single image cartoon which attempted humorous coverage of a topical issue of the day. These were in essence almost identical to the 'classic' political cartoon and the two could come together on occasions, with the boxing match a frequent element of the political cartoonist's repertoire.[8]

Amos and his imps

Local and regional sports cartoonists (and journalists, for that matter), with their pseudonyms and often quite low status within the wider newspaper trade, are often shadowy figures for historians. Amos Ramsbottom is, to say the least, a particularly elusive individual. His studio archive came to light some years ago and a number of works attributed to him have appeared in several auctions between 2000 and 2004. No reliable biographical information is available, although amongst auctioneers it is believed that (like the great twentieth-century political cartoonist, David Low) he was born in New Zealand in 1887 and apparently moved to Manchester aged ten and died there in 1967. Ramsbottom does not appear in the street directories of Manchester for the period under study here, although he may well have lived outside of the city centre. If this birth date is correct then Ramsbottom must have been only fifteen years old when his work began to be published, making him a particularly interesting subject.

What can be established is that the original ink drawings emerging at recent auctions bear a very similar signature and the same identifying device – the imp – to that which appeared on a wide body of sporting illustrations in three separate Edwardian papers within Edward Hulton's Manchester press empire, the *Athletic News*, *Daily Dispatch* and *Manchester Evening Chronicle*. Even here, however, there are slight inconsistencies. As can be seen in Figure 2, the signature on the player portraits studied here appears to read 'AR' with the date of drawing or publication underneath. However, the wider body of cartoons typified by Figure 5 normally sees a more mannered signature that might be read as 'AER', although the diagonal underscore on the 'R' can almost render the letter an 'M' on occasions, or a heart or a quasi-geometrical shape in others. The fact that the two genres, portrait and cartoon, are consciously drawn in slightly different styles, renders any search for telling stylistic similarity between the two more difficult. The presence of the imp almost certainly identifies the whole corpus of work as coming from the same hand, while differences in signature might be explained by a conscious commercial decision to distinguish one type of sporting illustration from another. For present purpose, all the material here will be seen as produced by Ramsbottom; given that the article seeks to open up the subject of sporting cartoons, exact knowledge of the authorship of the work surveyed is not a necessity. Nevertheless, it is possible that more than one artist was involved – 'Amos Ramsbottom' may even have been a collective name – and, hopefully, others might join in this search for greater biographical knowledge and certainty.

As is implied above, this case study is based upon two slightly different bodies of work. On one hand, this author has looked at a number of original colour master drawings of association footballers and similar masters of other match sketches and topical cartoons held either in the National Football Museum, Preston, or by the privately owned Priory Collection.[9] The study also looks at actual printed material from the three papers. In reality, this distinction makes little practical difference, although the eventual place of publication of the master copies is still not always known and thus our contextual knowledge can be sometimes limited.

By simple virtue of his having worked for the Hulton press empire, Ramsbottom takes on a considerable status within the ranks of Edwardian cartoonists. Edward Hulton always had 'a strong group of cartoonists working in the studio at his Withy Grove offices', and at least one of Ramsbottom's contemporaries, Percy Fearon (1874–1948), working under the name 'Poy', eventually attained national prominence in the inter-war period following a move to the London *Evening News* in 1913.[10] Ramsbottom worked quite widely across the Hulton titles. His earliest drawing yet discovered dates to the *Athletic News* of 2 June 1902 when he provided a topical cartoon on England's first cricket test match against Australia. His first football match sketch appeared on 15 December of that year and depicted incidents from Bury's home win over Newcastle United. From then on until the end of 1909 he provided a weekly match sketch during the football season and a topical cartoon during the cricket season, as well as caricatures and sketches of individual players. From 1910 onwards, *Athletic News* turned to photographs to provide the front page illustration and he moved to contributing three to four small topical cartoons per edition in 1910 and 1911. He first appeared in the *Daily Dispatch* in 1903, providing match sketches for Manchester United or Manchester City midweek matches. He also occasionally provided coverage of other sporting events such as Anglo-Japanese wrestling at the Manchester Theatre of Varieties in 1905.[11] From 17 December 1904 to 9 April 1906 he provided a weekly caricature of Association and Northern Union footballers and cricketers. His work first appeared regularly in the *Manchester Evening Chronicle* in the 1908 season, with a topical cartoon in the Saturday edition. (That the *Chronicle* felt it worthwhile to carry such an item demonstrates the depth of the roots that modern sporting culture was now developing.) He was also providing material for the *Manchester Evening Chronicle* football edition, examples of which were reproduced in the *Daily Dispatch*.

As this record implies, we are presented with a picture of a very busy and productive artist. In 1903 he produced a total of fifty-nine pieces for *Athletic News*, of which thirty-two were match sketches and sixteen were topical cricket pieces. In 1905 he probably produced a similar amount (approximately three months of *Athletic News* are missing for 1905) while producing fifty-nine pieces for the *Daily Dispatch*, including six match sketches and forty-one caricatures of individual players. A simple but easily overlooked point is that this work required a tremendous amount of travelling within the industrial north of England and sometimes beyond. Although there was a strong Lancashire emphasis in his coverage of matches for *Athletic News* – of the eighteen Association Football matches that he covered in 1903, eleven were of matches played in Lancashire, with all ten Northern Union games taking place in the same county – the same year also saw visits to Sheffield, Leeds and Bradford in Yorkshire,

Figure 1:
Ramsbottom satirizes the brass band contest. From the *British Bandsman*, probably 1913 (British Library)

Stoke in the Midlands, Glasgow (for the Scotland *v* England international at Hampden Park), Belfast and London, where he covered the FA Cup Final. That he managed to contribute material to three or four newspapers at a time was no mean feat and must have required considerable time management. Moreover, this was probably not the limit of his activities. He was certainly providing topical *political* cartoons for the *Manchester Evening Chronicle* in 1910 and items of his work can also be found in the brass-band paper, the *British Bandsman* (Figure 1).[12] It is highly likely that further research will unearth many more examples of his endeavours.

Player portraits

What makes Ramsbottom so suitable for a case study is that he drew in all of the formats discussed earlier. Probably the best examples of his sporting portraits are the eight original sketches of Association Football players owned by the National Football Museum at Preston and the further four held on loan from the Priory Collection. They are coloured pen and ink drawings measuring 6cm wide by 11.5cm high and were presumably the masters for published prints. They all date from the period 1905 to 1909 and are of leading players of the period. The earliest is of James Howie of Newcastle United (1905) followed by William Dunlop of Liverpool (1906), Tim Coleman of Woolwich Arsenal (1907), Jackie Rutherford of Newcastle, F. W. Mouncher of Fulham (1908), Colin Veitch of Newcastle United, James Ashcroft of Woolwich Arsenal, H. Middlemiss and Vivian Woodward both of Tottenham Hotspur, David Stokes of Bolton Wanderers, and Leigh Richmond Roose and Charles Thompson of Sunderland (all 1909).

COLEMAN.
Woolwich Arsenal.

Figure 2: Tim Coleman of Woolwich Arsenal, 1907 (National Football Museum)

Figure 2 is in many ways a typical example of a Ramsbottom player caricature. In the background is the silhouette of the ground and the urban-industrial backdrop that formed the settings of many football grounds in England. The constant inclusion of smoking chimneys behind the players might have reflected Ramsbottom's experience of conditions at Bank Street, home to Manchester United between 1893 and 1909. In describing a 1907 cup tie at the ground, the *Manchester Guardian* could record that 'all the time the struggle was waging the thirty Clayton chimneys smoked and gave forth their pungent odours and the boilers behind the goal poured mists of steam over the ground.'[13] In the bottom right-hand corner, Ramsbottom's trademark imp imitates the player's pose and provides a playful signature mark in addition to his initials.[14] In the top right-hand corner a silhouette of the player is also provided. Silhouettes of this type are not found in all the portraits, but when they do they add usefully to our understanding of players' individual styles and idiosyncrasies. Coleman's slightly stooping way of running, with his head well over the ball, is captured here. Similarly, the drawing of Leigh Richmond Roose, an amateur goalkeeper who played internationally for Wales as well as for six League clubs between 1901 and 1911, was particularly noted for his habit of bouncing the ball to the half way line, as the rules allowed until 1912. Ramsbottom's drawing has a silhouette of Roose bouncing the ball along at the run, indicating his familiarity with this quirk.

This facility is reinforced by Figure 3, a drawing of Jackie Rutherford of Newcastle United. This shows Ramsbottom's attention to the smaller details of his characters, in particular movement and facial features. Known as the 'Newcastle flyer', Rutherford was an extremely fast outside right with a particularly long running stride, neatly captured here. Rutherford was also superstitious, once refusing the captaincy whilst playing for Woolwich Arsenal because it would interfere with his routine of coming out last from the changing room. Perhaps one of his other superstitions was the rolling up his left sleeve whilst keeping his right one down. This detail, faithfully recorded by Ramsbottom, can be seen in contemporary photographs and drawings.[15] The enlarged head, a standard feature of the caricaturist's art, is well used here, as in all his drawings, to capture the receding hairline which characterised Rutherford from an early age. However, there is no malice in the use of this device; it simply allows the artist to capture the essence of a face or a head in a stylized but ultimately sympathetic way.

Figure 3: Jackie Rutherford of Newcastle United, 1909 (National Football Museum)

Ramsbottom's ability to portray the footballer in movement, something particularly difficult to render, is well demonstrated in Figure 4 which depicts Colin Veitch in mid-run, pushing the ball forward with his instep. Veitch was widely admired as an extremely versatile and skilful player and Ramsbottom captures his subject's grace of movement. Veitch appeared in every position bar outside left, left back and goalkeeper for Newcastle United during his career and played in four different positions in five FA Cup Final appearances. Perhaps his favourite position was at half back or midfield in modern terms. He played an attacking, creative game and this picture gives a little glimpse of what this Edwardian star looked like when he played.

Match sketches

Sketches of matches were Ramsbottom's principal contribution to the *Athletic News*. They were mainly of football, rugby and cricket (league as well as county and test) although many other sports could feature, as is demonstrated by the lacrosse sketch that ends this article (Figure 10). Figure 5 typifies the key features of Ramsbottom's style in this format. Depicting a Second Division match between Manchester United and Preston North End it is given the alliterative title of 'Proud Preston's peerless record.'[16] In the top right Ramsbottom notes the attendance of the Lancashire and England cricketer, Archie MacLaren. The rest of the piece is taken up with six incidents from the match, which is depicted as being played in heavy rain. Rather than providing a continuous narrative – the accompanying match report met that need – it offers, in effect, a montage of 'images' and 'incidents' from the game. They are, in televisual terms, more like the images used in the introduction to *Match of the Day* than the edited highlights that follow. (The cartoon version of the edited highlights approach probably emerged in the 1920s when cartoonists like 'Bos' of the *Sunday Sun* in Newcastle told the story of the match as well as selecting key incidents. More research is required, however.) Some of the images chosen obviously capture central moments from the game, which Preston won by two goals to nil. The Preston goalkeeper Peter McBride is prominent, probably due to a penalty save, and features

COLIN VEITCH.
Newcastle United.

Figure 4: Colin Veitch of Newcastle United, 1909. Note the ship masts in the right background, possibly suggesting some attempt to capture the detail of specific grounds (National Football Museum)

Figure 5:
'Proud Preston's
Peerless Record',
Athletic News, 23
November 1903

three times. Other aspects described seem to capture noteworthy
if less definitive moments in the game, likely to have amused or
captivated cartoonist and spectator alike. On the left-hand side we see
the referee about to administer first aid to an injured Preston player
by appearing to cover him with his jacket (referees wore jackets in
this period). In the bottom right-hand corner we see an interesting
example of on-field violence and foul play as the Preston defender
Hunter aims a retaliatory kick at an opponent.

Figure 6 shows a similar approach being taken to Wales's historic
3–0 win against New Zealand in the All Blacks' first tour of Britain
in 1905.[17] Before arriving in Wales, the All Blacks were undefeated,
having played twenty-seven matches, scoring 801 points and conceding
just thirty-two. There was an enormous build up of expectation

before this game and it is hardly surprising that Ramsbottom found his way to Cardiff Arms Park. An important addition to his style in this work is an early use of his signature imps, here placed in the top left-hand corner. Ramsbottom liked to dress them in appropriate national dress for international matches and we can see the Welsh imp forcing a leek down the throat of his New Zealand counterpart; perhaps the cartoonist's devilish accomplice could be allowed a level of celebratory excess denied to mere humans. Again, narrative is rejected in favour of a selection of incidents. The choices to be made must have been quite difficult, given the very low scoring involved. While the winning try clearly had to be depicted, he chooses generally to focus on Welsh players who contributed significantly throughout the game. Ramsbottom picks up amusingly on one of the game's key features, namely the constant penalization of the New Zealand

Figure 6:
'New Zealand's first defeat',
Athletic News, 18 December 1905

players for offside.[18] In a dryly witty reversal of standard roles, he has the New Zealand captain Dave Gallaher 'explain the game' to Scottish referee John Dewar Dallas.

The main features noted explicitly or implicitly above can be seen throughout his match sketches in the Edwardian period. The equivalent of the camera zoom-in on the crowd that captured MacLaren often tempted Ramsbottom's pencil. Female spectators attending rugby and cricket matches were an obvious source of interest. In 'Cheshire vs. Northumberland at Birkenhead Park' from 1903 he showed two alternative parasol styles for female spectators under the caption 'Studies in Millinery.'[19] In 1905 he again depicted well dressed ladies with parasols attending another Cheshire county match.[20] A different kind of female presence at an English League versus Irish League match was captured in 1905. This game was held at Manchester and it seems the pre-match team photos were taken by a woman. Ramsbottom added a small *double entendre* to his picture by captioning it 'a taking photographer'.[21]

As the picture of Hunter's retaliatory 'tackle' shows, Ramsbottom provides a good feel for the physicality of the game. In 'The Battle of Bramall Lane' in 1905 he covered the Derby match between Sheffield United and Sheffield Wednesday. Here, the United full back, Harry Thickett, is seen charging a Sheffield Wednesday player. Possessed of a weighty build, the full back appears twice as big as his opponent and easily knocks him off the ball. The sense of power and strength is increased by the humorous caption, 'Thickett presents a broadside to Simpson'.[22] Interestingly, match officials appear frequently in these sketches. There are two reasons for their appearance. Firstly, Ramsbottom picks them as central actors in the unfolding events. As we saw in Figure 6, a referee and his decisions could be questioned and debated by players. A disputed decision is wonderfully captured in his sketch of a match between Blackburn Rovers and Tottenham Hotspur in 1907. Under the caption 'The Spurs appealed in vain for a penalty', the referee can be seen moving purposely away from the incident, pursued by an animated crowd of Tottenham players.[23] He might also have to interact with the crowd. In 'A Battle Royal at Blackburn', Ramsbottom depicts the referee lecturing a section of the crowd with the caption, 'Referee Stark rendered advice to the crowd'.[24] Secondly, referees and linesmen also appeared as individuals with their own style and behaviour. In 'Scotland Victorious', Ramsbottom sketched a kilted linesmen at Hampden Park.[25] In 'Cheshire vs. Durham' the referee is depicted in a dramatic pose, sharply pointing to an infringement. The humorous caption makes play with a version of a line from Shakespeare's *Macbeth*, with a modern addition, 'Ha! What is that I see before mine eyes? Feet up!'[26]

Topical cartoons

The third and final category is discussed here with reference to three topical cartoons, one from the *Athletic News* and the others from the *Manchester Evening Chronicle*. These were intended to pass comment on a major event or issue within the contemporary sporting environment. Unsurprisingly, Ramsbottom clearly leans heavily in these works on the standard styles of contemporary political cartooning, offering a single picture inhabited by clearly identifiable figures.

THE FIGHT AT THE BRIDGE.

Then out spake Brave Horatius,
The Captain of the Gate:
To every man upon this earth
Death cometh soon or late.

Then how can man die better
Than facing fearful odds
For the Ashes of his country
And the Temples of his Gods?

Figure 7:
The 'Fight at the Bridge', *Athletic News*, 5 June 1905

Figure 7 celebrates the England cricket team's 213-run victory over the Australian tourists at Nottingham's Trent Bridge ground in June 1905 while Figure 8, perhaps unusually for a Lancashire-based newspaper, focuses on the nine wickets for twenty-three runs taken by Yorkshire bowler George Hirst in the 1910 'Roses' match at Leeds. While the choice of examples perhaps dictates the argument here, neither item has quite the fluidity and visual wit and dexterity of some the work discussed earlier. In the 'Fight at the Bridge', drawing inspiration from Macaulay's 'Horatius' from his *Lays of ancient Rome*, there is a concentration on making absolutely sure that England's key players can be celebrated and identified, even if the tactics involved in the later process are somewhat obvious and hackneyed. Bernard

Bosanquet, the so-called 'father of the googly' is shown packing away the 'weapons' that saw him take eight for 107 in the Australian second innings.[27] Similarly, England's leading run-scorers, Archie MacLaren (140 in the second innings), the captain F. S. 'Stanley' Jackson (eighty-two not out in the second innings) and J. T. Tydesley (fifty-six and sixty-one) have their achievements inscribed on their swords/bats. (The fact that both MacLaren and Tydesley were Lancastrians may have added to local readers' enjoyment of this cartoon.)[28] Figure 7, 'A Powerful Son of York', again belongs to the mainstream styles of

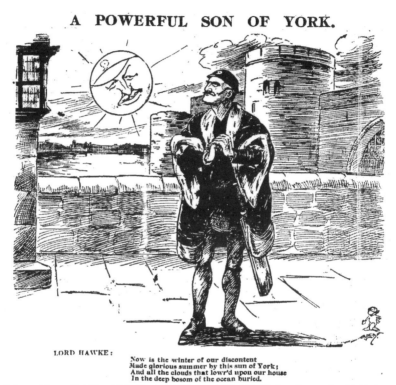

A POWERFUL SON OF YORK.

LORD HAWKE :

Now is the winter of our discontent
Made glorious summer by this sun of York;
And all the clouds that lowr'd upon our house
In the deep bosom of the ocean buried.

In the match between Yorkshire and Lancashire at Leeds, Hirst extracted the White Rose forces from an awkward position by taking nine wickets in Lancashire's second innings for 23 runs.

Figure 8: 'A Powerful Son of York', *Manchester Evening Chronicle*, 21 May 1910

political cartooning. Here, Yorkshire captain Lord Hawke basks in the rays of a 'sun of York' that bears the features of the bowling hero Hirst. For both of these cartoons, the humour and pleasure comes from the use and clever misuse of literary sources, an issue that will be returned to shortly.

A visual humour perhaps a little more akin to that found in the match sketches can be witnessed in the last of these three topical works, 'Drawing Room Football', another *Evening Chronicle* work from 1910 (Figure 9). As the script under the cartoon shows, the context here was the publication of an article suggesting that Northern Union players chosen to tour Australia and New Zealand in the summer of 1910 were 'taking it easy' in matches. Players saunter arm-in-arm, play tig as a substitute for tackling, and one leans on a goal-post reading a P&O cruise liner brochure. The normally hyperactive imp lolls in a sympathetic stupor. The combination of visual wit and slightly surreal imagination on show here in many ways demonstrates Ramsbottom at his best, offering much to smile about both to those who knew little about Northern Union and the followers of that most physical and un-drawing-room-like of games.[29]

Any detailed analysis of Ramsbottom's work and style would not be complete without some discussion of the imps which added enormously to the fun and pleasure generated by his work. Although his trademark, they could also be so much more than that. They both contributed to his sketches and cartoons and appeared as the main actors in more humorous pieces, large and small. As a visual device for use in humorous cartoons and sketches, the imp was well chosen. As a 'mischievous child' or 'little devil' in the *Oxford English Dictionary*'s words, the imp carried the imputation of mischief rather than malignant evil. Within the pages of *Athletic News* the imps appeared in a variety of roles. While in individual studies they tended to copy and reinforce the pose of the player, within the match sketch they could assume a variety of roles. An individual imp might be a spectator, perhaps applauding the play on display or holding a score-board informing viewers of the outcome of the event illustrated. In extreme weather conditions, an imp might be depicted as coping with, or suffering from, the conditions at hand. On one occasion,

DRAWING-ROOM FOOTBALL.

[A writer says that the Northern Union footballers selected for the tour in Australia have been taking things easy in recent matches.]

Figure 9: 'Drawing Room Football', *Manchester Evening Chronicle*, 6 April 1910

Ramsbottom has some gentle fun at the expense of his fellow artists (or perhaps himself). In 'Surrey's defeat' of 1907, the imp is depicted at a press desk, sketching away with a hip flask visible on his desk.[30]

Imps were also used to decorate *Athletic News* columns. Thus, in January 1909, the title 'The Fight for the Cup' was created by imps forming the letters in the manner of music hall acrobats. Several imps would form an individual letter, giving the paper a playful and creative feel.[31] Imps also adorned the title pieces of individual columns. In 1907 imps were depicted on bicycles in 'The Wheel World' and with hockey sticks for 'Hockey Notes.'[32] Finally, the imps might appear in their own right in the topical cartoon. In June 1908 they appeared in their own cartoon entitled 'Ye Wicked Imps at Old Trafford.' A band of imps were depicted engaged in various mischievous activities ahead of the coming test match. Preparations for this event included ploughing the field, planting croquet hoops, greasing the crease and setting dynamite.[33]

Reading sports cartoons

Sports cartoons and comic illustrations have much to tell us. As the work of both Constanzo and Huggins has shown in their considerations of women's sport and the cartoon, they can shed vital light on contemporary attitudes to controversial issues. Again, Huggins's analysis of the comic adventures upon England's sporting locations of that great *arriviste*, Ally Sloper, shows the source to be as valuable a tool for the exploration of the social intricacies of sporting life as a Surtees hunting novel. However, both of these writers have looked essentially at sports cartoons in non-sporting publications and it may be that the *specialist* sports press offers a somewhat different kind of commentary on a somewhat different range of topics. Certainly, there were major controversies that historians could well research through the medium of specialist cartoons. Just as the daily newspapers revealed their political sympathies in cartoons covering events such as strikes, so might sports newspapers reveal their political views on the issues of free trade and workers' rights in professional football in their attitude to, for example, the Players' Union and the proposed strike of 1909.

Nevertheless, in it is perhaps in their treatment of the day-to-day, less formal, aspects of sporting culture that these cartoons offer their particular reward. Ramsbottom's treatment of physical, even rough, play, noted above, might be instructive here. Hunter's retribution shown in Figure 5 is recorded in a way that is slightly comic – there is arguably something child-like in the action – but it carries no sense of moral censure. This aspect of the game, while in no sense condoned, appears at least to have been acknowledged and allowed to take its place amongst the variety of more or less entertaining things that happened in a match. This might provide some sense of how such play was viewed at the time. The hectoring of referees by players and crowds is perhaps another slightly 'hidden' part of sport that cartoons might illuminate. Obviously, cartoons need to be set against other sources – future work should see the cartoon and accompanying match report or article as in fruitful partnership, albeit not always an equal or mutually supportive one – but their value as an entry point into contemporary mindsets could be considerable.

Equally interesting ground might be opened up by looking at the role of cartoons within fan culture. By dealing with the 'hot' topics of the day, these illustrations will certainly have helped boost the already vigorous press-driven discussion that took place around sport, encouraging and allowing people to pass judgment on previous events or emerging stories. However, cartoons were ultimately concerned with amusing people and it is their humorous element that should most concern us here. Huggins argues that 'the humour that surrounds sport is a field ripe for further exploration' and Ramsbottom's work certainly shows this to be the case.[34] Much of our, admittedly limited, knowledge of humour within fan culture relates to the public sphere, to witty football chants, or terrace wisecracks.[35] However, sporting laughter could also take place in private or in group settings well away from the sporting arena. At the most basic but highly important level, looking at cartoons provided much straightforward pleasure. The cartoonist's skills were there to be admired. Some cartoons were intended to inform but the majority were enjoyable lampoons of sportsmen's idiosyncrasies or depictions of amusing incidents to be chuckled over. Extreme weather conditions were a common topic for comment. Fog featured prominently in the 'Cheshire *versus* Durham' rugby cartoon of 1903.[36] Depicting shadowy figures in the murk, Ramsbottom punned that it was 'a bit thick for the spectators', while in 'An abandoned tie at Burnley' from 1909, featuring an FA Cup match between Burnley and Manchester United ended by a snowstorm, he depicts a spectator entirely covered in snow and one almost feels cold looking at the drawing.[37] Attractive female spectators, footballers' dress – 'Cox's outfit scarcely conformed with the rules', he noted of a game at Liverpool in October 1905, in which a player risked unusually short shorts – and their distinctive physical appearance were similarly popular topics. Unsurprisingly, the bulky figure of the legendary goalkeeper, William 'Fatty' Foulke (six foot four inches and perhaps over twenty stone at stages of his career) was a magnet for Ramsbottom as it was for so many other of his contemporaries.[38]

Given the frequency with which Ramsbottom used literary or dramatic quotation with which to embellish – or even act as foundation for – his work suggests that the fun could be focused as much on the written as the pictorial. Puns on or cultural references to great literature have already been evidenced above through the usage of Shakespeare and Macaulay. Again, in his 'Mudlarks at Deepdale' in October 1909, Ramsbottom depicts one muddy and bedraggled player with the caption 'a credit to Kipling', a knowing nod to Rudyard Kipling's complaints about sports-crazed 'muddied oafs' in his 1902 poem 'The Islanders'.[39] This raises potentially very interesting issues about both the nature of the sports fan and the wider milieu in which sport and its associated culture was consumed. Superficially, these 'high cultural' references might suggest that the topical cartoons at least were aimed at a well educated middle-class audience. It is undoubtedly the case that individuals from such a background would have encountered the cartoons as part of the sporting culture in which they played such a significant part as players, spectators and administrators. However, the cost of the newspapers that Ramsbottom worked for (the *Chronicle* was priced at only a halfpenny, the *Athletic News* at one penny) indicates a far more broadly based audience. Perhaps the crucial point here is that 'high culture' was not in any sense a neatly defined or closed entity. Shakespeare had his devotees within the working-class community, while poets such as Macaulay and Kipling reached popular audiences in a variety of ways and may well have been popular choices for classroom recitation.[40] Sport should be seen as part of what might generally be termed a common culture that cut across and connected different social classes and areas of life in often surprising ways.

A final and crucial point is that cartoons and caricatures played an important part in making certain players extremely well known to the sporting public. Although alert to the prominence of some exceptional figures such as the cricketers W. G. Grace and Jack Hobbs, or footballers such as Dixie Dean or Alex James, most historians have tended to date national sporting stardom to the period after 1945. The assumption here is clearly that a fully mature mass media, with television as the central component, is required for sportsmen (and only recently women) to gain a media profile and recognition beyond more than their immediate locality or region. However, as Joyce Woolridge as argued in earlier work and I have tried to demonstrate in recent work on collectable football cards, the infrastructure for the emergence of 'stars' was quite clearly being established in the late-Victorian and Edwardian period.[41] The sporting cartoon played its role in this. Through a publication like the *Athletic News*, with a circulation that was, if not national, then certainly more than simply regional, certain individuals could gain quite high levels of exposure during their career.

With the mass production of cigarette cards, postcards and other collectable cards in the 1890s and 1900s, images of sporting stars were circulating in large numbers. Woolridge has demonstrated how historians might sensibly use listings of such material objects to attempt to measure the relative status of association players. To these we now might add caricatures and sketches as suitable additions to the litmus test of stardom. Ramsbottom's series of 'Famous Footballers' and 'Famous Cricketers' in the *Daily Dispatch* between 1904 and 1906 form an snapshot of sporting stardom at the point in time. My own current research into star footballers on cigarette cards between 1905 and 1917 indicates that many of the star players on these cards were being sketched by Ramsbottom in his series in the *Dispatch*. His sketches form an additional source when carefully examined.

Star players could appear several times within a single drawing as we have seen with, for example, Preston's Peter McBride in Figure 5. They could also appear at frequent intervals. Both Leigh Richmond Roose and Colin Veitch were the subject of Ramsbottom caricatures, as noted above, but they also featured in his other works. Roose, for example, appeared twice in a 1906 work called 'Stoke's Success'. The first image showed Roose being challenged as he attempted to gather the ball, whilst the second image was a side-on shoulder sketch of Roose with the caption 'Stoke's stalwart custodian'.[42] Similarly, Veitch's skills were the focus of 'A draw at Derby', where he is shown avoiding a tackle by jumping up with the ball between his feet under the caption 'fancy footwork by Veitch'.[43]

Interestingly, the *local* paper also played as significant a role here. As demonstrated by the two *Evening Chronicle* cartoons discussed above, a local paper did not concern itself solely with sport in the immediate environment and we should avoid viewing local papers as automatically parochial in their content. The pages of the local sports press, especially in larger cities like Manchester, were in some ways national pages. Ramsbottom was certainly pleased to celebrate the achievements of the city's sports teams and stars. In April 1910, for example, Ramsbottom's 'Fight for Promotion' depicted the race to escape the Second Division as a race between various bi-planes. Manchester City have landed safely, and captain Len Jones is shown shaking hands with an imp.[44] Nevertheless, he was also alert to the fact that the doings of the national cricket team, the halt to the march of the All Blacks, the build up to the FA Cup Final, the successes of a leading jockey and much else, were all of interest to some or all of his readers. Through his representation, the names, faces, characteristics and achievements of individuals from across the country, and even beyond, became part of the collective sporting knowledge and the emerging pantheon of sporting stars and heroes. The later twentieth century saw the nature of sporting stardom change dramatically and the extent of the phenomenon grow enormously, but a whole range of modest products were laying the basis for this and producing a recognizable category of 'stars' from many decades earlier.

Conclusion

This article can only scrape the surface of the vast amount of cartoon material to be found within both the Manchester mainstream and sporting press. Ramsbottom alone could keep us entertainingly busy. As more becomes known about him it would interesting to look

Figure 10: 'A test match at lacrosse', *Athletic News*, 6 May 1907 (The Priory Collection)

in more detail at the range and nature of his work in this period and the many decades ahead during which he was (presumably) an active cartoonist. Again, the numerous other artists at work in other papers might be studied, their opinions scrutinized and the changes in their approach and style analyzed. There are also questions to be asked about the changing place of cartoons in sporting culture more generally as they faced competition from photography within the press and had to hold their place in a world ever more influenced by an increasingly sophisticated electronic media. Preliminary work would suggest that it was in the 1960s that the staple cartoon match sketch or report finally fell from view, but close, detailed work could reveal this assumption and other suggestions made here to be wide of the mark. The critical point, however, is that cartoons can make comments and contributions of real interest. They should be seen as valuable in their own right, looked at alongside the text, of course, but not just as adjuncts to that text. There is much material 'out there' that can bring historical understanding as well as impish delight.

Notes

* I would like to thank Dave Russell for his help and advice on the structuring and organization of this article.

1. For its invaluable website, see http://library.kent.ac.uk/cartoons/about/aims.php. For a full cartoon historiography, http://www.rhs.ac.uk.

2. M. Constanzo, '"One can't shake off the women": Images of sport and gender in *Punch*, 1901–10', *International Journal of the History of Sport*, 19 (2002), pp. 31–56; Mike Huggins, 'Cartoons and comic periodicals, 1841–1901; a satirical sociology of Victorian sporting life', in Mike Huggins and J. A. Mangan, eds., *Disreputable pleasures: less virtuous Victorians at play* (London, 2004), pp. 124–52.

3. Huggins, 'Cartoons', p. 149.

4. Patricia Anderson, *The printed image and the transformation of popular culture, 1790–1860* (Oxford, 1991).

5. Peter Bailey, '*Ally Sloper's Half Holiday*: comic art in the 1880s', *History Workshop Journal*, 16 (1983), pp. 4–31; Huggins, 'Cartoons', pp. 142–9.

6. Alan Fowler and Terry Wyke, 'Tickling Lancashire's funny bone: the gradely cartoons of Sam Fitton', *Transactions of the Lancashire and Cheshire Antiquarian Society*, 89 (1995), pp. 1–53; and Alan Fowler and Terry Wyke, 'Cartooning King Cotton', *The Historian*, 5 (1997), pp. 17–20.

7. William Feaver and Ann Gould, *Masters of caricature from Hogarth and Gillray to Scarfe and Levine* (London, 1989), p. 110.

8. For example, http://www.cartoons.ac.uk/record/LSE1455/zoom, accessed 5 Dec. 2008. For a local example, see 'Rubber Down', *Manchester Evening Chronicle*, 5 May 1910.

9. http://www.priorycollection.com/.

10. British Cartoon Archive, biographies, http://www.cartoons.ac.uk/artists/percyfearon/biography, accessed 5 Dec. 2008.

11. *Daily Dispatch*, 22 Aug. 1905.

12. For political cartoons, see, for example, *Manchester Evening Chronicle*, 5, 7, 14, 19, 20 Apr. 1910. Interestingly, this crossing-over also saw the paper's mainstream political cartoonists tackle the occasional sporting topic. See John Harding, *Football wizard: the Billy Meredith story* (London, 1998), p. 145, for a 'Poy' carton, albeit on the topic of football trade unionism.

13. *Manchester Guardian*, 26 Jan. 1907, cited in Percy Young, *A history of British football* (London, 1968), p. 216.

14. Such trademark symbols were not uncommon. Lee Bennett's football caricatures in the *Liverpool Weekly Courier* featured a teddy bear in a football shirt mirroring the pose of the player in the bottom left-hand corner.

15. Paul Joannou, *United: the first hundred years* (Leicester, 1992), pp. 78–9.

16. Preston eventually won the Second Division championship that season.

17. Gareth Williams, *1905 and all that: essays on rugby football, sport and Welsh society* (Llandysul, 1991); for a remarkably full web history, http://rugbyrelics.com/Museum/exhibits/WvNZ.htm, accessed 8 Dec. 2008.

18. http://rugbyrelics.com/Museum/exhibits/WvNZ.htm, accessed 8 Dec. 2008. *The Times* match report, reproduced on the site, comments that 'Mr. John D. Dallas, the referee nominated by the Scottish Union, had a very difficult task to perform. He administered the laws of the game unflinchingly, and the New Zealanders had to pay dearly for sailing so near the wind on the question of off-side.'

19. *Athletic News*, 2 Nov. 1903.

20. Ibid., 13 Nov. 1905.

21. Ibid., 16 Oct. 1905.

22. Ibid., 14 Dec. 1905.

23. Ibid., 4 Feb. 1907.

24. Ibid., 22 Nov. 1909.

25. Ibid., 6 Apr. 1903.

26. Ibid., 7 Dec. 1903.

27. The 'googly' is a ball bowled by a leg-spin bowler. The leg-spinner's normal delivery when delivered to a right-handed batsman turns, on hitting the pitch, from the batsman's left to his right. A googly is delivered with the same action but spins the other way. In Australia, a 'googly' is often known as a 'Bosie' in recognition of Bosanquet's success with this style of delivery.

28. http://www.cricketarchive.co.uk/Archive/Scorecards/6/6707.html, provides full scoreboard details of this game. England did go on to win this 'Ashes' series.

29. England won both test series on this 35,000-mile, five-month tour.

30. See 'The Manchester Wheelers Meet' of 1907 in which an imp is depicted with a concerned face and equipped with an umbrella and mackintosh: *Athletic News*, 15 July 1907.

31. *Athletic News*, 18 Jan. 1909.

32. Ibid., 7 Jan. 1909.

33. Ibid., 22 June 1908.

34. Huggins, 'Cartoons', p. 149.

35. See, for example, Larry Bulmer and Rob Merrills, *Dicks out! The unique guide to British football chants* (Tunbridge Wells, 1992); and Rob Merrills, *Dicks out 2: you're not singing any more* (London, 1998).

36. *Athletic News*, 7 Dec. 1903.

37. Ibid., 8 Mar. 1909.

38. For example, ibid., 14 Dec. 1905.

39. Ibid., 25 Oct. 1909.

40. For example, Douglas A. Reid, 'Popular theatre in Victorian Birmingham', in D. Bradby, L. James and B. Sharratt, eds., *Performance and politics in popular drama: aspects of popular entertainment in theatre, film and television, 1800–1976* (Cambridge, 1980), pp. 65–89.

41. Joyce Woolridge, 'Mapping the stars: stardom in English professional football, 1890–1946', *Soccer and Society*, 3 (2002), pp. 51–69; Alexander Jackson, 'The Baines Card and its place in boys' popular culture between 1887 and 1922', in Robert Snape and Helen Pussard, eds., *Recording leisure lives: histories, archives and memories of leisure in twentieth-century Britain* (Bolton; forthcoming, 2009).

42. *Athletic News*, 15 Jan. 1906.

43. Ibid., 5 Feb. 1906.

44. *Manchester Evening Chronicle*, 30 Apr. 1910. The club eventually finished as champions.

Bowling for a living: a century on the Panel[1]

Hugh Hornby

This article is prompted by the 2008 centenary of the Lancashire Professional Bowling Association, more commonly known among crown-green bowlers as 'The Panel'. It provides an overview of the Association's history, with a special concentration on the period after World War Two. At that time, owing partly to its own popularity but mostly to government legislation on betting, the Panel expanded from its core territory between Bolton and Chorley to take in venues at many points between two east-west lines drawn from Manchester to Warrington and Burnley to Blackpool. The unpublished memoirs of Glen Howarth, a Panel player from the late 1940s to the mid 1960s, provide a substantial primary source from which to investigate specific issues such as the viability of a professional career in bowls and attitudes to gender in the sport at this time.

Crown green bowls

Bowls is perhaps Britain's senior 'pure' sport. Unlike archery, for example, it has no martial basis and it has been popular since at least the thirteenth century. There is a green in Chesterfield often said to date from 1294 (although without documentary evidence). More certainly, the Southampton Old Bowling Green has been in continuous use since 1299. That is now a flat green club, playing to the laws first written by William Mitchell in Glasgow in 1848. Before the Victorian urge to codify, bowls was subject to the same local variety noted in other sports, such as football.

The flat, or level green game, is the dominant form in Scotland, southern and eastern England, and South Wales. The alternative crown game, meanwhile, is played in northern England, the Midlands, North Wales, and the Isle of Man. Crown greens are usually defined as rising gently from the edges to a hump in the middle but it is equally useful to think of them simply as uneven or undulating.

The British Crown Green Bowling Association was founded in 1907. It includes the following sixteen 'counties' with a combined membership of 2,983 clubs:[2]

Lancashire (formed 1888 as Lancashire and Cheshire; split 1910)

Cheshire (1888, *see above*)
Yorkshire (1892)
Isle of Man (1892)
Warwick and Worcester (1897)
Staffordshire (1903)
Derbyshire (1910)
Shropshire (1912)
Potteries (1933 as part of Staffordshire; split 1964)
Wales (1936, originally North Wales)
North Midlands (1951)
Greater Manchester (1978, previously included in Lancashire)
Cumbria (1979, previously included in Lancashire)
Merseyside (1980, previously included in Lancashire and Cheshire)
South Yorkshire (1981, previously included in Yorkshire)
North Lancashire and Fylde (1984, previously included in
    Lancashire)[3]

The border between flat and crown territory is quite clear in most areas. For example, the Lake District is 'crown' as far north as Ambleside, but Penrith and Keswick are 'flat'. In Yorkshire, Harrogate is 'crown' but York is 'flat'. The only places where there is significant blending of the two are Birmingham and Coventry. In the former, for example, the Tally Ho! Club has both a flat and a crown green.

Other key differences are that the jack – the target for the other bowls – is biased in crown and unbiased in flat. In crown, the players may bowl in any direction; from corner to corner or along an edge, whereas in flat they must bowl up and down the same lane or rink for the duration of the match. In crown, singles is the normal make-up of play, with each person using two bowls each. In flat, fours is the commonest form of the game, where again two bowls each are used (but in singles, four bowls each is more common.)

The historiography of crown green bowls is not as full as the sport deserves. Only around ten dedicated books have ever been published and half of them focus only on how to play.[4] There is some coverage in books primarily about the level green code, but much of this history has been written from a flat (one might almost say a flat earth) perspective. James Manson in *The complete bowler* (1912) was particularly dismissive of crown green bowls as an upstart: 'The utmost that can be urged in favour of the crown-green pastime is that it yields a sporting, though not a scientific, game. Yet this admission must not be pushed too far. In a great pastime we have a right to look for qualities somewhat rarer and less fleeting than glorious uncertainty.'[5] The green, equipment and rules at Lewes Castle in Sussex, however, which have barely changed since at least the mid-eighteenth century,

closely resemble those of the crown code. It is probable that bowling on uneven and sloping ground, with the jack cast in any direction, was common throughout Britain before 1800, including Sir Francis Drake's famous game on Plymouth Hoe in 1588.

Bowling for money

Bowls and gambling have been linked for centuries. This was a major reason for bowls' frequent inclusion on lists of banned sports. On 20 April 1450, for example, the inhabitants of Halifax were informed 'that none, from henceforth, play at dice, bowls, or football, or other unlawful games, under pain of a penalty of 12 pence, for each offence.'[6]

The popularity of the sport among royalty and the aristocracy in the Tudor and Stuart periods was increased by its suitability for wagering. Henry VIII and Charles I were both keen players. King Charles is said to have lost £1,000 to Richard Chute of Barking Hall in one game. At a lower social level, bowling alleys were often secreted behind public houses.

Lancashire was the centre of professional bowling in the late nineteenth century. The top players, men like Gerard Hart of Blackrod and Bolton's Thomas Taylor, known as 'Owd Toss', were among the highest-paid sportsmen in the country. £50 was regularly put up as a prize, a year's wage for some labourers at that time. The games were long, to fifty-one, seventy-one and sometimes even 101 points with play split over two days. Pub landlords played an important role as promoters and stakeholders, with the Talbot Hotel in Blackpool the most famous venue. In 1900 James Rothwell played George Beatty at the Bamfurlong Hotel in Wigan. The stake was £340.[7]

Occasionally, pubs collaborated in the staging of a match. This advertisement appeared in the *Sporting Chronicle* in 1902:

> A bowling match will take place at the Chat Moss Hotel, Glazebury, and Farmers Arms, Padgate, between Robt. Nimmey and Novice and the brothers Roberts. Today, Wednesday, July 16th, game 61 up. First half (31 up) to be played at Chat Moss, comm. 2.00pm. The other 30 to be played at Farmers Arms 4.00 o'clock.
> J. Baron, Prop.

Such business arrangements were facilitated by the Lancashire Licensed Victuallers Bowling Green and Players' Protection Society. It promoted bowls as a spectator and gambling sport in the county and ensured that big matches did not clash. Betting was the driving force behind this top end of the sport. Inevitably, some bowlers needed little persuading to 'throw' a game, easily done in bowls where it is quite possible for a skilled player to miss the correct line by a couple of inches.

By the early 1900s, leading players had formed their own body, the Professional Bowlers' Association. In October 1908, shortly after the Players' Union for football was also set up in Manchester, they met with the Green Owners' Association in the same city. The *Sporting Chronicle* reported that 'the new association which will be formed will leave no stone unturned to purge the game from those undesirable elements which have crept into it'.[8] This body became the Lancashire Professional Bowling Association (LPBA), soon commonly known as the Panel after the group of players selected to perform.

Professional and amateur bowling were never totally separate worlds, with players allowed to move back and forth, unlike in rugby. Between the two World Wars, the LPBA sponsored an Annual Charity Handicap which was opened up to amateurs as well as its own members. The Springfield Hotel in Wigan was the usual venue. Indeed, charity fundraising was a constant aim of the Association, especially towards the provision of hospital beds. £10,000 was given to the Red Cross during World War Two. Panel men were allowed to enter the limited number of open competitions then organized as well. The biggest of these were the Talbot and Waterloo handicaps in Blackpool, and the *News of the World* tournament in Preston.

Miners made up a good proportion of the Panel's support. The regular venues for matches in Wigan, Bolton and Chorley were close to a number of collieries and many men came off shift at lunch-time and went to watch the bowls in the afternoon in the fresh air. There is a strong connection between mining, sport and gambling in other parts of Britain.[9]

The Panel

In the results round-up of the *Daily Telegraph's* sports supplement you will still find:

> Crown Green Bowling
> PANEL (Red Lion, Westhoughton)

The Red Lion, right in the centre of Westhoughton, is now the LPBA's headquarters. The Association bought the green for £12,000 in 2005 to provide a secure home. The green is across the road from the pub, behind a patch of waste ground. With only occasional forays to Blackpool, or other locations nearby if work is being done on the green, there are two matches here 250 days a year. The Panel operates Monday to Friday, whatever the weather. If it snows (not so common in the current climate) a lane is swept clear and the bowlers go up and down the same strip for the duration of the game.

A 1953 feature in the *Manchester Guardian* was headlined:

> *CATACLYSM STOPPED PLAY?*
> *Little Else Likely to Interfere With Professional Play*

The writer noted that: 'A few days earlier from the correspondent's visit, for instance, there was thick fog but the game went on. When bowlers could no longer see the jack a man in a white apron stood over it with a hurricane lamp. If the green is flooded they have a cobbing match, throwing the bowls instead of rolling them and spinning them so that they skim over the puddles.'[10]

The Panel has certain rules of play which differ from those of crown green bowling more generally. Most notably, the players are allowed a second attempt to send the jack if they bowl it off the green into the ditch the first time. Ordinarily, the other player would then send it in a direction and to a distance of his choosing. The players do not pick up the mat (on which they place one foot to deliver a bowl) at the conclusion of each end of play but rely on a marker, who follows them around the green, throwing down one of the several which are in use. This speeds the game up.

The most notable feature about the gambling is that bets can be laid as well as taken by anyone who is interested. Years ahead of internet exchanges like Betfair, Panel men were making both sides of a bet, competing for business by offering more generous odds. All bets are

The Red Lion: the stables are long gone and the Panel has yet to feature on Sky Sports (Peter Holme)

on credit, recorded in notebooks and settled at the end of a match. The ideal is to end up with 'two winners' by backing one player and then re-entering the market during the course of a match to bet on the opponent at long odds if their man takes a strong lead.

The Panel is split into two groups of players, known as the first and second panel. The stronger players are in the former and generally play others in the same group. All games are handicapped by the committee to make a close game more likely, with the outsider also given the jack at the first end.

Glen Howarth

Glen Howarth, born in 1902, was from Haslingden in east Lancashire and came to prominence as an amateur bowler there between the world wars. During the second of these, though, he was living in Manchester and working in a motor works at Knott Mill. His memoirs, written after he retired from playing on the Panel in 1966, are an honest account of his career, full of gripes as well as funny stories. They give a full and valuable account of Panel bowling halfway through its first century. Fifty years earlier, the top matchplay bowlers had been very well rewarded but Howarth describes a tougher economic climate in post-war Britain. The memoirs begin with his desire to play bowls for a living in the spring of 1944:

I don't know why I had this sudden thought to become a professional and I had a talk with the wife about it. She said it would be all right provided we had something to fall back to, provided I was not successful in the event of me going professional. She said that if we could get a small business which she could manage, it would be OK for both of us.[11]

Lacking the money to buy a business, Howarth entered a bowls competition in Stockport in July 1944, a 41-up handicap with 64 entries for a first prize of £50. He also backed himself with a bookmaker, staking £6 to win £100. He had never played in the area before. The competition was played on a number of different greens and Howarth made early progress before scraping through his semi-final at Hazel Grove 41–40:

I would like to say here that this handicap was well patronized and it was common for 200 people to be there, for there was a lot of betting went on quietly. In the final I had to play T. Kershaw, a well known bowler from Hyde. We played at the Crown Hotel, Stockport Road on July 28th before a very large crowd. I had been promised quite a few backhanders if I won, and I reckoned on clearing about £175 in the event of winning, which to me wouldn't be a bad nights work. I might add that every time I was due to play, I didn't go to work in the afternoon but went to bed instead.[12]

Losing 33–40 to Kershaw, Howarth's dreams of a new career were fading. However, he then chose to play a mark on which he had lost several ends in a previous round and 'ran out' (see Glossary) to win 41–40. His only disappointment was that none of the promised backhanders materialized:

It was now the turn of the wife to have a look round for a small business that would suit her, for she was the one who would have to attend to it, and after a bit of scouting round we eventually got one on the corner of Bland Street, Moss Side. It wasn't in what you might call a posh quarter but the business looked OK and it could be improved upon. We hadn't quite enough cash to buy it but with a little help from my brother Harry, we clinched the deal and moved in.[13]

After several trial matches, Howarth was accepted as a regular Panel player in 1945. He won thirty-eight of his seventy-nine matches that year. His goal was to take on the top men: Jack Rothwell from Rochdale and Albert Jackson from Leigh. The LPBA had around 600 members at this time, paying five shillings a year to join.

In fact it took several years for Howarth to establish himself as one of the strongest players. He had an emergency operation for a poisoned goitre in 1950 and moved out of Manchester to help his recovery, settling at Kearsley. As older men retired and his knowledge of the greens increased, he became more successful.

Jackson was warned off in 1951, under suspicion of losing games deliberately. Howarth finally made it to the first panel the following year:

> As I have said earlier the wages were nothing great so much so that when we came to live at Kearsley my wife had to go out to work so that we could keep appearances up. I didn't like the idea of her going out to work but as I was turned 50 I knew it wouldn't be easy for me to get a job if I gave up panel bowling for as I told the wife things would go better before worse.[14]

The Howarths finally moved back to Haslingden in 1963. They had acquired a car by then and Mrs Howarth acted as chauffeur for Glen's last seven years on the Panel:

> When we were there she attended to my food and during the game she always brought me a cup of coffee. If I was in front the fellows would tell her I didn't need it, but if I was behind they would ask her if she had put a few chalks in the cup. Another thing she always did was to see that my underclothes were aired if possible whenever I came off the green wet through.[15]

She would have been in a very small minority as a woman at the Panel. This gender bias has not changed.

Howarth's professional career culminated in his record 41–3 win over Jackie Grimes of Leigh at Belle Vue in Blackpool on 29 July 1964. Increasingly hampered by osteoarthritis in his knee, he retired from the Panel in 1966. He continued to play as an amateur.

Earning a living

Howarth and the small band he joined were in a marginal occupation. Outside association football, there were very few opportunities for a full-time career in sport. County cricketers, for example, were only employed during the summer months.

The closest sport to the Panel, in terms of geography and the social background of players and supporters, is Rugby League. In the 1950s and 60s, however, there were no professional players – all had other jobs to make up a living wage. As detailed by Tony Collins, Rugby League players in the 50s were also engineers, drivers, fitters and bricklayers, among many occupations.[16]

Clause 3 of the Rugby Football League's standard player contract stated that: 'the player shall have the right to refuse to play when called upon, if by his playing he would jeopardise his position at his ordinary work or be likely to lose such work.' [17]

With training a couple of nights a week and matches on Saturday afternoons, it was perfectly possible to combine a Rugby League career with a full-time job. Panel bowlers, however, had to be available to play from Monday to Friday, in the afternoons, all year round.

Howarth noted of 1958: 'In April our basic wage was raised to £3 per match. I should have mentioned earlier that owing to the shortage of greens and the poor crowds we had ceased to play on Saturdays for a good few years, but in June we started to play again on Saturdays which was a good thing from the bowlers point of view for it meant an extra match for 4 players.' [18] A percentage of the gate money was also paid to the players and there were bonuses for the best performers each month. On 6 July 1959, the games held at the Talbot in Blackpool were a long-service benefit for Howarth.

Jimmy Cunliffe, who was a goal-scoring left winger for Everton through the 1930s, became a Panel player in 1958 but took a long time to settle 'because he wasn't secure and he told me more than once that he was sorry he gave his job up, for as he said that on this Panel bowling there was no holidays with pay and there was no superannuation when you finished your career on the Panel.' [19] Some of the players had regular jobs which fitted in with their bowling. Vernon Lee from Chadderton had a milk round. His refusal to play on the Panel on Saturdays, his collecting day, was one of Howarth's bugbears. Jerry Cornwell of Chorley worked nights for Ribble Buses. [20]

Howarth regularly complained about the Panel's refusal to pay the players' 'stamp' for National Insurance. For example in 1947:

> This stamp business was a sore point with me, the reason being that the association told us who we had to play and where we had to play and when we had to play so I ask you how could we be classed as self employed. I wrote to the legal adviser of the *News of the World* on this matter and explained everything to him whereupon his reply was to the effect that in his opinion we were employed by the association and they should put the stamp on. [21]

The fact that income tax was deducted from the players' wages by the association only increased Howarth's frustration – they had to wait until the end of the tax year in April to claim back for travel, food, clothing and bowls. He never won this argument in over twenty years on the Panel.

From checking his diaries (1949's had been lost), Howarth reckoned to have played over 3,000 Panel matches on 115 different greens when he retired from the paid ranks in 1966, 'and as the average mileage for a game is between 3½ and 4½ miles it appears that I have covered in the region of 11,000 miles on the green, no wonder my legs are bad'.[22] He also remembered many stories about his time. These would have formed part of the banter of the regulars, still a major part of the attraction of the Panel and crown green bowling in general. For example:

> I have also known a few spectators die during the course of a game, but whether it was through excitement we shall never know. There was one case of a fellow who went in the toilets at Irlam and tried to cut his wrists with a razor blade because he had lost his cash and from what I heard later it was only a matter of £3. It's a good thing that everyone who loses at this game don't try to commit suicide or there would be no one coming some days.[23]

Howarth mentions the many sets of bowls he owned to suit different greens and weather conditions, 'from 2lb 15oz down to 2lb 6oz and bias from 2½ to 3 full. [The standard now is 2 full bias, meaning that the bowls are 'weaker' than of old and curve less as they travel.] I had about 8 sets of bowls and that wasn't many compared with some of the players.'[24] He goes on:

> Of course some of the other players who had not so many sets would occasionally borrow a set from you. The worst offender for this was [Johnny] Featherstone for I don't think he had above two sets of bowls and he knew when he came into the game that he would require more bowls but he would rather borrow than buy … The story I am going to tell may seem hard to believe but it is true. I was matched to play Featherstone at Robin Hood and I had no intention of playing these good set of bowls so Featherstone asked me could he borrow them but I said no as I was playing with them. But Featherstone wasn't going to be outdone and he waited until I went on the green to start the match and then he went in my bag and got these bowls and he came on the green with them and he beat me with those bowls.

Bowls has always been known for its characters. Glen Howarth remembered one from Bolton, Harry Peers:

> Now this chap was about 24 stone and 6 foot and he was good to get on with. He used to like a pint of beer and it is said that he made a wager that he could drink 50 pints of beer between 7 o'clock and 10 o'clock and he won his wager. He was also a very good eater as also was Albert Jackson and these two had an eating contest at Moor Park Conservative Club [Preston] which Jackson

Two current Panel stars: Chris Morrison delivers while Noel Burrows watches (Peter Holme)

won by a piece of cake ... Another time the domino men were having a session at Farnworth Con Club and they felt a bit peckish so they gave Harry some money and sent him out for some grub. Now it happened to be Wednesday which was early closing day at Farnworth and the only thing Harry could get was 4½ lb of tripe which he duly brought back to the club. Of course the domino players wanted something more substantial than tripe and they told Harry what to do with the tripe whereupon he sat down and ate the lot.[25]

The 1947 dispute

Howarth's early years on the Panel included its biggest crisis. There was a long break in matches in the first quarter of 1947, caused by police investigation of the relevance of the 1934 Betting and Lotteries Act. Panel members were suspected of gambling illegally on the outcome of matches. Unfortunately, the LPBA minutes have been lost and the story is therefore based on Howarth's recollections and a few pieces by the *Sporting Chronicle's* regular Panel correspondent, Jack Davies, who wrote under the name 'Touchwood'. Howarth had his own ideas about the origin of the dispute, noting:

> there was trouble brewing amongst the officials which was to turn out bad for the panel for a good few months. At the General

Meeting H. Martin lost his position as President to be replaced by C. Yates, from Horwich and H. Martin didn't take his defeat too well. It may have been a coincidence but soon after H. Martin lost his position as President the panel ceased to play for a month or two owing to the intervention of the Police who implemented the 1934 Betting Act which meant that the panel could only play 8 times a year on any one green.[26]

Previously, around a dozen greens had been used much more frequently, including the Yarrow Bridge and Robin Hood at Chorley and the Seven Stars, Standish.

The winter of 1947 was one of the worst of the century. Manchester had snow cover on every day except three from 27 January to 16 March.[27] This turned the already serious post-war fuel shortage into a national emergency. Representatives of the major spectator sports – football, rugby, horse-racing, greyhound racing, speedway and ice hockey – were summoned to London on 10 March to discuss a ban on midweek sport.[28] The government's concerns were aired by the Home Secretary, Chuter Ede, and the Minister for Fuel, Manny Shinwell. In addition to the need to conserve fuel directly by not staging fixtures, there was a feeling that absenteeism, particularly by miners wishing to watch sport, was affecting productivity. A ban was announced from Monday 17 March and plans were made to move key events, like the Grand National steeplechase at Aintree, to a Saturday. There followed days of uncertainty over how to finish the football season, given that hundreds of matches had already been postponed because of the weather. The status of amateur and junior sport was also unclear. Dewsbury Rugby League club announced its attention to defy the ban by playing Wakefield Trinity as scheduled. The Rugby Football Union then declared its opposition too. The ban never really started.

In such a situation, it is perhaps not surprising that the Panel took such a long time to resolve its own problems. On 12 March, 'Touchwood' wrote in the *Sporting Chronicle*:

> Apart from yesterday's talks on the future of mid-week sport, the Lancashire Professional Bowling Association yesterday sent a deputation to the Home Office and also to contact certain Members of Parliament. Theirs is a complaint that there is undue interference by certain local authorities with their panel match games, and they are trying to find out if such instructions emanate from the Home Office or from local authorities. This interference takes the form of hints to green-owners that their public-house licence might be jeopardized if they allowed the use of their greens for certain matches. Both the Home Office and the contacted Members of Parliament will be reminded of official promises made

when the 1934 Betting and Lotteries Act was passed that sports and games, such as bowls, would not be affected by the Act.[29]

On 21 March the Association secretary James Stratton, and committee member William Frost, took a petition to the House of Commons, supported by legal advice.

'Touchwood' noted: 'The LPBA are faced with either a test case or an amendment of the 1934 Betting and Lotteries Act to absolve their greens being classed as "tracks"'.[30]

By 9 April, there was no progress. Howarth and his colleagues still had no income. 'Touchwood' reported:

> The LPBA may decide to apply for a licence under this Act which would permit 108 promotions per year [sic] on a particular green. This could be repeated with other greens and so make up the daily round as before. That, however, would mean the abandonment of the original claims, which have stood so well for nearly 12 years, namely:– (1) That bowling and bowling greens do not and were never intended by Parliament to come within the scope of the 1934 Act. (2) That wagering on bowling was legal because it was on credit, and not in or on a 'place' within the meaning of earlier Acts.[31]

However, legal advice included concern that, in the words of 'Touchwood', 'several transactions repeatedly turned over at a small percentage either way [...] might be construed to be professional bookmaking.' The article went on: 'The old-timers remember the advent of this type of wagering about 25 to 30 years ago. It was the invention of a bowling follower with the appropriate nom de guerre of "Puddin' of Bury"'. It seems that this was the nub of the problem. The Association was reluctant to apply for licences for a handful of greens because this would be an admission that it was bound by the terms of the 1934 Act. However, the nature of the gambling which went on at the Panel, with spectators offering odds and engaging in multiple bets, was a worry to the committee. In early May it was decided to restart on the basis of only using a venue eight times a year. This effectively meant a policy of moving around the whole north-west region.

Play recommenced on Whit Monday, 26 May, at the Hulton Arms, Four Lane Ends near Bolton.[32] Jack Rothwell beat Albert Jackson 41–40, with both men starting off scratch; then Tom Mayor from Bolton, receiving one start, defeated Harry Winstanley from Wigan, again by 41–40.

'Touchwood' reported in the *Sporting Chronicle* on 31 May: 'The resumption of rationed Panel match bowling was a big success. Many other venues are being prepared under the "eight dates per green per year" order and soon three or four days per week will be scheduled.' The Secretary now had to apply to the relevant police force in writing, at least seven days in advance, for the use of a green. Not surprisingly, it took some weeks for a full programme to be organized and initially there was a reliance on the old favourite venues. See, for example, the June 1947 programme:

Mon 2 Springfield Hotel, Wigan
Wed 4 Red Lion, Westhoughton

Mon 9 George & Dragon, Whelley
Wed 11 Robin Hood, Chorley
Thu 12 Springfield Hotel

Mon 16 Hulton Arms, Four Lane Ends
Wed 18 George & Dragon
Thu 19 Springfield Hotel
Fri 20 Robin Hood

Mon 23 Yarrow Bridge, Chorley
Tue 24 Red Lion
Wed 25 Robin Hood
Thu 26 George & Dragon

Glen Howarth did not look back fondly on 1947. 'I only drew £75 for the whole year and I had to pay expenses and put a stamp on out of that so there wasn't much left, and it was a good job I had a small business or else Panel bowling would have gone by the board, and I

An advert for a charity bowling match (Manchester Archives and Local Studies, Central Library, M06775)

didn't want that to happen so soon.'[33] (An unskilled manual worker earned around £300 a year at this time.) He also made reference to the new system: 'If it didn't suit the police they would not allow us to play, also when we did play the police would come to the match and enquire how many spectators were there.'[34] Attendances at the Panel dropped as it entered new territory, further from its regular supporters. A coach firm from Chorley began to run a bus to the venue every day. This service was copied in Bolton, Leigh and Manchester.

New licences

In March 1957, the landlord of the Robin Hood at Chorley, with the support of the LPBA, applied for a licence to hold 104 matches a year.[35] It was granted and from then on, this was the venue every Monday and Thursday. This move, ruled out by the Association in 1947 during the long dispute, now saved the secretary at least some of his work.

Despite the change of tack, it was another four years before four other places followed suit, prompted by the shutting down of the Robin Hood in February 1961. These were the Hulton Arms at Four Lane Ends on the western edge of Bolton, the Springfield Hotel at Wigan, the Red Lion at Westhoughton, and the George and Dragon at Whelley. On Mondays, Wednesdays and Thursdays, the first two were used during one month and the last two the next. Finally, the Panel was able to settle back fully into its favoured area of Lancashire again, for the first time since the war.[36] With the requirement to use a large number of greens and adhere to the eight-times-a-year maximum rule, the geography of the Panel had thus extended far from its heartland – the triangle between Chorley, Bolton and Wigan – in the fifteen years after World War Two. Games were played as far west as Southport, as far north as Nelson, as far east as Hyde and as far south as Fearnhead on the edge of Warrington.

This was a test for the players, since they liked to get to know the greens well. The backers and layers were quick to voice their discontent if the bowls were sprayed around and this was more likely on a strange green. Although the regulars were inconvenienced by having to travel further, it brought the Panel and its leading players within reach of new fans. Don Lyons, editor of Howarth's memoirs, was just taking up the game in 1955, aged twenty-one. He travelled to the London Hotel in Southport for one of the extra evening matches then being held. Glen Howarth was playing Seth Wane of Bolton:

> As far as I was concerned it was very much an eye opener. It was the first time I had ever seen so much fast striking in one game and

I had never seen ends being played along the edges of a green for at that time in the amateur game as distinct from the professional one, the four-yard markers were in operation. It was an illegal mark if footer and jack were four yards from the same edge. As if that was not enough, the shouting by bookmakers and punters really took me by surprise, particularly as I did not understand any of it.[37]

The future of the Panel

Despite the problems of 1947 and the ensuing need to use many different venues, this was still a successful period for the Panel, as it was for many sports. The end of World War Two encouraged attendance. Crown green bowls was colourful and entertaining.

A new generation of players appeared on the Panel in the late 1960s after Howarth retired, including Norman Fletcher from Leigh, and Brian Duncan from Orrell. The standard of play in this period was reckoned to be extremely high, with Cunliffe still hard to beat. Winning players now received £8, and losers £6.[38] Duncan is considered to be the greatest-ever crown-green player, having won five Waterloo Handicaps.

There is some gloom about the future in the LPBA's centenary year, although that is true of the sport as a whole. With increasing numbers of leagues and small competitions, people are playing crown green bowls more but watching it less. It was always the crowd which 'made' the Panel and numbers today rarely reach three figures. With rising prosperity and less shift work around, fewer of the top men in the game are now willing or able to join the Panel. The Association now *charges* every player £10 a match, so only the winner, who gets £30, is sure to make anything. There is certainly not enough money available for a man to live on his Panel income as Glen Howarth did, with the notable support of Mrs Howarth.

Appendices

i) **Scoring**: the normal length of a match in crown-green bowls is '21 up', that is to say the first player to reach 21 points, in a combination of ones and twos, is the winner. The player whose bowl is nearest to the jack scores one point. If both his bowls are nearer the jack than either of his opponent's, he scores two. Unlike some other sports (table tennis, badminton, volleyball), there is no requirement to be two points clear and 21–20 is a common outcome.

On the Panel, longer games have always been preferred. 31, 41 and 51 have been the most common winning scores and 41 up is now the

The score is 21–20: game over in most crown green bowling but not on the Panel (Peter Holme)

standard. The longer duration allows for more fluctuations in fortunes and therefore more betting opportunities.

ii) Locations/greens used by the Panel (1947–61): There is a marked difference in the type of bowling clubs prevalent in crown- and flat-green bowling. The latter now relies largely on private clubs, with bigger memberships on average. Public-house greens remain much more common in crown green, along with those at political and works' clubs. The list of greens used by the Panel during its enforced wanderings reflects this balance.

Pub greens are, however, also much less secure than privately owned ones. Many, including most of those listed here, have now been turned into car parks, beer gardens or building extensions. The Yarrow Bridge on Bolton Road at Chorley now has a Premier Travel Inn behind it instead of a bowling green. In Blackpool, the Talbot, Belle Vue, and No 3 greens have all been lost.

Pubs

London Hotel, Southport
Railway Hotel, Ainsdale
Cambridge Hotel, Burscough
Waterloo Hotel, Talbot Hotel,
    Raikes Hall, Belle Vue, No 3
    and Highfield, Blackpool

Pickups Arms, Church
Horse and Farrier, Rochdale
Birches Head, Whitworth
Railway, Bury
Robin Hood and Yarrow Bridge
    Hotel, Chorley

Park Hotel, Higher Ince
George and Dragon, Whelley
Queens Arms, Orrell
Bryn Hall Hotel, Bryn
Hare and Hounds, Radcliffe
Wagon and Horses, Adlington
Lord Nelson, Hindley Green
Springfield Hotel, Wigan
Westwood Hotel, Poolstock
Caledonian Hotel and Bay
    Horse, Ashton-in-Makerfield
Red Lion, Westhoughton

Hulton Arms and Sunnyside
    Hotel, Bolton
Seven Stars, Standish
Crown Hotel, Worthington
Brown Cow, Winton
Lord Nelson, Pendlebury
Star Inn, Failsworth
Grapes, Hyde
Railway, Cadishead
Phoenix, Heywood
Belmont, Pendleton

Political social clubs
Parkfield Labour, Preston
St Paul's Labour, Leigh
Rawtenstall Conservative
Coppull Conservative
Adlington Conservative
Ashton-in-Makerfield
    Conservative
Westhoughton Conservative
West Leigh Conservative
Dunscar Conservative, Bolton

Farnworth Conservative
Little Lever Conservative
Cadishead Conservative
Hurst Conservative,
    Ashton-under-Lyne
Whitefield Conservative
Failsworth Liberal
Prestwich Liberal
Swinton Liberal

Working Men's Clubs
Stacksteads
Outwood, Radcliffe
Blackrod

Hindley Green
Uppermill, Oldham

Clubs with other affiliations
Platt Bridge British Legion
Eccles British Legion
Empire Services, Preston

Huntley Unionist, Bury
Westhoughton Reform
Holy Family, Platt Bridge

Works' Clubs
Lowerhouse
Church, Accrington
Stubbins Paper Mill
Clock Face Colliery Recreation,
    St Helens

Garswood Hall
Lancashire Steel Recreation,
    Irlam

Independent Bowling and Social Clubs

Frenchwood, Preston

All Springs Cricket and
    Subscription, Great Harwood

Old Brass Band, Nelson

Woolfold, Blackford Bridge,
    Blackthorn Bridge and
    Fishpool, Bury

Withins, Outwood, Prestolee
    Stoneclough and Band,
    Radcliffe

Platt Bridge Bowling Club

Lowton Village Club

Leigh Bowling Club

Hinsford Botanical Gardens

Farnworth Cricket and Bowling

North Chadderton

Rhodes, Middleton Junction

Stalybridge Recreation

Locations without a specified green

Whittle-le-Woods

Bacup

Fearnhead (Warrington)[39]

Glossary

Bias – the slight difference in shape on one side of a bowl which causes it to curve as it runs

Chalk – point

End – one end comprises the sending of the jack and then two bowls by each player, alternately

Footer – the mat

Jack – the small bowl sent first to act as the target

Mark – a section of the green on which a bowler plays back and forth until losing an end

(Playing off) scratch – starting a match from a handicap mark of zero

Run out – when a player comes from behind to achieve victory with a single break of points

Striking – sending a bowl at high speed in an attempt to knock the jack, or an opponent's bowl, off the green

Notes

1. The author would like to thank Don Lyons for providing a copy of the Glen Howarth memoirs and his generous assistance with this article.
2. *British Crown Green Bowling Association official handbook* (2007).
3. *British Crown Green Bowling Association 1907–2007* (2007).
4. www.booksonbowls.co.uk has a fuller listing than the British Library catalogue.
5. J. Manson, *The complete bowler* (London, 1912), p. 145.
6. Town records, noted in F. Magoun, *History of football from the beginnings to 1871* (Cologne, 1938), p. 13.

7. J. Vose, *Corner to corner* (Omagh, 1969), p. 6. This book is recommended for its coverage of the Panel and leading players.

8. Ibid, p. 71.

9. See, for example, A. Metcalfe, 'Potshare bowling in the mining communities of East Northumberland, 1800–1914', in R. Holt, ed., *Sport and the working class in Britain* (Manchester, 1990), pp. 29–44.

10. *Manchester Guardian*, 23 Dec. 1953.

11. G. Howarth memoirs 1944–66, ed. D. Lyons (unpublished typescript), p. 5.

12. Ibid., p. 6.

13. Ibid.

14. Ibid., p. 32.

15. Ibid., p. 118.

16. T. Collins, *Rugby league in twentieth-century Britain* (London, 2006), app. 6.

17. Ibid., p. 46.

18. Howarth memoirs, p. 57.

19. Ibid., p. 62.

20. Ibid., p. 94; *Manchester Guardian*, 23 Dec. 1953.

21. Howarth memoirs, p. 17.

22. Ibid., p. 94.

23. Ibid., p. 46.

24. Ibid., p. 53.

25. Ibid., p. 119.

26. Ibid., p. 16.

27. See http://www.winter1947.co.uk for details.

28. *Sporting Chronicle*, 11 Mar. 1947.

29. Ibid., 12 Mar. 1947.

30. Ibid., 22 Mar. 1947.

31. Ibid., 9 Apr. 1947.

32. Ibid., 27 May 1947.

33. Howarth memoirs, p. 15.

34. Ibid., p. 17.

35. Ibid., p. 54.

36. Ibid., p. 72.

37. Ibid., p. 44 (editor's note).

38. B. Duncan, *Crown king* (Chorley, 1995), p. 133.

39. Compiled from *Sporting Chronicle*, and Howarth memoirs, passim. Specific greens are not always mentioned in reports and there may be other locations to add to this list.

'They shall grow not old': mourning, memory and the Munich air disaster of 1958

Joyce Woolridge

On 6 February 1958, an aeroplane carrying players and officials of Manchester United Football Club, along with accompanying journalists and other passengers, crashed on take-off at Munich Riem airport. Twenty-three people died as a result, including eight footballers.[1] 2008 marked the fiftieth anniversary of what has become known as the Munich air disaster, and Manchester United announced its intention to commemorate the occasion by constructing a new memorial 'both significant and easily accessible to all who visit the ground', in addition to the original commemorative plaque and clock which had been erected by 1960.[2]

Since the 1980s, the public commemoration of the accident has enjoyed something of a revival – a resurgence of interest which Dave Russell, in one of the few academic studies of commemoration in football, has attributed to a 'new culture of memorialization within football'.[3] Elsewhere, Gavin Mellor has discussed how the disaster has helped to construct a 'community' of Manchester United supporters.[4] Both these analyses largely situate the Munich crash within the 'football world'. This examination will focus on how those who died were mourned in the years immediately afterwards, placing it in the wider context of the development of the culture of mourning and commemoration in England in the second half of the twentieth century. It will argue that the material culture of mourning and commemoration – from the impermanent, such as the funerals and tributes, to those intended to be more permanent memorials, for example, gravestones and monuments – allows an opportunity for an investigation of contemporary attitudes to grief and remembrance during what has become a neglected period.

The crash took place only thirteen years after the end of the Second World War. Although there is an abundance of writing by historians of mourning and commemoration about the response to death in the First World War, the late 1940s and 1950s have not received the same attention. A major academic preoccupation has been to identify when 'modern' attitudes to death and remembrance replaced those essentially identified with the apogee of the cult of death in the reign of Victoria. Paul Fussell's study of poetry led him to conclude that the consolatory certainties expressed in the high diction of the Georgian poets were shattered by the experiences of the 1914–18 conflict.[5] Jay Winter and others have contested this interpretation, arguing instead for the continuity and robustness of traditional responses to death and commemoration. In a highly influential essay, David Cannadine contended that the Second World War had lifted the pall of death which shrouded inter-war Britain. 1945, according to Cannadine, saw no repeat of the inter-war cult of the dead, no great government or public concern for permanent commemorative monuments, no myth of the 'lost generation'. Remembrance Day, though it survived, and was changed to remember the dead of both wars, never recovered its previous 'intensity of significance'.[6] Thus, the assumption has been that 1945 marks the beginning of 'modern' practices of mourning and commemoration.

Albert Scanlon visited in hospital by his wife. Despite a fractured skull, broken leg and kidney problems he was back in action at the start of the 1958–9 season (Manchester Archives and Local Studies, Central Library, M74154)

This analysis will argue that the mourning and commemoration of the footballers who died in 1958 can only be understood in the context of the post-war climate where there was a sometimes submerged, but nevertheless vigorous, continuation of commemorative traditions. Although it draws heavily upon the literature concerning mourning

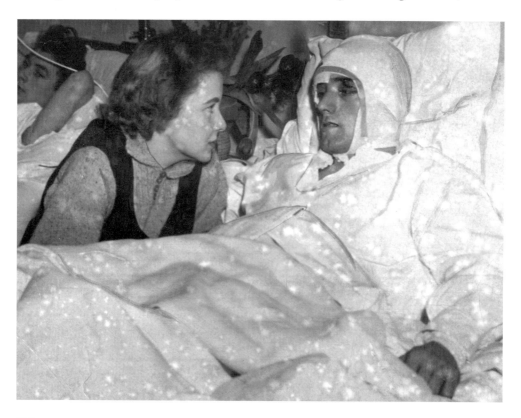

and commemorative practices established during and after the Great War, it recognizes that there is a important difference between the grief of individuals who suffered direct, personal bereavement – the relatives, friends and colleagues of those who died in the war and also in the Munich crash – and those thousands who participated in the public mourning and commemoration of the footballers and others who perished. Nor does it propose a 'psychic universalism' which assumes a uniform response to the tragedy.[7]

The Second World War and the 'suppression of mourning'

Historians generally accept that there was a suppression of mourning between 1914–18 promoted by influential public figures who were concerned that a mass outpouring of grief would affect morale and future support for the war. What followed the end of hostilities was a prolonged period of 'delayed mourning'. There have been few similar claims for the Second World War. Tony Walters has suggested that the 1950s and 1960s saw a 'sweeping of the loss under the carpet' – but otherwise there has been little challenge to Cannadine's argument.[8] However, reconsideration of some of the evidence suggests that the diminished public concern for new 'stone memorials' that Cannadine perceived was not necessarily indicative of a lack of enthusiasm for permanent commemoration.

Mark Quinlan's study of the papers of the War Memorial Advisory Council, established as a result of a meeting about war memorials at the Royal Society of Arts in April 1944, reveals that the explanation for why no second English national war monument was constructed owed much to government opposition, but also the cultural importance that the Cenotaph had assumed. Sir Fabian Ware, founder of the Imperial War Graves commission, was a powerful influence in the decision only to add new dates to the Cenotaph, rather than erecting 'any competing monument'. The government circumvented the War Memorial Advisory Council's consultations on a national monument by setting up the National Land Fund to purchase land, property and works of art for the nation. This did not signify that the impulse to memorialize the dead had diminished. The Advisory Council was endorsed by fifty leading societies connected with the arts and social welfare, as well as many prominent individuals.[9] There was a strong progressive agenda from 1944 onwards which supported the building of utilitarian monuments, expressed in Mass-Observation's influential November 1944 bulletin, entitled 'No Stone Memorials'.[10] The bulletin claimed that 'most people wanted a memorial which would be <u>useful or give pleasure to those who outlive the war</u>', such as scholarships, utility buildings, clinics or memorial halls. Similar ideas were aired in two feature films, *Vote for Huggett* (1949) and *Silent Dust* (1949). In the latter, a businessman is forced to abandon his plan to dedicate a cricket pavilion to his son, wrongly believed killed in action, so it becomes instead a memorial for all the village's dead, espousing the 'People's War' discourse of commemorating communal rather than individual sacrifice.

In the Mass-Observation bulletin and in these two films there is strong support for some form of commemoration. The distinction which was drawn between utilitarian and artistic monuments was not new, but was one which, according to Alex King, had been 'established mainly in the late-Victorian period'.[11] More utilitarian monuments were built after the First World War than the Second and it is wrong to see a preference for utilitarian forms as indicative of a decline in the commemorative impulse, or of the beginning of a more 'healthy', less obsessive mourning after 1945. 'Stone memorials' already existed all over the country to which new names were added, a practice which the Advisory Council strongly endorsed and which reflected the common opinion, expressed by its President, Lord Chatfield, that eventually, 'these two wars will appear like one war in two parts'.[12] The estimated 700 new memorials built between 1945 and 1995 tend to commemorate those groups without existing memorials, or, flying in the face of the discourse of communality, remembered individuals.[13] Artistically, many of these used First World War iconography and texts, a tendency which Alan Wilkinson suggests was particularly strong in the north of England, though he offers no supporting evidence for this contention.[14] The powerful influence exerted by the language and symbolism of Great War commemoration is apparent in the mourning and commemoration of the Munich air disaster. The scale and nature of contemporary reactions are compelling evidence of the deeper significance of the impact of the deaths, in particular, of the eight young footballers.

The mourning of the Munich air disaster: 'For the fallen' and the 'lost generation'

The actions of the Football League and Manchester United in the days after the crash followed forms of mourning established since 1918, as well as earlier traditions. The League ordered a two-minutes' silence at all games on Saturday 8 February, together with the wearing of black armbands and the lowering of flags to half-mast. There was a precedent in international football. When thirty-one footballers and officials of the Torino Football Club were killed in an aeroplane crash in the Superga disaster of May 1949, the FIFA Executive Committee ordered a one-minute's silence.[15] However, the League's 'official silence' was preceded at a Hallé Orchestra concert in Sheffield on 7 February. The audience stood as the orchestra played Elgar's 'Nimrod Variation', 'the musicians' traditional tribute for colleagues who have died', as an *in memoriam* which was followed by the observation of a minute's silence.[16] After its inception in Britain on 11 November 1919, as a central part of Remembrance Day, the two- (or one-) minutes' silence had rapidly become adopted as a popular means of showing respect. The first instance recorded in *The Times* of a silence held outside the Armistice Day ceremonies was on 13 May 1921 when the internment of the cinematography pioneer William Friese Greene was marked by a two-minutes' silence in cinemas.[17] Since then it had been widely used to mourn deaths of groups or individuals in sporting and non-sporting contexts. In football, the death of the Arsenal manager Herbert Chapman in January 1934 was marked by a minute's silence at most Football League grounds. At Highbury (Arsenal's stadium), the influence of the Armistice Day rituals was underlined by the sounding of the 'Last Post'.[18]

In some quarters even the solemnity of a two-minutes' silence throughout sporting England was considered insufficiently respectful. Alan Hardaker, Secretary of the Football League, came under criticism for not suspending the League programme. The *Manchester Evening Chronicle* claimed that the 'vast majority' of Manchester people wanted professional football called off the following Saturday.[19] Some footballers had made similar representations to Cliff Lloyd, Secretary of the Players' Union. However, Hardaker had consulted Harold Hardman, the Manchester United chairman, who backed his decision to carry on as 'the best way of playing tribute to the players concerned in the tragedy'.[20] A suspension would have exceeded the respect shown by the Football League upon the death of the last two kings, where football matches were played as normal, after a silence had been observed.

On the night of 10 February, remarkable demonstrations of public mourning accompanied the return to Old Trafford (United's stadium) of the bodies of the dead players and Manchester United officials which had been flown back to Manchester. Although the aeroplane arrived late, at midnight, and it rained heavily, the twelve-mile route from Ringway airport to the stadium was lined, according to the *Daily Express*, by a quarter of a million onlookers, although *The Times* reduced the figure to a still-impressive 100,000.[21] The bulk of the spectators comported themselves in the respectful manner expected of those who gathered at the Cenotaph or at major state funerals, standing to attention in orderly ranks or maintaining a 'silent vigil' as the coffins passed. Others demonstrated their sorrow more openly: 'women knelt and men wept'.[22] The attendance of such large numbers in difficult conditions suggests that the participants were not only present because the 'homecoming' had become a 'media event' or as followers of Manchester United and others saddened by the deaths of such talented young footballers. This may have been such an important occasion for some of the many mourners because it satisfied a deep-rooted psychological need. It has been well documented how relatives of the Great War dead lobbied the government unsuccessfully for the repatriation of bodies so that they could be buried in Britain and there was a widespread feeling of being unable to mourn properly in the absence of a grave to visit. The Tomb of the Unknown Soldier was partly a symbolic response to this demand. Pilgrimages to war graves had reached 140,000 a year by 1931 and 160,000 by 1939.[23] After the Second World War, the general dislocation in Europe and elsewhere made such pilgrimages difficult, but much later these became, and still continue to be, very popular. The 'repatriation' of some of the dead to Old Trafford was thus a significant moment in the grieving for those lost in the crash, but it may have had deeper resonance as a symbolic homecoming for those war casualties whose bodies remained overseas or missing. One of those who joined the vigil directly evoked the war: 'This is the most terrible thing that has happened since the Blitz and the least we can do is to pay our respects'.[24] Women were prominent in the crowds of mourners, as they were on Remembrance Day, reflecting perhaps partly the pin-up status of the 'Busby Babes', but also symbolically mourning the loss of sons, brothers and husbands in wartime. Mrs Betty Clarke, interviewed outside the ground, said poignantly, 'I stood in the rain for three hours to see them last night … I never knew them personally, but they were to me every mother's ideal of a son'.[25] The United gymnasium under the main stand had been converted to a temporary chapel of rest. Here the desire of a few to get close to the coffins overwhelmed decorum. Weeping fans tried to burst through crash barriers.[26] One of the policemen responsible for watching over the coffins during the night remembers people banging on the doors trying to gain admittance.[27]

Harold Hardman turned to the 'high diction' of the traditional poetic language of war to express grief for the dead and to console the living. The cover of the first club programme issued after the crash carried an address written by Hardman, entitled 'United Will Go On …'. 'We mourn our dead', he concluded, 'and grieve for our wounded'. It also carried a tribute to the (then) seven dead players (Duncan Edwards lived until 21 February), which consisted of head-and-shoulders photographs of each man introduced by a stanza of Laurence Binyon's 'For the fallen'.[28] Binyon's poem was read at the Cenotaph on Remembrance Day, and was the most popular poem at other memorial services. Its concluding lines were chosen by those bereaved in the Great War as 'supremely appropriate' for soldiers' headstones:

> They shall grow not old,
>   as we that are left grow old ...
> At the going down of the sun,
>   And in the morning
> We will remember them.[29]

The poem's longevity and popularity in the late 1950s and beyond is an indication of the continued consolatory importance of the sentiments it expresses. Fussell has commented how the high-Georgian imagery of Binyon's poem represented 'a constant reaching out towards traditional significance ... an attempt to make some sense of the war in relation towards inherited tradition'.[30] Its evocation here by Manchester United indicated how the club intended the footballers who died should be remembered. The 'Busby Babes' were to become the 'lost generation' of football's gilded youth. The 'myth of the lost generation' which Cannadine saw as a notable absence after the Second World War, resurfaces in the story of the shattering of the 'Babes' team at Munich and continued to be developed in its later commemoration. Arthur Walmsley expressed it eloquently in his tribute on Duncan Edwards's death:

> Of all the glittering gems in the Manchester United treasure chest of talent, Duncan Edwards was the brightest jewel of them all. His loss to club and country is irreparable, for it is only once in a generation that a footballer of Duncan's staggering ability comes to full flower.[31]

Manchester United had been one of the football clubs to embrace a 'turn to youth' after the Second World War, a policy which was very much in tune with the emphasis upon education and inculcation of moral values, promoted by the government and other interested parties as part of the planned Welfare State. Under their manager, Matt Busby, the 'Babes' became the most successful of those young teams much feted by the press. It has been suggested that the dead 'Babes' took on an even greater significance as martyrs. 'It was Europe that had made Matt Busby's young Manchester side into heroes before Munich turned them into martyrs ... The sight of their broken plane lying in the snow was on every television screen.'[32] The traditional justification for death in war had been to cast the dead as making a redemptive sacrifice for those who came after.[33] At Duncan Edwards's funeral service the Revd Catterall shared his belief that Edwards's death had been such a sacrifice, providing inspiration and an example for future generations. 'The mark of sacrifice and genius

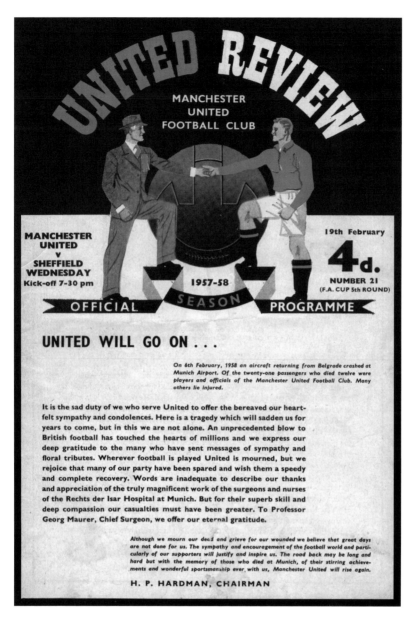

UNITED REVIEW

MANCHESTER
UNITED
FOOTBALL CLUB

MANCHESTER
UNITED
v
SHEFFIELD
WEDNESDAY
Kick-off 7-30 pm

1957-58

SEASON

OFFICIAL

19th February

4d.

NUMBER 21
(F.A. CUP 5th ROUND)

PROGRAMME

UNITED WILL GO ON . . .

On 6th February, 1958 an aircraft returning from Belgrade crashed at Munich Airport. Of the twenty-one passengers who died twelve were players and officials of the Manchester United Football Club. Many others lie injured.

It is the sad duty of we who serve United to offer the bereaved our heart-felt sympathy and condolences. Here is a tragedy which will sadden us for years to come, but in this we are not alone. An unprecedented blow to British football has touched the hearts of millions and we express our deep gratitude to the many who have sent messages of sympathy and floral tributes. Wherever football is played United is mourned, but we rejoice that many of our party have been spared and wish them a speedy and complete recovery. Words are inadequate to describe our thanks and appreciation of the truly magnificent work of the surgeons and nurses of the Rechts der Isar Hospital at Munich. But for their superb skill and deep compassion our casualties must have been greater. To Professor Georg Maurer, Chief Surgeon, we offer our eternal gratitude.

Although we mourn our dead and grieve for our wounded we believe that great days are not done for us. The sympathy and encouragement of the football world and parti-cularly of our supporters will justify and inspire us. The road back may be long and hard but with the memory of those who died at Munich, of their stirring achieve-ments and wonderful sportsmanship ever with us, Manchester United will rise again.

H. P. HARDMAN, CHAIRMAN

'We mourn our dead and grieve for our wounded'. Harold Hardman's 'high diction'. Cover of *United Review*, 15 February 1958. Photograph by arrangement of Manchester United Museum.

is deeply imprinted on this [...] community.' Edwards's death had been used by God 'that all that is best in His sons may be revealed. He uses a dark February day that [...] the last courageous fight of Duncan Edwards might be a fitting epilogue to his years of high endeavour and vision.'[34] To raise money for the Disaster Fund, *Carve her Name with Pride* (1958), the poignant story of Violet Szabo's wartime sacrifice (captured while working as a British agent in Germany, she was shot by the Nazis) was given its northern premiere at the Gaumont on Oxford Street.[35]

The subsequent funerals of journalists, United officials and players saw similar reactions from the public. During what the Manchester *City and Suburban News* called 'the black week of mourning' hundreds of thousands of people lined the streets.[36] An official United statement passed on a request by the families of the deceased that the funerals should be a private matter, but the funeral itineraries were printed in the papers.[37] Organizers had to make contingencies for the numbers of onlookers, and sometimes police had to control the crowds, though people's behaviour was generally very respectful.[38] Local businesses felt obliged to allow their workers time off to attend some of the funerals; when one box-making firm sacked twenty-seven people who went to watch the cortege of Eddie Colman, the Salford-born winger, one woman claimed it was her duty to attend and the firm hastily reversed its decision.[39] Thousands lined the route, silent in orderly ranks; some even stood on the roofs of the buildings in Cemetery Road. Reports of all the funerals emphasize the large numbers of floral tributes. There were 160 wreaths at Colman's funeral; the gardens of Tommy Taylor's former home in Barnsley and those of neighbouring houses were covered in wreaths.[40] Although many were from football clubs or other official bodies, florists in Stretford reported that there was a huge demand for flowers 'mainly from ordinary people', and extra supplies were flown in from Holland.[41] One fan expressed the desire to 'carpet the playing pitch [at Old Trafford] with flowers'.[42] Memorial services organized by Manchester United had huge attendances. More than 6,000 took part in a Roman Catholic mass at Belle Vue, where a wooden crucifix was erected in the centre of the cavernous King's Hall, one of four services for various religious denominations organized in Manchester on 22 February. Canon William Sewell, Matt Busby's parish priest, told worshippers, 'No single disaster, even in the darkest days of the war, made such an impact in the minds of the general community'.[43]

There were dissenting voices. Such highly demonstrative outbursts of public grief were at odds with the official burden of Hardman's pronouncement that the best memorial was for the club and its supporters to carry on. Bobby Charlton, who survived the crash, recounted later how, prostrated by grief, he only began playing again because a doctor, who had served in the RAF in the war 'gave me a short and kindly lecture on picking up the threads and knuckling down to the business of living again'.[44] When some businesses in Manchester refused to fly their flags at half-mast, one letter writer defended them for resisting the prevailing 'mass hysteria'.[45] These objections were exceptional and usually roundly condemned. Indeed, most contemporaries did not see such behaviour as hysterical, but as a fitting mark of respect. Most criticism seems to have been excited by

They shall grow not old . . .

as we that are left grow old,
Age shall not weary them,
     nor the years condemn.
At the going down of the sun,
          and in the morning
We will remember them.

LAURENCE BINYON

ROGER BYRNE

EDDIE COLMAN

BILL WHELAN

MARK JONES

GEOFF BENT

TOMMY TAYLOR

DAVID PEGG

Photos by P. A. Reuter, Manchester Evening News, Manchester Evening Chronicle, The Daily Herald, The Daily Mirror.

the continuing perfervid atmosphere at Old Trafford, particularly as the hastily rebuilt Manchester United team progressed against the odds to the FA Cup Final. Writing nine years after the crash, Arthur Hopcraft opined that after a week or so, 'much of the genuine shock and grief in Manchester had naturally lifted, to be replaced by a maudlin and too deliberate mourning, in which the newspapers mostly wallowed with more business acumen than taste'.[46] An examination of the local newspapers suggests, in contrast, that, following the funerals and the 'black week', the coverage of the crash was scaled down, apart from the additional tributes when Duncan Edwards died. Most of the mourning of ordinary people was decorous in the extreme, although not without sentimentality.

'For the Fallen'. Tribute to the 'lost generation', *United Review*, 15 February 1958. Photograph by arrangement of Manchester United Museum.

The commemoration of the Munich air disaster: 'We will remember them'

The dead were commemorated in the longer term in a variety of ways, many of which once again reveal the influence of mourning practices developed after the First World War, and thus the importance and resonance of the young players' deaths for contemporaries. Some relatives of the dead players maintained their own commemorative 'shrines' in their homes, collections of shirts, caps and medals, as well as other mementoes, which they showed to visitors. The journalist John Roberts was still able to see these 'shrines' twenty-five years after the crash.[47] These displays echoed the photographs and medals of war of those who were killed in the First World War which dominated the homes of inter-war Britain.[48] Manchester United was presented with two illuminated 'rolls of honour', a Great War practice which endured after the Second World War and was promoted by the War Advisory Council. One from prisoners in Pentonville carried the RAF motto, 'Per ardua ad astra', another, listing the names of the dead, came from an ex-servicemen's club in Stretford. A third, 'Coggan's Memorial to the Ambassadors of Sport', is still displayed, like many military rolls, in a Cheshire church: St Luke's, Dukinfield.[49]

The graves of some of the players became sites of unofficial pilgrimage. A Salford man claimed to have visited Eddie Colman's grave every week 'because he was our local star'.[50] In October 1959, Santiago Bernabeu, the chairman of Real Madrid, took his players to Salford's Weaste Cemetery to lay a wreath on Colman's grave – as Roger Byrne was cremated and the other dead players were not Mancunians, it was the closest to Old Trafford. The courage shown by Duncan Edwards in his unavailing two-week struggle for life won him a special place among the dead. Edwards's father, Gladstone, became caretaker at Dudley's Queen's Cross cemetery where his son (and infant daughter) were buried, and guided visitors to Duncan's grave. A 1967 tribute reported that, 'Even now ... there are sometimes 20 pilgrims a day at his grave in Dudley Cemetery'.[51] Both Colman's and Edwards's graves reflected their role as footballers, and as such offered those who came as pilgrims to the graves images of the two men immortalized as vital social beings. Standing at the side of Colman's headstone was a marble statuette of the player in his kit with a ball at his feet, but it was removed later because of damage by vandals and kept in his grandfather's house along with other mementoes. This was not the only memorial of the disaster, intended to be permanent, which suffered later harm or neglect, the significance of which is considered below. Edwards's headstone, unveiled by Matt Busby at a special ceremony on 5 October 1958, bore his portrait, a continental European tradition rarely seen on English graves.[52] The *Dudley Herald* described the design as 'unusual, to say the least'.[53] In the idealized image, Edwards is taking a throw-in, his eyes elevated, as if raised towards heaven. He is portrayed as eternally youthful and vigorous, a representation which appears to have resonated with the many visitors to his tomb since 1958.

Edwards was further commemorated individually in his local parish church, St Francis's in the Priory, Dudley. The Revd A. Dawson Catterall, the 'Sporting Parson', who had delivered Edwards's funeral oration, was responsible for organizing the installation of two lights in a chapel window, depicting Edwards in the dual role of Manchester United and England player. The stained glass transforms the footballer into the perfect, humble, Christian knight, serving God and his country. In one light, Edwards kneels below St Francis of Assisi. In the other, clad in England kit, he kneels underneath St George in his guise as dragon slayer, crowned with the arms of Manchester and Munich. The design is highly reminiscent of a number of stained glass windows, erected by the families of those who died in the Second World War in defiance of disapproval about memorials to individuals, which cast the deceased as a Christian knight. A window in St Mary's Church, Sparham in Norfolk, in memory of an airman killed in 1944, depicts St George with the inscription 'Tranquil you lie, your knightly virtue proved'. David Pegg's neighbours donated a less ostentatious memorial to St George's Church, Highfields, Doncaster, a chair in the chancel, which matched one opposite, dedicated by his parents to a young man who died while serving in the RAF in the war.[54]

The Revd Catterall struggled to raise the money for the window. However, his problems do not necessarily show a lack of popular support for a memorial of this kind, but probably stemmed from asking Football League clubs, which had already contributed to the official disaster fund, to sponsor it. Many may well have looked askance at an additional demand from a private individual, albeit a clergyman. Once his dilemma was publicized, the money was raised easily. The vicar was also heavily involved in the fund-raising for a utilitarian memorial to Edwards in Dudley, intended to be a youth club so that future generations of local youth would benefit from his example and legacy. Of those players who lost their lives at Munich, Duncan Edwards has been publicly commemorated most extensively and continuously, although not in Manchester, but in his home town, a reflection of how he has become a focus for Dudley's civic pride.[55]

The memorials at Old Trafford

The day after the accident, the Lord Mayor of Manchester, Leslie Lever, launched a disaster fund – which was to raise over £52,000 – and announced that some of the money collected would be used to provide a permanent memorial.[56] He intended to seek public opinion about its form. On 11 February he again publicly discussed a memorial in terms which closely echoed the wartime debates: 'It will be a permanent memorial, and an essentially useful one which the community, and particularly the younger members, can use and remember with affection and gratitude those who served this city and country so well.'[57] During the next few weeks, the local newspapers carried a selection of the large number of letters they received on the subject. Many supported a utilitarian tribute. Some suggestions were for dressing rooms for sports teams playing in the Manchester parks; donations to the Munich hospital which had cared for the crash victims; and travel scholarships for German nurses. There was even a proposal for the equivalents of a 'poppy day', where red and white rosettes would be sold, and of Remembrance Day, a 'Sportsmen's Sunday' to be held at churches around Manchester. Others wanted some kind of monument, whether it was a memorial chapel in each community to which the dead had belonged; the transformation of Piccadilly sunken gardens in the centre of Manchester into a 'Place of Remembrance'; a symbolic statue of a 'fleeting figure intent on the ball' to be erected in Albert Square with the inscription, 'They lived and died for Manchester United'; or a 'magnificent memorial bridge' across the railway at Old Trafford 'suitably inscribed and surmounted at each corner with an imposing monument'.[58] However, there was to be no official city memorial, but not because there was no support for one. Manchester United later said that they would like to choose and pay for the memorial themselves, and the £52,000 in the Lord Mayor's Fund was distributed among dependents of the dead and survivors.[59]

The 'official' club memorial was not unveiled until 25 February 1960 and the delay caused complaint. In a letter to the *Manchester Evening News*, 'a United fan' protested,

> It is now 16 months since Munich, and still nothing has been done about erecting a memorial to those who died. Surely after all their wonderful works in the field of sport, both at home and overseas, some sort of memorial should be erected as a permanent tribute to the Manchester United lads whose lives were so tragically cut short.[60]

Three days later, Manchester United released details of their proposed monument. This was to be a memorial plaque in the shape of a complete plan of the ground to scale, seen from overhead, 'a field in stone'.[61] The original plans and notes of its designer, a local architect, J. Vipond, appear not to have survived, but it is obvious that he drew on many influences and the monument's features are highly allusive of a range of commemorative traditions, not least the memorial plaques which proliferated after the Great War.[62] The Manchester United directors' minutes, although laconic, do suggest that considerable thought was given to its nature for nearly two years.[63] £2,100, then a large sum, was spent on its construction. The club programme, the *United Review*, of 5 March 1960, devoted a page to 'Our Munich Memorials' and is the main piece of information extant about the memorial plaque. Vipond's design was realized by Messrs Jaconello

(Manchester) Ltd., a small firm based in the Pendleton district of Salford. A variety of different materials were used in its construction. The central pitch, which bore the inscription, was made from green slabs of faience (a ceramic), as were the terraces, gangways and steps, in mauve and grey, which formed part of the outer border of the plaque. The pitch markings were inlaid gold glass. The stand roofs and perimeter paths of the stadium were carved from quartzite, and the whole was enclosed by the boundary walling of the ground, worked in red Balmoral granite.

The green pitch symbolized 'the evergreen memory of those whose names it bears'.[64] The programme describes the choice of mauve and grey as 'a memorial colour', but the colours of some of the other materials also have particular associations of which Vipond at least as an architect would have been aware. Red is associated with the doctrine of redemption because of its connotation with the blood of Christ.[65] The football stadium itself, which represents Manchester United, supporters and officials, encircles and supports the memorial inscription. The message of communal mourning and remembrance is emphasized by the figure group, standing on top of the memorial and carved in teak by Manchester firm Bond and Hall. These represented 'players, officials and spectators standing with bowed heads and outstretched hands'.

The dead are commemorated by the recording of their names, an act which had immense significance. The list of names was intended to be a still, calm focal point, not distracting from the essential action of commemoration.[66] The simple inscription set into the pitch in black glass read: 'In memory of the officials and players who lost their lives in the Munich Air Disaster 6th February 1958', followed by the names of the three dead club officials, Walter Crickmer, Tom Curry and Bert Whalley, and then of the eight players. Their enduring memory was emphasized by the two bronze torch lights, flanking the plaque, which were added to the design and agreed by the Board of Directors on 12 January 1960. After the First World War, the image of an upturned torch signifying a life extinguished – a classical funerary symbol – was transformed into a burning torch that could be passed on, thus connoting the need to continue the struggle of the fallen.[67]

The memorial was unveiled, along with two others, in a ceremony on 25 February 1960 which was unpublicized as it was felt that 'thousands of spectators would try to attend'.[68] The *Manchester Evening Chronicle* observed that the unveiling would bring a measure of closure to the mourning. 'Quietly [...] the closing chapters were written [...] to the tragedy at Munich.'[69]

The Supporters' Club Ground Committee paid for a rectangular illuminated clock inscribed 'FEB 6th 1958' above, with the single

Busby unveils the memorial plaque to the victims of Munich at Old Trafford. It is still a moving sight today

'A fitting and lasting tribute'. Matt Busby unveils the Munich plaque, 25 February 1960 (Lance Bellers, Steve Absalom and Simon Spinks, *The unseen archives: a photographic history of Manchester United* [Bath, 1999], p. 59. Copyright Mirror Group)

word 'MUNICH' below in black capitals. With no record of their deliberations, it is only possible to suggest their purposes in choosing this type of memorial. The functioning clock is both a utilitarian monument, as well as a traditional *memento mori*, exploring the 'double certainties of the passage of time and the arrival of death'.[70] Anecdotal evidence suggests that something of the latter metaphor reverberated with some visitors, as a mistaken belief grew up that it was stopped at 3.04pm, the time of the crash. The directors blocked plans for a plaque underneath explaining its significance, though did not record why they refused. A third memorial, a bronze tablet paid for by the Football Writers' Association to commemorate the journalists who were killed, was fixed in the press box.

The later commemoration of the Munich crash: a lessening of concern?

The plaque was sited above the directors' and players' entrance at Old Trafford, high upon the wall where the directors hoped it 'would be a fitting and lasting tribute, worthy of the Club'.[71] It appears not to have become the focus for the laying of flowers on the anniversary of the disaster, whether because of its position above the entrance doors or for some other reason. Fragmentary anecdotal and retrospective evidence suggests that it did serve its function of preserving the memory of those it named. Fans leaving the Stretford end 'headed for the forecourt via the main entrance, you'd ALWAYS look up to the plaque … and momentarily quietly pay your respects to the great ones whom tragically met their fate'.[72] However, some of the memorials to the dead of the Munich crash suffered from neglect and vandalism. The Munich plaque at Old Trafford proved to be one of the most vulnerable, despite the hopes expressed on its unveiling. In the mid 1970s, the plaque was to be moved to enable the construction of executive boxes. The club later stated that a decision was reluctantly made to leave it in situ because it was impossible to take it down without causing damage, and it was obscured subsequently by the new building work. However, it was not treated so respectfully. One fan recalled seeing 'a huge hole cut out of the plaque with a concrete beam going straight through it'.[73] A replica, far simpler and smaller, not in the expensive materials of the first, was made and erected at the front of the ground. A third plaque, more faithful to the original, though still in cheaper materials, was placed next to the new statue of Matt Busby in 1996.

The current version of the Munich clock is also not original. The larger replacement was made quite crudely from two sheets of metal with the clock dial represented as a dotted circle and with different hands, though the form of the inscription is preserved. One of the sides is now rusting and buckled. The bronze press-box plaque, now in the press briefing room, is also a replica. The original was stolen in the 1980s. Whether the treatment of the original memorials reflects the wider growing disdain discerned in society for formal monuments, for example the widespread neglect of cemeteries which began in the 1970s, is unclear. The principle of the memorials was maintained by the making of these copies, even if they are of inferior quality. The minute's silence on the anniversary of the disaster continued to be observed, although not in 2003 as the nearest home game was against

Manchester City, and there were fears that it might be disrupted. The twenty-fifth anniversary in 1983 was marked by a special supplement in the programme. When the club museum was extended in 1991, a large display about the tragedy was included. There was greater attention to the fortieth anniversary of the crash. A service was held at Manchester Cathedral on 6 February 1998, and a small ceremony of remembrance carried out on the Old Trafford pitch the following day. Eight wreaths were laid in the centre circle and the players formed a line, linking arms and bowing their heads during the minute's silence. A delayed benefit match for the Munich Disaster Fund was staged at Old Trafford on 18 August which raised nearly one million pounds, although the payment of over £90,000 in expenses to Eric Cantona for his appearance in the game, and other deductions, led to controversy.

The fiftieth anniversary commemorations in 2008 were extensive and elaborate, carefully planned by Manchester United who consulted supporters about the form these should take. On 6 February, a memorial service, to which relatives of the victims, survivors and their families, current Manchester United players and officials, as well as fans chosen by ballot, were invited, was conducted at Old Trafford by the club chaplain. The service was televized free on the club's subscription channel, MUTV, and relayed live to the estimated 1,500 people who had gathered outside, many around the Munich plaque, then surrounded by flowers, wreaths and other supporters' tributes. A minute's silence was held before a permanent, free exhibition about the crash was opened in the South Stand tunnel, renamed 'Munich Tunnel'. The FA had revoked their initial decision not to accede to United's request to hold a minute's silence before the friendly international against Switzerland at Wembley because of fears that it would be disrupted. However, the referee, obviously acting under instructions, truncated the silence after thirty-two seconds when whistling and shouting began in a small section of the crowd. In contrast, the minute's silence held before the nearest home game to the anniversary, the Manchester derby on 10 February, was impeccably observed, despite widely aired speculation that some Manchester City fans would be similarly disrespectful. There have been complaints since the 1990s that the official remembrance of the anniversary is inadequate, and alternative, unofficial commemorations have been organized. The 'Flowers of Manchester', an anonymous folk song in the style of a soldiers' lament, written in 1958, was regularly sung at 3.04 on 6 February below the Munich plaque. In 2008, a major concern of certain sections of the support was that the ceremonies should not be exploited for commercial gain. Hence the special '1958-style' kit worn by United's players carried no sponsor's logo and was not mass produced for public sale. There were protests when the impressive giant photograph of the 'last lineup' of the Busby Babes team, next to a verse from the Manchester United calypso and unveiled above the main entrance to the stadium, was found to display the sponsor's logo prominently.

Conclusion

Hundreds of thousands of people in Manchester and its environs, as well as throughout the rest of the country, participated in some manner in the mourning for those killed in the Munich air crash. Contemporary observers considered the depth of the response extraordinary, and for a week in February 1958 crowds attending the 'homecoming' of the victims and their funerals filled the streets, bringing traffic to a standstill. The response to the Munich disaster was remarkable, possibly because it had a metaphorical significance, allowing for public expression of grief not only about the death of highly popular young footballers who lost their lives in tragic circumstances, but also because it may have, for some people, allowed a space for the mourning of the loss of life during the war which had been constricted, if not denied, by the rhetoric and demands of post-war reconstruction. A few of those mourners explicitly linked the deaths of the eight young players with the suffering of wartime, and the 'lost Babes' quickly became a symbol of the sacrifice of the finest of their generation.

This examination of the response to the Munich disaster seems to suggest, in line with other studies which have concentrated on the analysis of the material culture of death and mourning, that rather than a major attitudinal shift occurring after the Second World War, there was a much more varied reaction characterized by the robust continuance and modification of some long-established traditions and practices. Rituals developed following the Great War were clearly highly significant for many who participated and sought consolation from their observance. There was no lack of interest in the design and erection of permanent memorials in Manchester and elsewhere, whether 'stone monuments' or utilitarian memorials. Peter Jupp and Tony Walters have pointed instead to the 1960s and 1970s as the period when British psychiatrists promoted the definition of healthy grieving as a process of letting go of attachments to the dead and 'secularism, rationalism and an emphasis on youth, progress and consumerism' curtailed grave-visiting and other traditions as obsessive and morbid.[74] Although this analysis has briefly considered the commemoration of the crash in the subsequent decades, it is beyond its scope to say whether the 1960s and 1970s did mark such a watershed, and the evidence is somewhat contradictory.

Indeed, although the revival of interest in commemoration, generally discerned since the 1980s, has been attributed pejoratively to a post-modern confusion in which a 'museal sensibility' replaces authentic emotion, it could be seen rather as a re-emergence of important rituals and traditions deeply rooted in popular culture.[75] As Dave Russell has pointed out, the Munich disaster was an 'exceptional tragedy' which 'broke the mould' of the mourning of football deaths as essentially a private business.[76] It was not until the 1980s that large public ceremonies and displays of mourning connected with football became commonplace, a trend which has since continued. What is clear is that such displays and some of the accompanying 'rituals', as in the mourning after the deaths of ninety-five Liverpool supporters at Sheffield Wednesday's Hillsborough ground on 15 April 1989, sometimes derided as 'modern' inventions, inappropriate and mawkish, were in evidence in 1958.[77]

Notes

1. The eight footballers were Geoff Bent, Roger Byrne, Eddie Colman, Duncan Edwards, Mark Jones, David Pegg, Tommy Taylor and Liam (Billy) Whelan. Duncan Edwards survived the crash, but died later from his injuries. Manager Matt Busby spent months recovering in hospital in Munich.

2. David Gill, quoted in 'United plan new memorial', http://www.munich58.co.uk/articles/new_mufc_memorial.asp accessed 27 Apr. 2007.

3. Dave Russell, '"We all agree, name the stand after Shankly": cultures of commemoration in late twentieth-century English football culture', *Sport in History*, 26 (2006), pp. 1–25.

4. Gavin Mellor, '"The Flowers of Manchester", The Munich disaster and the discursive creation of Manchester United football club', *Soccer and Society*, 5 (2004), pp. 264–84.

5. Paul Fussell, *The Great War and modern memory* (Oxford, 1977).

6. David Cannadine, 'War and death, grief and mourning in modern Britain', in Joachim Whalley, ed., *Mirrors of mortality: studies in the social history of death* (London, 1981), pp. 187–242.

7. See T. G. Ashplant, Graham Dawson and Michael Roper, 'The politics of war memory and commemoration: contests, structures and dynamics', in idem, eds., *The politics of war memory and commemoration* (London, 2000), pp. 3–85.

8. Tony Walter, 'War grave pilgrimage', in Ian Reader and Tony Walter, eds., *Pilgrimage in popular culture* (London, 1993), pp. 63–91.

9. Mark Quinlan, *British war memorials* (Hertford, 2005), pp. 57, 138–9.

10. 'War memorials', Mass-Observation bulletin, Nov. 1944.

11. Alex King, 'Remembering and forgetting in the public memorials of

the Great War', in Adrian Forty and Susanne Kuchler, eds., *The art of forgetting* (Oxford, 2001), pp. 147–69.

12. Lord Chatfield, 24 Oct. 1944, quoted in Quinlan, *British war memorials*, p. 132.

13. Derek Boorman, *For your tomorrow: British Second World War memorials* (York, 1995), p. 1.

14. Alan Wilkinson, 'Changing English attitudes to death in the two world wars', in Peter C. Jupp and Glennys Howarth, eds., *The changing face of death: historical accounts of death and disposal* (London, 1997), pp. 149–63.

15. Paul Dietschy, 'The Superga disaster and the death of the Great Torino', in Paul Darby, Martin Johnes and Gavin Mellor, eds., *Soccer and disaster* (London, 2005), pp. 174–85.

16. *Manchester Evening Chronicle*, 7 Feb. 1958, p. 33.

17. *The Times*, 14 May 1921, p. 8.

18. Dave Russell, '"We all agree"', p. 3.

19. *Manchester Evening Chronicle*, 7 Feb. 1958, p. 12.

20. *The Times*, 8 Feb. 1958, p. 6.

21. *Daily Express*, 11 Feb. 1958, p. 1; *The Times*, 11 Feb. 1958, p. 5. The coffins of those killed in the Superga crash were also taken through the streets in Turin, following a memorial service. See Alexandra Manna and Mike Gibbs, *The day Italian football died: Torino and the tragedy of Superga* (Derby, 2000), pp. 107–8.

22. *Daily Express*, 11 Feb. 1958, p. 1.

23. Cannadine, 'War and death', p. 231.

24. *Manchester City and Suburban News*, 14 Feb.1958, p. 7. This weekly prided itself on reflecting the views of local people and its reporters mingled with the crowds to gather opinions.

25. *Manchester Evening News*, 11 Feb. 1958, p. 11.

26. *Daily Express*, 11 Feb. 1958, p. 1. One local shop reportedly sold out of black ties in a day: John Roberts, *The team that wouldn't die* (London, 1988), p. 58.

27. 'Busby Babes: end of a dream', ITV, broadcast 1 Feb. 1998.

28. *United Review*, 19 Feb. 1958, pp. 7–8.

29. Fussell, *Great War*, p. 56.

30. Ibid., p. 57.

31. *Manchester Evening Chronicle*, 21 Feb. 1958, p. 1.

32. Richard Holt and Tony Mason, *Sport in Britain 1945–2000* (Oxford, 2000), p. 99.

33. See Wilkinson, 'Changing English attitudes to death', p. 157, for a discussion of the ancient belief that 'redemption could only be achieved by the shedding of blood'.

34. 'Last farewell to "One of the Immortals"', Dudley Archives Newspaper Cuttings 14, p. 77. A newspaper cuttings folder about Duncan Edwards is kept by Dudley Archives. Articles do not always have the full date and

name of newspaper attributed and if so are hereafter identified as NC with the page reference of the folder. Thanks to the Dudley archives and local history service for providing copies.

35. *Manchester Evening News*, 19 Feb. 1958, p. 7.

36. *Manchester City and Suburban News*, 14 Feb. 1958, p. 1.

37. *Manchester Evening Chronicle*, 10 Feb. 1958, p. 1.

38. *Manchester Evening News*, 13 Feb. 1958, p. 7.

39. Quoted in Russell, '"We all agree"', p. 4.

40. *Manchester Evening Chronicle*, 14 Feb. 1958, p. 2.

41. *Ibid.*, 11 Feb. 1958, p. 7.

42. *Ibid.*, 13 Feb. 1958, p. 4.

43. *The Times*, 24 Feb. 1958, p. 3.

44. Bobby Charlton, *Forward for England* (London, 1967), p. 44.

45. Quoted in Mellor, 'The Flowers of Manchester', p. 272.

46. Arthur Hopcraft, 'The lost heroes', *Sunday Times* colour supplement, 29 Jan. 1967, p. 8.

47. Roberts, *The team that wouldn't die*, p. 118.

48. Wilkinson, 'Changing English attitudes to death', p. 156.

49. See 'Carl's Cam: Memorial to the Munich air disaster in St Luke's church, Dukinfield, Cheshire', http://www.carlscam.com/dukinfield/munich.htm, accessed 16 Mar. 2007.

50. Mike Sweeney, quoted in Max Arthur, *The Busby Babes: men of magic* (London, 1998), p. 26.

51. Arthur Hopcraft, 'The lost heroes', p. 8.

52. See Harold Mytum, *Mortuary monuments and burial grounds of the historic period* (New York, 2004), p. 79. A memorial silk tapestry commissioned by Santiago Bernabeu which carried the named portraits of seven dead players, as it was made before Edwards died, was hung in Real Madrid's stadium chapel until sold privately in 2001: Jeff Connor, *The lost Babes: Manchester United and the forgotten victims of Munich* (London, 2007), p. 210.

53. *Dudley Herald*, 4 Oct. 1958, in NC, 16, p. 80.

54. *St George's church, Highfields, golden jubilee, 1913–1963 souvenir brochure*, Doncaster Archives P53/4/G1. Thanks to Dr Charles Kelham for finding this and other material relating to David Pegg.

55. Memorials to Edwards included a sports pavilion, opened in 1969; a special display of shirts and trophies at the Dudley leisure centre; Duncan Edwards Close, opposite the cemetery; and his statue in Dudley market place, erected in 1999. In 1980, the stained glass windows were repaired using money partly donated by Manchester United fans.

56. £52,000 was also the sum raised for the Lord Mayor's fund launched in Bolton following the deaths of thirty-three spectators at the Burnden Park ground during on the FA cup-tie of 9 Mar. 1946. Although this was recognized as one of the worst tragedies in British football, and financial

assistance was offered, it did not generate the same public displays of grief.

57. *Manchester Evening News*, 11 Feb. 1958, p. 1.
58. Ibid., 13 Feb. 1950, p. 7; 14 Feb. 1958, pp. 8, 20.
59. Ibid., 2 June 1959, p. 6.
60. Ibid.
61. Ibid., 5 June 1959, p. 5.
62. Thanks to the staff of Salford, Trafford and Manchester Local Archives who searched in vain for any archival material relating to Vipond and the design of the memorial. Mark Wylie, curator of the Manchester United Museum, confirmed no detailed records survive at Old Trafford.
63. Manchester United Board of Directors Minutes, 9 Dec. 1958. Thanks to Mark Wylie for his kindness and considerable efforts to provide this information.
64. *Manchester Evening Chronicle*, 25 Feb. 1960, p. 15.
65. Nigel Llewellyn, *The art of death: visual culture in the English death ritual c. 1500–c1800* (London, 1991), p. 59.
66. King, 'Remembering and forgetting', p. 161.
67. King, *Memorials of the Great War*, p. 130.
68. *Manchester Guardian*, 26 Feb. 1960, p. 5.
69. *Manchester Evening Chronicle*, 25 Feb. 1960, p. 15.
70. Elizabeth Hallam and Jenny Hockey, *Death, memory and material culture* (Oxford, 2001), p. 51.
71. *United Review*, 5 Mar. 1960, p. 5.
72. 'The Munich plaque at Old Trafford', http://www.munich58.co.uk/memorials/plaque/plaque_history.asp, accessed 14 June 2007.
73. 'The Munich plaque'. Manchester United have since disclosed that the plaque suffered serious damage: Letter to the author, 26 Mar. 2007.
74. Peter C. Jupp and Tony Walter, 'The healthy society, 1918–98', in P. C. Jupp and Clare Gittings, eds., *Death in England: an illustrated history* (Manchester, 1999), pp. 256–82 at p. 274.
75. A. Huyssen, *Twilight memories: marking time in a culture of amnesia* (London, 1995), quoted in Hallam and Hockey, *Death, memory and material culture*, p. 206.
76. Russell, '"We all agree"', p. 4.
77. See Tony Walter, 'The mourning after Hillsborough', *Sociological Review*, 39 (1991), pp. 599–625, for the argument that the mourning rituals this tragedy engendered were part of the re-emergence of traditional Victorian mourning practices maintained by the working-class, celtic, Catholicism of the city.

MUSEUMS
The National Football Museum

Kevin Moore

The National Football Museum is the leading football museum in the world, holding the world's finest collection of football artefacts, including the FIFA Collection. The National Football Museum represents a new direction for museums in the twenty-first century, by addressing a popular culture theme which has very wide public appeal.[1]

England was the birthplace of the modern professional game of football, the world's most popular sport. Football is an important part of England's heritage, its people's way of life and sense of identity. The National Football Museum collects, preserves and interprets this unique heritage for the public benefit. There is a comparable museum for Scotland, and a national collection has been established in Wales. The Museum operates to the highest professional museum standards and has achieved National Museum Registration status with the Museums, Libraries and Archives Council (MLA), the Government body that promotes standards in the museums, libraries and archives sector in the UK.

The Museum is for everyone, regardless of age, gender, disability, sexuality, religion or any other factor. It seeks to explain the meaning of football in society: what deeper truths about us as human beings can the fascination (or revulsion) for the game reveal? The Museum exists to explain how and why football has become 'the people's game', a key part of England's heritage, and also aims to explain England's place in the sport.

The National Football Museum opened in 2001, following a £15-million capital project to construct the Museum and establish its initial collections. The Heritage Lottery Fund gave grants totalling £9.3 million, and the North-West Regional Development Agency £2.3 million, with the balance being raised from a range of other sources.

Deepdale Stadium, Preston, was chosen as the location for the Museum as both the stadium and the city have played a key role in the development of the modern game. Preston North End Football Club was a founder member of the world's first football league, winning the Football League in its first season, 1888–9. Preston has been playing at Deepdale Stadium since 1878, making it the oldest Football League ground in the world still in use today. The Football League established offices in Preston in 1902 and still has its headquarters in

the city. There could therefore be no more appropriate home for the National Football Museum.

The Museum holds the world's finest collections relating to the history of football, including the FIFA Collection; the Football Association Collection; the Football League Collection; the People's Collection – over 5,000 items donated by members of the public; and the Littlewoods Collection – over 5,000 items relating to the history of the leading football pools company. At any time, around 1,500 items from the Museum's collections are on display, with a further 30,000 items held in storage. The Museum continues to collect historical items, and also collects material relating to football today.

The Museum is a registered charity, governed by a board of independent trustees. The Board comprises a chair and trustees drawn from each of the museums and heritage sectors; the football bodies; the business community; and key stakeholders. The Museum reached the final shortlist for European Museum of the Year in 2003 and was named Large Visitor Attraction of the Year at the 2005–6 Lancashire and Blackpool Tourism Awards.

The National Football Museum is breaking new ground in terms of the audiences for museums.[2] It is the leading museum in terms of the success of the government's policy of free admission to national museums. Since the introduction of free access to the Museum in March 2003, visitor numbers have risen by 177 per cent, to over 100,000 each year – compared with an average 87 per cent rise at

Trying on costumes at the National Football Museum (National Football Museum)

the national museums as a whole. It is also the leading museum in attracting new audiences in terms of people from socio-economic groups C2, D and E. At the National Football Museum, 42 per cent of visitors are from socio-economic groups C2, D and E, which is more than twice the national average for museums funded by DCMS (19 per cent). As well as welcoming over 500,000 visitors in Preston since 2001, the Museum has reached an audience of over one million visitors from elsewhere in the UK by holding, or contributing to, exhibitions at forty-five other museums.

The Museum is also a pioneer in terms of social inclusion, reaching out to new audiences and addressing the needs of disadvantaged sections of the community. In particular the Museum has worked with young Asian Heritage women; women's groups; young people with learning difficulties and disabilities; people with a range of disabilities; the gay and lesbian communities; children from schools in areas of relatively high social deprivation; and prisoners and young offenders.

As the leading football museum in the world, the National Football Museum has held or contributed to twenty exhibitions overseas, in Germany, Belgium, Portugal, Brazil, China, Switzerland and Japan. The Museum created the FIFA Centenary Exhibition, opened by Joseph S. Blatter, President of FIFA, at the Museum in September 2004. The Museum was also invited by UEFA to work in partnership to create the UEFA Jubilee exhibition, which opened at the European Parliament in Brussels in September 2004, before moving to the National Football Museum. In partnership with UEFA, to celebrate the UEFA Euro 2005 Women's Football championship in June of that year, the Museum created the world's first exhibition dedicated to women's football, 'Girls Allowed: The History of Women's Football'.

The Museum has attracted very favourable reviews in the media. For example, in the *New Statesman*, Hunter Davies, commenting on his first visit to the Museum, wrote 'I spent five hours, dazed by all the wonders, and can't wait to go again. It's brilliant ... I honestly, sincerely think it is amazing.' A review in *The Times* described the Museum as 'a fantastic place. Yes, fantastic'.

The ball used in the 1966 World Cup final, one of the exhibits at the National Football Museum (National Football Museum).

Frank Skinner writing in *The Times* concluded that the Museum was 'Brilliant.'[3]

The Museum has attracted a number of major reviews by academics. Johnes and Mason have commented that 'The NFM is ... taking forward the game's public history and helping it develop a more reflective and informed character that extends beyond nostalgia and an obsession with records and statistics [...]. The NFM encourages fans to feel some ownership over the game's past and that can only encourage them to feel the same over its future too'.[4] Brabazon and Mallinder have contrasted the success of the National Football Museum with the failure of the Sheffield Pop Music Centre while Brabazon has described the Museum as 'flawlessly constructed, innovative in method and considered in its selection of items' and 'a brilliant, evocative, interactive celebration of football'.[5]

In partnership with the University of Central Lancashire the Museum has established the International Football Institute (IFI). This seeks to advance research on all aspects of football and to make this research available to the widest possible audience, nationally and internationally. A number of major IFI research projects have been completed and many are underway. IFI has held two major international academic conferences, including the world's first conference on women's football, 'Women, Football and Europe', during the UEFA Euro 2005 championship. IFI has produced over fifty publications to date, including volumes of the papers from the two international

A family enjoying one of the many activities provided by the Museum (National Football Museum)

Never too early to introduce a new generation (National Football Museum)

conferences.[6] Current IFI research projects include a PhD studentship funded by the Arts and Humanities Research Council (AHRC) and jointly supervised by Leeds Metropolitan University, entitled 'Football's Consumer Culture and the Construction of Fan Identities, c1880 to c1960'. Undertaken by Alexander Jackson, this primarily involves a detailed study of the Museum's collections relating to football fandom.

Future plans by the Museum include a major project to improve the literacy skills and self confidence of disadvantaged children, using football poetry and literature to stimulate their interest. A further project and exhibition will focus on football in the gay and lesbian communities, linked to the 2008 International Gay and Lesbian Football Association (IGLFA) world championships. The Museum helped to create a major exhibition in Vienna during the UEFA Euro 2008 Tournament and is working with partner museums in South Africa to create exhibitions during the 2010 FIFA World Cup in South Africa. The Museum will also make a significant contribution to the UK's celebration of hosting the Olympics and Paralympics in 2012 by creating the first major exhibition on the history of football in the Olympics and Paralympics.

Contact details and opening times

The National Football Museum
Sir Tom Finney Way
Preston PR1 6PA
Tel: 01772 908442
Fax: 01772 908433
E-mail: enquiries@nationalfootballmuseum.com
http://www.nationalfootballmuseum.com/
The Museum is open from Tuesday to Saturday, from 10am to 5pm and on Sunday from 11am to 5pm. Admission is free.

(Please note that opening times vary on days when Preston North End are playing. To avoid disappointment we suggest you contact us before setting off on a long journey, particularly on Saturdays during the football season [August – May]. For midweek evening games the Museum stays open later until kick off.)

Notes

1. K. Moore, *Museums and popular culture* (Leicester, 1997).
2. K. Moore, 'Marketing sports museums: attracting new audiences?', pp. 29–32; and K. Moore, 'The People's Museum of the Peoples Game? The National Football Museum, England', pp. 33–43, both in *Revista de Museologia* 22 (2001); K. Moore, 'Attracting new audiences: the National Football Museum, England', in *M: Museums of Mexico and the World*, 2 (2004), pp. 22–31.
3. *New Statesman*, 23 Sep. 2002; *The Times*, 14 Oct. 2002, 4 Nov. 2002.
4. M. Johnes and R. Mason, 'Soccer, public history and the National Football Museum', *Sport in History*, 23 (2003), pp. 130–1.
5. T. Brabazon and S. Mallinder, 'Popping the museum: the cases of Sheffield and Preston', *Museums and Society*, 4 (2006), pp. 96–112; T. Brabazon, *Playing on the periphery: sport, identity and memory* (London, 2006), p. 71; and T. Brabazon, 'Museums and popular culture revisited: Kevin Moore and the politics of pop', *Museum Management and Curatorship*, 21 (2006), p. 285.
6. J. Magee, A. Bairner and A. Tomlinson, eds., *The bountiful game? Football, identities and finance* (Oxford, 2005); M. Atherton, *The theft of the Jules Rimet Trophy* (Oxford, 2007); J. Magee, J. Caudwell, K. Liston and S. Scraton, eds., *Women, football and Europe: Vol. 1: Histories, equity and experience* (Oxford, 2007); J. Magee, G. Baldwin and G. Kelly, eds., *Women, football and Europe: Vol. 2: Contemporary perspectives* (Oxford, 2007).

LIBRARIES AND ARCHIVES
Sporting collections in Manchester and sources for its sporting history

Richard Cox

Manchester has a rich sporting heritage that is a significant part of its extensive and influential socio-cultural, economic and industrial history. As indicated in a recent and extensive study by Jason Wood, 'over the past 200 years, Manchester has been, at one time or another, a leading centre for archery, crown green bowling, cycling, football, greyhound racing, lacrosse, real tennis, rugby, speedway and water polo'.[1] In recent times it has hosted several world championship events plus the 2002 Commonwealth Games. Today it is estimated that Manchester has in excess of 10,000 sports clubs and over a million regular participants in sport. It is home to more national sports organizations than any city outside London and some of the nation's finest facilities and stadiums. Not surprisingly, therefore, it has an extensive sporting archive and literature on which to draw for the purposes of historical research. This article is in two distinct sections. Part One below outlines the sporting content of archives and libraries in Manchester and discusses sources for the history of sport in Manchester. Part Two is a listing of manuscripts in archive collections and a bibliography of secondary sources on the history of sport in Manchester. This part is to be published separately on the *Manchester Region History Review* website (http://www.mcrh.mmu. ac.uk/pubs/mrhr.htm).

The sporting content of archives and libraries in Manchester

As one might reasonably expect in a city the size of Manchester, there are numerous resources for the historian of sport. Only a couple of these collections focus entirely on sport, these being the historical collections at Old Trafford, namely Lancashire County Cricket Club (LCCC) (http://www.cricketarchive.co.uk/Lancashire/) and Manchester United Football Club (http://www.manutd.com). A decade ago, the LCCC honorary librarian and archivist, The Revd Malcolm Lorimer, wrote a piece for this journal in which he described the collection at Old Trafford Cricket Ground.[2] Today, it can boast over 5,000 items and (subject to prior arrangement by writing to the Hon. Archivist and Librarian there) can be made accessible for

purposes of research to outsiders as well as members. The collection embraces national, county and local club histories, biographies, tour records and scrapbooks. Many of these contain newspaper cuttings surrounding individuals, clubs and leagues. One such bound collection of original cuttings is the work of Walter Lawton of Rochdale who maintained a comprehensive scrapbook on LCCC for the years 1888 to 1913. Archival material includes the original score books of the Club's forerunner, the Manchester Cricket Club, from 1850 to 1855; the LCCC's minute books from its founding in 1865 to the present day; score books, and many photographs. It has a growing periodical collection including a complete set of *Wisdens, Lilleywhites, Cricket* (1882–1913), *The Cricket Field* (1892–1895), the *Journal of the Cricket Society* (1961 to date), *Wisden Cricket Monthly* (1979 to date), and *Cricket Quarterly* (1963 to date) plus numerous league and club annuals. The museum at Manchester United's Old Trafford ground was not created until 1986 and is largely confined to a collection of artefacts such as shirts, cups, medals, pennants, programmes and other memorabilia. This collection and displays have been described by the Museum's curator, Mark Wylie:

Road runners of both sexes, presumably on a training run, 1956 (Manchester Archives and Local Studies, Central Library, M07716)

The overwhelming impression of the museum display is one of 'glory, glory, glory', with little mention of the downside. There is no mention of the 1915 match-fixing scandal that rocked the club, the twenty-six year championships wait, the Docherty Affair or the terrible reputation that their travelling supporters gained in the mid 70s. However, the collection is growing apace and will be of interest to many historians of sport as well as soccer (Manchester United) fans.[3]

What some readers may not have previously appreciated is that it is the more general archive and library collections that hold the most material concerning sport, including the perhaps not-so-obvious University of Manchester (John Rylands) Library (http://www.library.manchester.ac.uk/). This library houses the William Brockbank Cricket Collection, bequeathed to the library by former Dean of Clinical Studies at the university, and avid cricket enthusiast. The collection, containing over 1,000 volumes, is organized within its own classification scheme covering bibliographies and reference works, periodicals, general history, biography, laws of cricket, technique, club cricket, county cricket, test cricket, fiction, verse and prose. As these headings show, the range of the collection is diverse and in each category includes works of great value and rarity, as well as items of a more popular and ephemeral nature. The periodical collection includes an almost complete run of *Wisden* (lacking 1869 only) and Samuel Britcher's *A complete list of all the grand matches, 1790–1804*, the latter described by cricket bibliographer David Rayvern as exceedingly valuable in its role as precursor of other annuals such as *Lilleywhites* and *Wisden*, and as objects surviving (very few copies are know to exist anywhere in the world). This collection is described more extensively by John. P. Tuck.[4]

The Rylands Library's sporting collection does not end with cricket. Notable collections include books on cycling, water-sports and an eclectic collection of all sports bequeathed by another Manchester doctor, Thomas Windsor. These volumes range in date of publication from 1799 to 1909 and comprise many different genres including treatises and instructional manuals, descriptive works and travel writings, price lists and periodical parts. Some rare books were once part of the University's Physical Education Department Library integrated into the main library in the mid 1980s. Examples include Izzack Walton's *The compleat Angler* (1760); Henry Altkens's *The national sports of Great Britain* (1903); J. C. F. Guts Muths's *Turnbuch für die Söhne des Vaterlandes* (1817); Edward Whyper's *Scrambles amongst the Alps* (1893), plus many more, including early issues of the Manchester-based *Athletic Review*. Similarly, the library holds many general periodicals which frequently had sporting content, ranging from the gentlemen's magazines of Victorian England such as *Contemporary Review* and *Macmillan's Magazine* to the *Illustrated London News* and *Vanity Fair*, both of which frequently carried sporting content. There are various indexes to some of these periodicals (for example, *The Waterloo Directory of Periodicals 1824–1900*), their contents (for example, W. E. Houghton's *Wellesley index to Victorian periodicals 1824–1900*), as well as a collection of their articles on sport.[5]

The John Rylands Library's special collections section also hosts a number of large national collections such as the archives of the *Guardian* and the *Daily Mail*. The *Guardian* archive collection includes notes made by the cricket correspondent Neville Cardus (B/C34/1441). According to a survey in 1955, 33 per cent of the *Daily Mail* was filled by sporting content. The photograph library of the *Daily Mail* includes literally hundreds of photographs on sporting topics at home and abroad such as local organizations like the Agecroft Rowing Club, and a valuable set of photographs taken at the 1936 Olympic Games which help capture the mood of the occasion. The library has full runs of over twenty other national newspapers which, although not unique to this collection, can be valuable to the modern historian of sport. *The Times* is indexed throughout its existence, copies of which can also be found in the library. For local sport, the *Manchester Evening News* is an invaluable resource. Back copies are to be found in several locations within and outside the city, including the Central Reference Library.

Readers might be even more surprised to find the odd interesting item on sport in other less obvious collections within John Rylands. One such example is a manuscript within the Methodist archive calling for the abolition of cruel sports such a bull-baiting. The late S. G. Jones, Mancunian and PhD graduate of the University of Manchester, published his study of sport and organized labour in 1988.[6] This book reveals the vast scope of source material for the history of sport in the Labour Party archive, held at the Manchester-based People's History Museum (http://www.phm.org.uk). The Professional Footballers' Association was founded in Manchester in 1907, albeit under a different name, and has retained its headquarters in the city ever since. Its archives are also held at the People's History Museum. They were extensively used by John Harding in his history of that organization and an exhibition mounted by the museum.[7] A valuable collection of Labour Party news cuttings and pamphlets is also held at John Rylands and a scan of the in-house index to the collection reveals a significant amount of material relating to sport.

More locally centred records within the Rylands Library are those of some of the large estates within Manchester and surrounding areas

such as Dunham Massey. Within their records are manuscripts relating to shooting and hunting, and for more modern times, documents that illustrate how the tenth Earl of Stamford (Roger Grey [1896–1976]) supported and encouraged many local clubs and teams in sports as diverse as angling, cricket, golf, football and rugby. The issue of Sunday golf at Bowden Golf Club figures large in his correspondence of the 1920s and even becomes the subject of a village referendum. The records of the University of Manchester itself contain some sporting material in the form of Athletic Union records. These relate largely to inter-varsity sport and club activities but also include material relating to the facilities once owned and managed by the Athletic Union, including the sports grounds in Fallowfield. This was the venue for many national championships and the training ground of Reg Harris, one of Britain's most famous cyclists. He won the world amateur sprint title in 1947, two Olympic silver medals in 1948, and the professional title in 1949, 1950, 1951 and 1954. It is not generally well known that the pitch inside the racing track also hosted the 1893 FA Cup final between Wolverhampton Wanderers and Everton FC. It was the first time that the initial match for the cup final had been held outside London. The stadium was demolished to make way for student housing in the late 1990s. Some of the larger university sports club had their own archive and library collection, also housed in the Rylands Library, such as those of the University of Manchester

Mountaineering Club. This was a pioneering club in its day and helped establish the Manchester region as something of a breeding ground for rock-climbers and mountaineers.

So far, mention has only been made of sport in the modern world but many activities, of course, go back further in history and in the Library are Greek papyri which include items of sporting interest; papyrus 93, for example, has a list of athletes dating from the third century. Finally, it would be remiss of me not to mention the large number of higher degree theses and dissertations completed at the University of Manchester and now available for consultation within the library. These included theses submitted to the History Department but more numerous are those completed in the department of physical education. This was the first university in the UK to teach a Masters degree (MEd) in this field and was largely down to the work of physical education historian David McNair. These theses covered many topics including local studies and can be identified in Part Two. Also owned by the University of Manchester is the Manchester Museum on Oxford Street. In respect of sport, this is well known as the home of the Simon Archery Collection, perhaps the most significant archive of archery material in the British Isles and possibly the English language. The collection contains a vast array of books, periodicals and manuscripts, all of which are listed in F. Lake and H. Wright's *Bibliography of archery*, published by the Simon Foundation in 1974.[8] The museum also mounted a special exhibition on sport in support of the unsuccessful Manchester Olympic bid. Finally, it is worth noting that from 7 June to 19 October 1990 the Library mounted a special exhibition *A Summer of Sport* in connection with the Olympic festival and the (unsuccessful) Manchester Olympic bid. It was at the same time and with similar purpose that the Greater Manchester Museum of Science and Industry mounted a similar exhibition *Everyone's a Winner: The History of Sport In and Around Manchester*. A companion booklet with the same title edited by Alison Taubman, Pauline Webb and Jenny Wetton was also published. This volume illustrates the vast range of material, mainly artefacts, still in private hands with items loaned from such organizations as the Manchester Tennis and Racquets Club, Northern Lawn Tennis Club, Salford Rugby League Club, Sale Harriers, Reg Harris, and sporting Mancunians such as Ron Hill (athletics), Harry Hill (cycling), and Paula Thomas (athletics).

Manchester Metropolitan University hosts the North West Film Archive in Chorlton Street (http://www.nwfa.mmu.ac.uk/). This collection grew out of a research project into the history of the local film industry established in 1977 by Manchester Polytechnic and the North West Arts Association. The emphasis was on the films that recorded the life of the North West population, or film made by its inhabitants. Today, the archive houses a mainly non-fiction collection of over 400,000 feet of archive film on all gauges and qualities, and ranges from film taken in the pioneer days of the 1890s to local television material of the past two decades. A few films are entirely about sport, football matches, college sports, bowling tournaments, and the Co-op's Sports and Recreation ground, but most sporting activities appear within films of other events, such as cadets swimming while on camp; golf as a part of a film publicising Southport; and so forth. The University of Salford library contains significantly less material on sport but some significant and unique collections such as the nearby Working Class Movement Library (http://www.wcml.org.uk/) may have material relevant to some studies of sport. The University also hosts its own Sporting Hall of Fame, comprising commissioned paintings of famous local sportsmen and women. It is currently housed in the Staff House.

Manchester has many other private museums and archives of a more specialist nature that sometimes carry individual items relating to sport, but also valuable material for setting the wider socio-cultural scene of which sport was a part. These include the Police Museum (http://www.gmp.police.uk/mainsite/pages/history.htm), the People's History Museum (http://www.phm.org.uk), and the Jewish Museum (http://www.manchesterjewishmuseum.com/) many of which have been dealt with separately in previous editions of this journal. The Jewish Museum's major exhibition of 2007 entitled *Scenes Around Us* featured sport quite heavily.

Within the public sector, Manchester Archives and Local Studies (http://www.manchester.gov.uk) on the first floor of the Central Library in St Peter's Square is home to a wide range of materials on the history of sport in Manchester, its buildings, clubs and its people. Manchester Archives houses the records of several sports clubs. These are listed in the second section of Part Two of this survey. Club records tend to comprise largely of minutes and accounts, the value of which can be variable, often being full of much procedural waffle and some of unnecessary notes of an annoying nature. Occasionally, however, one may come across sets of club rules, fixture lists, posters, programmes, honours lists, scorebooks, certificates, membership lists, articles of association, ledgers and even cuttings books. Photographs, particularly of teams, are sometimes included but usually without any supporting information. There are, of course, many other useful sources depicting sporting facilities in the collection such as maps, plans and photographs. A valuable feature of this Manchester collection is the computerized local-image collection (http://www.images.manchester.gov.uk). Many of the 77,000 images concern sport of one form or another in and around Manchester. Commercial directories appeared in many local regions from the eighteenth century onwards, recording the commercial and topographical details of communities and listing the principal inhabitants and their occupations. Although they provided little information on sport until the 1860s, thereafter the Post Office and other directories for various local towns provide potted histories of clubs, details of their facilities, membership and officials. A number of provincial directories are held in the Central Library.

As with central government, it was not until recent years, mainly since local government reorganization in 1974, that many authorities set up separate committees for sport and recreation. Swimming baths usually came under Baths and Wash Houses; outdoor recreation areas under Parks, Gardens and Cemeteries; indoor sport under Education. Copies of annual reports and published minutes of the various committees are held in the Central Library, with unpublished documents in the Greater Manchester County Record Office (http://www.gmcro.co.uk/). The format and detail contained within these documents varies immensely. The annual reports of the local education authority's school medical officer (appointed in 1910), contained within the more general annual report for education, include a report by the organizer, inspector or advisor for physical education which mentions developments in local schools, evening play-centres and school camps. The book collection has a number of school histories, especially of

Chorlton-cum-Hardy Lacrosse Club, 1933. One of the many illustrations of local sporting clubs in the Manchester Local Image Collection (Manchester Archives and Local Studies, Central Library, M07668)

the more prominent Manchester schools such as William Hulme and Manchester Grammar School, which have sections devoted to sport. The book collection also has many of the club histories, listed in Part Two of this survey, plus other important publications and reports such as the official 1996 Manchester Olympic Games bid document and the official report of the 2002 Commonwealth Games. Many of the towns surrounding Manchester also have valuable local studies collections and archives containing similar materials, such as those for Bolton and Bury.[9]

The strong emotional and sensual side to sport has been well illustrated by the use of oral evidence. Rogan Taylor's BBC documentary on the history of football published as *Kicking and screaming: an oral history of football in England* in 1995 focussed heavily on north-west clubs and exhibits the importance of the individual perception and interpretation of events, and the value of oral evidence in supporting a history-from-below approach. A special edition of *Oral History* (vol. 25, no. 1, 1997) focussed entirely on sporting themes and mainly in the North West.[10] There are sound recordings of sportsmen (few women) in several of the archives mentioned above but the most significant collection is at The North West Sound Archive in Clitheroe (http://www.lancashire.gov.uk/education/record_office/about/archive.asp). Also further afield, but worthy of note within the context of Greater Manchester's sporting history are the National Football Museum in Preston, discussed elsewhere in this publication, and the Mass-Observation archive housed at the University of Sussex Library. This research project was set up to create what they called an 'anthology of ourselves'. One of the Mass-Observation's interests was how people spent their leisure time and their studies therefore touch on sporting activities in many different ways throughout the 1938–50 period. It is worth mentioning here because this was based on people living in Bolton (http://www.sussex.ac.uk/library/massobs/general.shtml).

Finally, many sports figured in the painting of several artists, some of which can be found in the rich collections in and around Manchester. C. S. Lowry's *Going to the Match* is a renowned work of art for a multitude of reasons. The work of a Salford artist, it graphically depicts the Saturday afternoon scene in a grim northern industrial town, and set a new record for a Lowry work of art (just under £2m in 1999). It is owned by the Professional Footballer's Association and sits on display in the boardroom of its headquarters in Manchester. Perhaps less well known is Lowry's *Cricket Club Outing* which I understand to be in private hands and not on public display. Various Manchester galleries, public and private, have staged displays on a sporting theme. At the time of the European Nations Championships in 1996, Manchester City Library, Manchester Art Gallery and the Cornerhouse Eye Gallery all staged important exhibitions on the history of football expressed through the pictorial record. Brochures and catalogues were produced for most of these.

The collection of family album photographs now housed at the Greater Manchester Record Office (http://www.gmcro.co.uk) is of special note. It contains many unusual sporting pictures, mainly between the years 1880 and 1940. There are street scenes, buildings, pictures of people as individuals, groups such as sports teams, and events such as school sports-days, all portraying the social life of the district. This project was originally funded by the Manpower Services Commission in the early 1980s and overseen by the Manchester Studies Unit of Manchester Polytechnic. It was one of many similar worthwhile projects that helped document historical evidence whilst offering work experience to the unemployed.

A listing of individual manuscripts within the record collections mentioned above is published in Part Two. This is not exhaustive in the sense that some records will be held in The National Archives at Kew in south-west London (http://www.nationalarchives.gov.uk/). These are items concerned with Manchester, but part of a larger collection reflecting the work of a government department. Some club records remain in private hands and are not always accessible, even to the academic researcher. Unfortunately, some will have also been lost. If the club was registered as a company (limited or unlimited), as is the case with professional clubs, then statutory records including details of capital, names and addresses of shareholders and directors, annual accounts and auditors reports will be deposited with Companies House (http://www.companies-house.gov.uk). Unfortunately the satellite branch in Manchester no longer exists. The files of defunct companies are kept by the Register of Companies until they are about twenty years old and then transferred to The National Archives. The files of dissolved companies are located in PRO classes BT31 and BT41. Researchers may be interested in sports-related industries and again Manchester companies were prominent in some fields. Simon Inglis, in his *Played in Manchester*, published by English Heritage in 2004, mentions Salford as the manufacturing base of most turnstiles used in sporting venues in the UK and even further afield.[11] Some may have taken out patents to protect their rights to the benefit from their inventions and these too can be a valuable source of information. Similarly, buildings of architectural interest are detailed in the archives of the British Institute of Architects and can be consulted at their London headquarters. Readers interested in researching more specialist topics of this nature are advised to consult Richard Cox's *History of sport: a guide to sources* (1994).

Secondary sources

Although there is not space to discuss the full range of the secondary literature on Manchester's sporting history, it is useful to give some key pointers. The range and scope of secondary literature on Manchester sport is well documented in this author's *History of sport in Britain to 2000: a bibliography of publications to 2000*, published by Frank Cass in 2003. Volume One, devoted to national histories, has a number of nationwide case studies that include detail of developments in the Manchester region. Richard Holt's *Sport and the working class* has a chapter by Stephen Jones, 'Working class sport in Manchester between the wars'. In respect of nationwide histories of individual sports, Manchester is well represented. It goes largely without saying that no history of football, for example, could be complete without mention of at least some developments in Manchester. The city had two large professional clubs, City and United, from the early years of the League which set the pace for others to emulate throughout the twentieth century. Lincoln Allison's essay 'Association football and the urban ethos' makes comparisons on an international scale and Tony Mason's pioneering history of professional football, *Association football and English society, 1863–1915*, draws on many examples from both the United and City clubs.[12] Cricket at Old Trafford is well served by G. Hudd and D. Mortimer's respective studies of test cricket at the ground.[13] Andrew Hignell takes an unusual perspective on the ground when he investigates the impact of the weather at Old Trafford in 'A look to the heavens', in the 1999 *Lancashire cricket yearbook*, and his *Rain stops play: cricketing climates*, published by Frank Cass in 2002.

Volume Two of my *British sport: a bibliography publications to 2000* lists specific regional and local histories of sport, histories of individual clubs, competitions and organizations, arranged topographically first by county (using the pre-1974 boundaries and names) and then by town. Within the general section of the county of Lancashire are such publications as the Victoria County Histories. Lancashire was one of the first counties to be included in the series. Volume Two, edited by W. Farrer and J. Brownbill and published in 1908, has a fairly extensive section on sport (see pp. 467–506). Although there is a strong emphasis on rural sports in the county as a whole, examples from many sports pertain to developments in Manchester and its environs. As the major industrial and financial city of the county of Lancashire, many county-wide histories of sport also make a focus on events in Manchester. Several university history theses on sport in Lancashire have touched on sport in and around Manchester, including, for example, D. J. Hill's *The growth of workin-class sport in Lancashire, 1870–1914* (MLitt thesis, University of Lancaster, 1975).

Much of what many regard as 'south Manchester' (defined here by where the local population tend to look for shopping, work and entertainment) is strictly in Cheshire, of course, and so it is important to consult this section of the bibliography too. M. K. Sykes focuses on the west side of the county but occasionally has something to say about districts that many would regard as 'south Manchester'.[14] The same does not apply so much to the other neighbouring counties, although towns like Glossop (Derbyshire) and Todmorden (Yorkshire) tended to look towards Lancashire and even Manchester for certain sports, competitions and teams. In respect of countywide histories of individual sports, R. W. Lewis embraces Manchester in his study of the development of professional football in Lancashire, as does B. W. Prose in his study of the control of Lancashire football crowds.[15]

Finally, biographical studies of individual sporting personalities, be they player, coach, or administrator vary enormously in both scope and scholarship. With few exceptions, most are predictably boring about goals scored and championships won, with no analytical substance. Their real value, however, lies when read between the lines. Insights into personalities, motives, influential events *et al* can often be identified. Many who made their name as players for Lancashire or Bolton or Manchester were not Mancunians or even British. Frenchman Eric Cantona, for example, figures largely in the history of Manchester United folklore, and Clive Lloyd in the recent history of LCCC. And some Mancunians, of course, made their name with other clubs, contributing further to the city and the region's sporting reputation.

Notes

1. Jason Wood, *A sporting chance: extra time for England's historic sports venues* (pilot study, internal report for English Heritage Consultancy Services, July 2002).
2. Malcolm Lorimer, 'Lancashire County Cricket Club library', *Manchester Region History Review*, 10 (1996), pp. 77–80.
3. Mark Wylie, 'Manchester United Museum', *Manchester Region History Review*, 10 (1996), pp. 81–4.
4. John. P. Tuck, 'Some sources for the history of popular culture', *Bulletin of the John Rylands University Library of Manchester*, 71 (1989), pp. 164–6.
5. Martin Polley, *The history of sport in Britain, 1880–1914* (5 vols., London, 2003). See also Richard Cox, *History of sport: a guide to sources* (Frodsham, 2005).
6. Richard Holt, *Sport, politics and the working class: organized labour and sport in inter-war Britain* (Manchester, 1988).
7. John Harding, *More than a game: the official history of the PFA* (London, 1991).

8. F. Lake and H. Wright, *Bibliography of archery* (Manchester, 1974); W. E. A. Axon, 'Archery in Manchester in the sixteenth and seventeenth centuries', *Transactions of the Lancashire and Cheshire Antiquarian Society*, 18 (1901), pp. 61–9.

9. http://www.oldmancunians.org/html/news/current The%20First%20 Medical%20Officer%20_illustrated_.pdf; http://www.bolton.gov.uk/portal/ page?_pageid=367, 129972&_dad=portal92&_schema=PORTAL92; http:// www.bury.gov.uk/LeisureAndCulture/Libraries/Archives/default.htm.

10. See, for example, L. Oliver, '"No Hard Brimmed Hats or Hat Pins Please!" Bolton women cotton workers and the game of rounders, 1911–39', *Oral History*, 25 (1997), pp. 40–5.

11. Simon Inglis, *Played in Manchester* (London, 2004), pp. 65–9.

12. Lincoln Allison, 'Association football and the urban ethos', in J. D. Worth and R. L. Jones, eds., *Manchester and Sao Paulo* (Palo Alto, CA; 1978); Tony Mason, *Association football and English society, 1863–1915* (Brighton, 1980).

13. G. Hudd, *Test cricket at Old Trafford, 1884–1998* (Warrington, 1999); and D. Mortimer, *Old Trafford: test cricket since 1888* (Stroud, 2005).

14. M. K. Sykes, *The development pattern of physical recreation in the county of Chester and its rural districts in the nineteenth century with particular reference to the period 1875–1900* (MPhil thesis, Coventry University, 1996).

15. R. W. Lewis, 'The development of professional football in Lancashire, 1870–1914' (PhD, University of Lancaster, 1994); B. W. Prose, 'The control and accommodation of Lancashire football crowds, 1885–1914' (MA thesis, University of Manchester, 1981).

LONG REVIEWS

John Dickinson

Misericords of north-west England: their nature and significance Lancaster: Centre for North-West Regional Studies, University of Lancaster, 2008. viii+128pp. ISBN 9781862202047.

The north-west of England has many ecclesiastical treasures, amongst them a considerable number of misericords, largely remaining in sets that can still be studied and appreciated as composite wholes. Lists of them are readily available, most notably in G. L. Remnant's *Catalogue*. The present work, a product of the author's obvious enthusiasm for his subject, treats the major sets in a manner at once topographical and thematic. The churches are dealt with individually, each providing occasion for a selection of a few more interesting misericords and a treatment of some subject matter well represented in them: folklore, perhaps, or foliage, or fun. Despite the need for cross-references, on the whole this scheme appears to serve its purpose. Based on those misericords that he illustrates, the author gives short accounts of the many forces he considers to have inspired the production of individual works in the period 1340–1520: clericalism, anti-feminism, the rise of scientific observation, the printing revolution, and so on.

Most, perhaps all, previous treatments of misericords, while celebrating their delightfully varied subject matter, have assumed that their craftsmen themselves chose subjects, presentation and execution for these minor works half hidden in darkness. Dickinson firmly states that he does not accept this. His view is that the subject of each misericord was chosen by 'the monks' (what precisely is meant by this phrase is never explained) and that the finished works were intended as, and

were indeed used as, starting points for meditation. For this reason the bulk of the text consists of hypothesis and speculation about what might have motivated the choice and what might have been the subject of the meditation.

It is an interesting idea. After all, a set of stalls with misericords was an expensive fitting; and from the modern viewpoint at least one might expect that payment for the work would necessarily imply control over it. That model seems to govern contemporary thinking about the work of universities or the BBC, but Dickinson gives no apparent consideration to whether it would always have been how a late-medieval craftsman worked with his ecclesiastical patron. Besides, whatever may be said about the original choice of subjects, the proposal that the misericords could have subsequently been the object of intelligent contemplation by 'the monks' is not easy to understand. During services the participants were necessarily in a position that made inspection of the misericord impossible, and even if they had at other times the inclination to potter round the church admiring artwork it is surely unlikely that they would have been particularly drawn to these secretive carvings, which must have been even more difficult to see and interpret when the only illumination was daylight filtered through coloured windows. Stalls cannot be thought of as planned like the sculptural programme of a church's west façade, which certainly was intended both to be seen and to teach.

Context is everything. In order to establish his difficult thesis, the author would need to look not only at the context in which individual works were created, and the context in which they might thereafter be observed. He would also need to consider other works not intended for the public eye – for example caricatures and baboonery in the margins of manuscripts – and explain why different considerations apply (or perhaps argue that here too each individual subject was chosen by the patron). He would need to consider each misericord not in isolation or in conjunction with a few others in the same place, but as part of a whole. Why should a patron anxious to convey a message confine himself to only a few of the misericords? What do the others mean? Alternatively, why commission a set of misericords without any holistic programme? By considering only misericords, and only a few from each church, Dickinson excludes the rigorous contextual analysis that his proposal requires.

There is a further problem. Whether or not sharing the concerns already expressed, the reader to whom the author's novel ideas are addressed may be less likely to accept them from a writer who thinks that *decani* means 'the deacon's side', that the 'Decorative' style of architecture was sweeping the nation when Carlisle Cathedral was being rebuilt, that the viewers of the stalls in St Mary's, Nantwich would have been monks (it is not a monastic foundation), or that clergy celebrating memorial masses required 'a choir (or chancel)'. In explaining that 'the North West' is a modern construct, Dickinson states 'all the churches and abbeys considered in this book were under the Archdiocese of York'. The vocabulary here is inappropriate or anachronistic; the sentiment ignores the role of the diocesan authorities, in particular of Carlisle; and the statement is simply wrong: half the buildings considered were until 1541 in the diocese of Lichfield and Coventry (under various names) and within the Southern Province. That references are given for these and other solecisms merely means that the author has misunderstood his secondary material; he appears to have deliberately avoided using primary sources.

With or without Dickinson's commentary and ideas, what the misericords demand of the modern viewer is to be studied. There are many discoveries and interpretations still to be made. Dickinson follows others in treating N5 at Lancaster as a baptism, but medieval representations of that sacrament generally show at least a priest and a baby, whereas here there is neither, and the structure illustrated does not look much like a font. N7 at Whalley does not in fact show a maiden holding the wodewose's beard as the text suggests: the creature has his head, fashionably divided beard and all, firmly resting on his own hand in an attitude of rapt admiration. These details are clear from Dickinson's excellent illustrations. If his work does nothing more than challenge the reader to look at those with care and then extend his study to the misericords themselves it will have been a job worth doing and a service to the appreciation of regional culture.

Mark Ockelton

Margaret Lynch (leader; edited by members of the Ranulf Higden Society)
Life, love and death in north-east Lancashire, 1510–1537: a translation of the Act Book of the ecclesiastical court of Whalley Manchester: The Chetham Society, 2006. ix+283pp. ISBN 0955427606.

This volume is an English translation of the Act Book of the ecclesiastical court of the Cistercian Abbey at Whalley, which was dissolved in 1537. A transcription of the original Latin manuscript (located at Stonyhurst College) was edited by Alice M. Cooke and published by the Chetham Society in 1901.

The court of Whalley Abbey was an ecclesiastical peculiar which held jurisdiction over the royal forests of north-east Lancashire – Blackburnshire, Bowland, Pendle, Rossendale and Trawden – and which was exempt from the authority of the Diocese of Coventry and Lichfield. After the Acts of Supremacy (1534) and Suppression (1536) the jurisdiction of the ecclesiastical peculiar was transferred to the royal courts in August 1536. Visitations were placed under royal supervision and legal administration was effectively transferred from the Church to the Tudor state. As such, the Act Book provides a fascinating insight into the daily lives of people living in these isolated rural communities on the eve of, and during, the Henrician Reformation. As Alice Cooke wrote in her introduction to the 1901 edition, 'no hint of approaching change breaks the quiet monotony of the record of the Abbey Court' (pp. iv–v). The Act Book's importance is all the more significant as the diocesan records have been lost.

The court dealt with a variety of offences during its visitations, including many examples similar to those cited in Ralph Houlbrooke's all-encompassing work, *Church courts and the people during*

the English Reformation, 1520–1570 (1979), on the ecclesiastical courts of the Dioceses of Norwich and Winchester during the Reformation. Many of the cases in the Whalley Act Book concern sexuality and morality – an issue long under the domain of the Church. Between 1510 and 1537, misdemeanours cited included: adultery, bastardy, concubinage, domestic violence, forced marriage, fornication, and illegitimacy. The Act Book demonstrates that the process of marriage formation was an especially significant one during this period, as the exact words of a betrothal could have long-term repercussions. A couple seeking an annulment might cite the following in an attempt to end their marriage: consanguinity and affinity – how closely related a couple were; forced marriage; or a prior betrothal or marriage. Annulments were relatively unusual, and cruelty and infidelity were not sufficient grounds for annulment. Rather, separation *a mensa et thoro* was the far more common consequence of marital breakdown.

Church records provide valuable insights into the lives of individuals who have otherwise been unrecorded. One of the most memorable and well documented cases is that of Agnes Houghton of Pendle, who fled the marital home, claiming she was being beaten for refusing sexual relations with her husband John Bulcock. Agnes sought an annulment, alleging that she had only married under threat of disinheritance. Agnes's words are recalled in local dialect during the testimony of a witness: 'I am undone, For myne Frendes wole nedes compell me to have John Bulcok, and by myne trouth I had lever dy then have hym, For I never loved hym ne never wyl do' (p. 71). Whether Agnes received her annulment is not recorded. Many of the cases remain unresolved; leaving the reader wondering what happened to the people whose lives we have been given such a tantalizing glimpse of.

Despite the presence of annulment cases, such examples remain distinctly unusual. A far more common sight in the Act Book is the citation of sexual miscreants. One of the most notorious sexual offenders recorded is Hugh Whittaker of Pendle, who fathered at least four illegitimate children. He was reported for 'behaving suspiciously [with Margery Crankshaw] in *lez barne* of Hugh's mother' (p. 176). Indeed, the barn was not the only location for liaisons: Agnes Aspenhalghe accused Emmote Whittaker of being 'a hoore with hir husband' in the 'swyncote of Edmund Whittaker' (pp. 48–9).

An intriguing point, raised by John Swain in his introduction, is the prevalence of adultery and fornication cases cited in Pendle. Was there more sexual misconduct in Pendle or were the local residents simply more assiduous about reporting it? Interestingly, given the region's later associations with witchcraft, an accusation is also recorded that the wife of John Herryson of Pendle 'makes charms and tells fortunes' (p. 53). Christopher Haigh's research on Lancashire has highlighted the prevalence and persistence of medieval Catholicism in the county (see *Reformation and resistance in Tudor Lancashire* [1975]; and *The last days of the Lancashire monasteries and the Pilgrimage of Grace* [1969]), so perhaps Pendle informants might be cited as examples of the heightened piety which existed within that isolated region.

Whatever the reason, the locality certainly appears to have been more morally sensitive than other areas under the court's jurisdiction.

Cases regarding the enforcement of religious uniformity were also brought before the court. Non-attendance at church services and working on Sundays and Holy Days were the most common misdemeanours. Sunday 'work' could include gardening, harvesting, or washing clothes. Non-payment of tithes is also reported; John Swindlehurst was excommunicated for his determined refusal to pay tithes on his lambs. Some families were persistent offenders, such as the Marcrofts of Rossendale who were presented for: gossiping and swearing during services; usury; defamation; illegitimacy; and keeping a bawdy house. The penances imposed for those found guilty of transgressions varied. Usually the guilty party was fined costs and required to join the church procession on one or more Sundays, barefoot, in undergarments only, and carrying a penitent's candle. Other punishments included whipping, public apology, or recitations of the rosary.

The world described in the Act Book is a decidedly medieval one with the parish church at the centre of the community – Eamon Duffy's *The stripping of the altars* (2nd ed., 2005) in action. The abrupt cessation of the records in 1537 is a timely reminder of the impact of the Henrician Reformation – Whalley Abbey was dissolved and its abbot executed on charges of complicity in the Pilgrimage of Grace.

Life, love and death in north-east Lancashire is a fascinating and compelling read which would be a valuable addition to any library. The work would be of great interest to students of cultural, legal, religious, and socio-economic history, as well as to general readers of local history. Undoubtedly the Act Book of Whalley will continue to be a valuable resource for academic historians and that its translation into English will make it accessible to a much wider readership.

Christina Brindley
Manchester Metropolitan University

Kevin McPhillips

Joseph Burgess (1853–1934) and the founding of the Independent Labour Party Lampeter: The Edwin Mellen Press, 2005. xii+244pp. ISBN 0773460683.

Kevin McPhillips has written a solid and useful account of the journalist and ILP activist Joseph Burgess, but one not without some problems. Burgess's story is one of erratic occupational, geographical and social mobility allied to an irritating and unaccommodating personality and self-confidence. As presented by McPhillips, far from celebrating his 'prominent role in the process of creating both the Independent Labour Party and later the Labour Party' (p. 1), Labour would have lost little and gained much if he and his type had not existed. It is worth noting that in David Howell's definitive *British workers and the Independent Labour Party*, Burgess features fleetingly on scarcely seven of 522 pages.

McPhillips's emphasis is on Burgess's career rather than his thought. Burgess's father – a weaver – was a restless drinker, gambler and fighter who was able to open – but not keep open – a pub with his winnings on the Chester Cup. The need to find work kept the family on the move around Oldham. Joseph acquired what education he could in dame and religious schools but started mill work at twelve. His arrest for gambling in public and the death of a work colleague appear to represent an existential turning-point (p. 20). Joseph signed the pledge, took to the Oldham Mechanics Institute, observed debates at the 'local Parliament' and got his dialect verses in the manner of Edwin Wright published. After 1881 he never worked in a mill again and was a journalist, first as a reporter and later editor on the Liberal *Oldham Evening Express*, then from 1884 editor of the *Oldham Operative* and other ultimately unviable titles. Though he never pins this down beyond reasonable doubt, McPhillips does hint that from then on Burgess's political stance had as much to do with finding a political formula to keep a succession of struggling newspapers afloat as ideological conviction. Thus, the *Workman's Times*'s advocacy of 'direct labour representation' in the early 1890s perhaps reflected the impact on Burgess of socialists on its staff (p. 51), but was also certainly an attempt to mop up the readers of failing socialist papers and supporters of the new ILP (p. 64). Whatever else he was at this time, Burgess was also – of necessity – a capitalist entrepreneur. This obviously complicates the selflessness of the key claim that Burgess 'certainly deserves a special place in Labour history' (p. 69) for his part in arranging the founding conference of the ILP.

Thereafter, as McPhillips demonstrates, Burgess was an undisciplined and wayward ILPer. One could point to three main instances of this. First, his behaviour as a parliamentary candidate. The Bradford

Conference 'did little to enhance the position of the *Workman's Times*' and in late 1893 Burgess was urging the party to give him £500 to enable the paper to survive. The money was not forthcoming and the paper folded, whereupon Burgess became an itinerant lecturer for the ILP for the next twenty years. His parliamentary candidacy for Leicester in August 1894 saw him refusing to attack the Lib-Lab Henry Broadhurst, to the annoyance of some party workers. On the other hand, his selection as candidate for Glasgow Camlachie saw Bernard Shaw criticize him for so alienating local Liberals that they refused to observe an electoral pact. Though Howell's analysis of the Leicester election uncovers a degree of complexity not evident in McPhillips's, Burgess does not emerge as an asset in either account.

Second, his abandonment of free trade. McPhillips suggests that the origins of this lie in a newspaper comment that, had Burgess been willing to support tariff reform, he could capture sufficient Tory votes to win at Montrose (p. 110); but this seems too slender a basis for what became an obsession for the rest of his life. With no training in economics, he set about finding a third way between free trade and protectionism whereby the export of British capital would be prevented and instead invested at home to eliminate unemployment and fund a socialist society. The instruments to achieve this were a draconian tax on overseas investments and Labour taking 'the earliest opportunity that presents itself to impeach as traitors British capitalists who thus finance foreign competition' (p. 112). When his critics inside and outside the ILP called into question his taxation plans, Burgess regarded this as an act of sabotage: he attacked J. A. Hobson for having stabbed

him in the back 'at a most critical point in my career' (p. 120).

Third, by mid 1915, he had shifted his allegiance from the ILP and its anti-war stance to Victor Fisher's Socialist Nationalist Defence Committee (which became the National Socialist Party) and published *Homeland or empire?*, which restated his economic ideas and sought to 'weld together the forces of Nationalism and Socialism' (p. 113). McPhillips sees this as 'just another example of acting on impulse' (p. 153), but it saw the Bradford ILP passing a motion of censure and Burgess attacking his former Labour colleagues, especially Snowden – even presenting himself as a NSP candidate for Blackburn in 1917. When the NSP unravelled in 1918, Burgess had nowhere to go. Eventually he rejoined the Labour Party in 1925, whereupon, as he put it in his autobiography, he 'resumed the task of educating it' in 'Burgess Economics'. All in all, the *Manchester Guardian*'s assessment when Burgess died, which McPhillips quotes and does not fundamentally dissent from, seems just: 'As a politician, Burgess for all his enthusiasm and force, was the despair of his friends ... He was in perpetual opposition to his party' (p. 185).

McPhillips narrates and evaluates this life clearly and carefully on the basis of all the existing sources. Nonetheless, Howell's analysis of the Leicester situation raises the suspicion that other episodes too were more complicated than they appear to be here. Again, it is a matter of regret that so little can be known of his private life: it seems clear that behind this erratic man stood an impressive third wife whose money enabled his political 'career' to take its course and who was willing to speak alongside him in Blackburn in 1917 (p. 157). It is also frustrating that the book does little to pinpoint *precisely* the origins of his ideas and the *character* of his 'socialism'; instead we are offered many hints. Thus, Burgess had 'scant knowledge of Socialist doctrine and preferred the emotional approach favoured by many in the movement' (p. 2); 'Over the years Blatchford probably had more influence on Burgess than any other politician' (p. 59); in his memoirs he wrote that 'Blatchford's *Merrie England* is the only book on economics I have read' (p. 111). His abandonment of free trade in particular requires more careful explanation than it receives here. Finally, the book needed more careful copy-editing than it evidently received. Given the author's conscientiousness in tracking down an impressive array of sources, it is a pity that the presentation too is not always exemplary.

Andrzej Olechnowicz
Durham University

Michael Nevell and Norman Redhead

Mellor: living on the edge: a regional study of an Iron Age and Romano-British upland settlement Manchester: Manchester Archaeological Monographs, Volume I. The University of Manchester Archaeological Unit, The Greater Manchester Archaeological Unit, and The Mellor Archaeological Trust, 2005. 126pp. ISBN 0952781360.

Mellor is a straggling village on the western gritstone fringe of the Peak District. Up to 1936 it was in Derbyshire before being transferred to Cheshire. John and Ann Hearle live in the old vicarage adjacent to the parish church, and the house and church are sited on a wonderful eminence from which there is a stunning view over the Manchester region and Cheshire plain. On a fine day, the mountains of north Wales are in view.

In the dry summer of 1995 they noticed brown and green patches on the lawn and a green arc running across an adjacent field. When Dr Peter Arrowsmith of the University of Manchester Archaeological Unit studied the photographs and inspected the site, he remarked 'This is old; I know it's old', and how right he was! A resistivity survey was carried out in spring 1998, and in the summer digging commenced. Immediately, Roman and Iron Age pottery fragments were found and then, in the 'surreal situation' of the old vicarage lawn, part of an Iron Age ditch cut into the local coal measure sandstone, the Woodhead Hill Rock. In the following years this superb ditch proved to be 4m wide and 2.1m deep. Since then excavations have revealed that there are two enclosure ditches, inner and outer, dating from Late Bronze Age to Iron Age. A round house was discovered within the inner ditch and other roundhouses between the two ditches. Full scale archaeology has continued each year and has shown that there has been a remarkable continuity of occupancy back to the Early Mesolithic period, c8,000–10,000 years ago, when there was a knap site or seasonal camp occupied by hunter-gatherers. Among the very many artefacts found are a polished Late Neolithic flint chisel, a group of bronze brooches, a nearly complete Iron Age vessel (known as the Mellor pot) and in 2004 a very fine and rare (for the region) Early Bronze Age flint dagger. Analysis of artefacts indicate a substantial and prolonged settlement during the first to fourth centuries AD, although little structural evidence has yet been found. Quern-stone fragments, spindle whorls and loom weights suggest a predominantly civilian Roman domestic settlement.

What is exceptional about this project is the role played by the local community and land-owners in association with the professional archaeologists. In 1999, the Mellor Archaeological Trust was formed and, later, Friends of the Trust. In 2001–2 an award of £25,000 was received from the Heritage Lottery Fund, and in 2003–5 a further £50,000. With an annual grant of £5,000 from Stockport MBC, the Trust has been able to fund an important programme of radiocarbon dating of deposits and features and employ three archaeologists from UMAU, who are needed to train and supervise the volunteers of which there are over sixty. Each September an open weekend is arranged for members of the public to learn from the professional and volunteer guides the story of the site and its recent excavations. A fortunate coincidence was the conversion in 2000 of the old Mellor school adjacent to the church into a parish centre which can used for displays and talks. Overall, the pattern of this project, set over the last ten years, is one which, where appropriate, can be recommended for community archaeology.

This fine volume of ten chapters, seventeen authors, 105 photographs, line drawings, graphs and tables, and a valuable bibliography of over 250 sources, reviews the history of the excavations, the finds and their significance to the regional context of north-west England and the broader conceptual understanding of what Robina McNeil describes as 'an exceptional archaeological phenomenom'. It is the first volume in the new Manchester Archaeological Monographs series. The standard set here makes one look forward to the next two volumes which will provide an overview of the excavations on Roman Manchester since 2000, and a report of the proceedings of a major conference on the archaeology of the Lancashire textile industry held in 2004.

Derek Brumhead

Pam Savage

Knutsford: A Cheshire market town, c1650–1750: its life and people Goostrey: INTEC Publishing, 2003. 205pp. ISBN 1899319212.

As with many Cheshire towns, Knutsford has received little attention from historians. Indeed, the only other detailed work with which I am familiar is H. Green's *Knutsford, its traditions and history* which was first published in 1859 – about time. Pam Savage's book is therefore a welcome addition to recent articles and books on Stockport, Nantwich and Northwich.

Following a general chapter on the town's ancient origins and development, the layout of the book is thematic with chapters on the town and its population, the manor courts, religion, local families, poverty, the medical scene, inns and innkeepers and work and leisure. As one would expect from a scholar who has spent many years researching her subject by using original archive sources, the work is packed with facts and figures about the townships of Nether Knutsford and Over Knutsford and the people who lived and worked in the environs. Added to this it is lavishly illustrated with photographs, charts and maps which all add to the interest that this book will no doubt generate.

I was particularly interested in the chapter dealing with medical matters, as this covers an important topic which is not often referred to in town histories. I also enjoyed reading the chapter on the Antrobus, Swinton and Birtles families and wish that there had been space more about the town's residents and their means of livelihood. Chapters are nicely divided into sections with sub-headings and these are listed in the contents – a useful feature. However I was disappointed with the index which I found it to be rather limited. At least there is one, which is not always the case with local history publications.

Whilst reading the book I found myself feeling somewhat uncomfortable with the overall presentation and the flow of the narrative. At times it seems somewhat disjointed, for example in the chapter on the manor courts, reference is made to the various town officials and their responsibilities, and yet the constable is not dealt with in any detail until a further eight pages on, and after some other topics have been dealt with. I would like to have read more about the work of the manor court and its administration of the town and considered that it might have been appropriate to insert some additional sub-headings in this chapter. I also consider that the larger tables that appear at the end of chapters or sections, for example the lists of schoolmasters and school charities, would have been better brought together as appendices at the end of the book. On the subject of Knutsford School, surely that is a subject which deserved a separate chapter or else being placed somewhere more appropriate than midway through the chapter on the manor court. I should also have liked to have seen a more detailed bibliography rather than a brief mention of sources which occur either at the end of the chapters or, in some cases, midway through a chapter. The merits of this book are the wealth of information it contains and yet the facts are not referenced sufficiently to allow those with an enquiring mind to pursue a particular topic for their own research.

Despite a few reservations, I have to say I did enjoy the book and believe that it makes a significant contribution to the study of Cheshire's historic market towns. It will appeal to a great many people who both reside in or visit Knutsford. I congratulate Pam on her hard work and perseverance in producing this book.

Tony Bostock

SHORT REVIEWS

Mary Presland, Ken Wilcock and Allan Moore, eds. *From acorn to oak: a history of Sutton Harriers and Athletic Club (St Helens)* St Helens: St Helens Association for Research into Local History, 2007. 144 pp. Illus. £9.99. ISBN 9780953690411.

This lively and very well illustrated work has been produced by an editorial team headed by Mary Presland on behalf of the St Helens Association for Research into Local History. It traces the history of the Sutton Harriers from its foundation in 1899 as an all-male (and, it would appear) largely working-class cross-country running club into an all-purpose athletic club open to both sexes and with a broad social mix. The book proceeds in a broadly chronological fashion and provides much detail of the club's many successes at collective and individual level. However, this narrative is thoughtfully broken up by a series of personal memories and pen pictures of key figures in the club's history. These add much to the value of the book, offering both raw material to future historians of amateur athletics (a sport that is surprisingly understudied by professional sports historians) and serving to capture the appeal of amateur sport to participants and followers. The hard work, the sense of mutuality – collections were held in 1938 when two runners had to find thirty shillings toward their expenses when selected for their national teams – and the sheer good fun that goes with a well run voluntary organization are everywhere apparent.

The book might have benefited from a little more consideration of some of the links between the club and the wider society. Was the arrival of women – a 'Ladies Section' was founded in 1949 – in any way controversial? What exactly was the chronology of the broadening of the club's social background that clearly took place? However, the main intention was to record and celebrate the club's achievements and in that the book works extremely well. It is to be hoped that the St Helens local historians might be sufficiently inspired by their work on this book to venture into other sporting territories and that their counterparts in other towns might be inspired to follow suit.

[this review by Dave Russell]

[Heritage Works Building Preservation Trust.] *All work and no play: an Ancoats scrapbook* Manchester: Heritage Works Preservation Trust, 2007. 76pp. Illus. ISBN 9780955609404.

The Ancoats area of Manchester was one of the most densely populated areas of inner city Manchester with industry and residential property in close proximity to each other. During the latter half of the twentieth century, a combination of industrial change and slum clearance meant that many of those who had originally lived there moved or were moved away, thus destroying the sense of community that once existed in the area. An oral history project carried out during 2005 and 2006 aimed to record life in Ancoats as seen by those who lived during the twentieth century and one result of this has been this publication. This well illustrated book concentrates on the lives of those who lived there, covering such topics as living conditions, education and their leisure time activities. It is a book that should appeal not only to all former residents of Ancoats, but also to those interested in Manchester's social history as well.

C. Edge and T. Wyke *The cotton church: a history of St Peter's, Ancoats* Manchester: Heritage Works Buildings Preservation Trust, 2007. 44pp. Illus, maps, diags. Bibliog. ISBN 9780955609411.

In the nineteenth century, Ancoats was one of the most densely populated parts of Manchester with terraced houses crowded close to factories, mills and workshops. This book is an account of how St Peter's church came to be established in the heart of Ancoats in the middle of the nineteenth century and the work that its clergy and organizations did amongst those who lived in its shadow. The book is well illustrated with photographs of the surrounding area together with copies from the registers, entries from directories and recollections of some of those who either attended the church or lived close to it. This book will be a valuable addition to the literature not only on Ancoats, but also the history of the Anglican Church in Manchester.

J. Aldred *The Steam Hammer Man: James Nasmyth (1808–1890)* Eccles and District History Society, 2008. 61pp. Illus, maps, bibliog. ISBN 9780900999192.

During the nineteenth century, Manchester and the surrounding towns were richly endowed with engineers who made important contributions not only to the area's prosperity, but also to the development of engineering generally. One of these was James Nasmyth, regarded by some as the 'Father of the Steam Hammer', whose factory was on the banks of the Bridgewater Canal at Patricroft. This short but informative biography traces Nasmyth's life from his birth in Scotland to Patricroft via London. Aldred outlines Nasymith's engineering achievements before examining the controversial matter of Nasmyth and the development of the steam hammer. As Aldred points out, it is difficult to say for certain who was the first to make a steam hammer, a situation which relates to many other nineteenth-century developments. This biography is an ideal introduction to the life and work of this important engineer.

M. Simpson and F. Broadhurst *A building stones guide to central Manchester* Manchester: Manchester Geological Association, 2nd. ed., 2008. 45pp. Illus, maps. £5.

This book consists of four walks around central Manchester pointing out the various types of stone that have been used on specific buildings. There is a sketch map for each walk which details the route and the location of the buildings mentioned in the text. The text itself draws attention to the stone, where it might have come from and features that can be used to identify it that would often not be noticed by the casual observer. This new and enlarged edition includes colour illustrations of some of the stones used and the detail to be found on them and is a useful supplement to the information in Hartwell's architectural guide to Manchester.

P. Kilvert *Weaste Cemetery heritage trail* Friends of Salford Cemeteries, 2008. 20pp. Illus, map.

Walking through a cemetery and looking at the various gravestones, one can sometimes find graves of well known local personalities as well as those of ordinary people. This interesting publication takes the reader on a walk through Weaste Cemetery in Salford and points out the locations of the final resting places of thirty-three people who were prominent in Salford's history. For each entry, there is a short biographical note about their lives and achievements whilst the key at the end of the publication enables the location of the graves to be identified.

G. Taylor and B. Dodson *Accrington acclaimed* Blackpool: Landy Publishing, 2008. 72pp. Illus. £8. ISBN 9781872895789.

Although there have been previous books of illustrations published on Accrington and its surrounding area, many of the illustrations in this book have never been published before, coming from the private collection of one of the authors. Many aspects of life in Accrington are depicted in this book either through the use of photographs, handbills or advertisements, many of which are accompanied by informative and well researched captions, which adds to the interest of the book and to the information available on the history of the town. This is a book that should be on the shelves of all those interested in Accrington's history.

Janet Rigby *Life on the Lancaster Canal* Blackpool: Landy Publishing, 2006. 112pp. Illus, maps. £8. ISBN 1872895662.

When the carrying of cargoes by canal boats ended in the mid twentieth century, there also disappeared a way of life that had existed for well over a century, namely that of those who used to work the boats. This book looks at the way of life of those who lived and worked the boats on the

Lancaster Canal up to the end of freight-carrying in 1947. The author has provided a fascinating insight into the lives of those who earned their living by carrying freight on the Lancaster Canal in the early decades of the twentieth century, drawing not only on her personal experience and knowledge, but also on the memories of those who worked on the canal in the first half of the twentieth century. This is a book that should appeal not only to those interested in the areas served by the canal, but by all those interested in canal and canal life.

Janet Rigby *The Lancaster Canal in focus* Blackpool: Landy Publishing, 2007. 60pp. Illus. £7. ISBN 9781872895727.

In many respects, this is a follow-up of Janet's previous book on the Lancaster Canal. This time, she has compiled a photograph album of views of the canal, many of which depict working boats, the boatmen and their families as well as basins, warehouses, trips and even 'disasters'. Each illustration is accompanied by an information caption, adding to the interest of the book and in some cases comple-menting the information in 'life on the Lancaster Canal'.

D. Brumhead, K. Rangeley and J. Rangeley *The Kinder reservoir and railway* New Mills: New Mills Heritage Centre, 2008. 93pp. Illus, diags, maps. £14.95.

This book is the story of the construction of the reservoirs at the head of the Kinder valley above Hayfield between 1899 and 1912 and the problems that were encountered during its construction. Although there were geological and technological problems, a major problem was access and moving equipment and materials onto the site. The book consists of two main parts, the first dealing with the construction of the reservoirs and the railway to supply it whilst the second consists of over 120 well captioned photographs of the construction work and the railway built to get materials to the site. For those wanting to trace the line of the now-disappeared railway, the book includes a walk of around five miles following its line. This book should appeal to those interested in the history of the area and walkers as well as those interested in industrial archaeology and the history of water supply.

J. Ali *Our boys: the Great War in a Lancashire village* Blackpool: Landy Publishing, 2007. 96pp. Illus. £8. ISBN 9781872895765.

Although much has been written on the First World War, there is relatively little written about its effect on individual communities, especially on the lives of those who lived in such communities whose men-folk died in action. In this book, Jonathan Ali traces the effect of the war on the village of Hawkshaw, between Bury and Ramsbottom. He makes full use of personal stories, press reports and other information that he was able to discover whilst setting the deaths of local men against the background of what was going on at the front. There are biographical details about those who died in action or as a result of wounds received, and extracts from letters, both personal and official, which add much to the poignancy of this book. The book concludes with a 'Complete Roll of Honour' for Hawkshaw, listing not only those who died, but also those who enlisted and returned home, their regiments, addresses and occupations. If you want to discover more about the effect

of the war on a Lancashire village, then you can do no better than read this book.

K. Warrender *Underground Manchester: secrets of the city revealed* Willow Publishing, 2007. 167pp. Illus, maps, diags. £15.95. ISBN 9780946361410.

Manchester, like many other cities, has many stories about secret passages and underground tunnels, many of which cannot be confirmed or denied. In this book, the author states that his aim 'is to reveal many surprising things which lie below the city. Here, for the first time, are the collected accounts of many people who have seen it for themselves, which put together with information from other sources, will be a revelation to many'. This he succeeds in doing, pointing out that whilst many such tunnels are passages is well recorded and documented by official bodies, there are many whose origins and even existence is in secrecy. The author has made extensive use of newspapers and other articles on the subject as well as information provided by those who have examined some of these passages and tunnels. The book is well illustrated with photographs, diagrams and plans. It is a valuable contribution to the history of Manchester, especially on an aspect that is subject to much discussion and even argument. It is a book that should be read and the reader should make up his own mind about a particular tunnel or passage.

M. Garratt *Images of England: Stockport revisited.* Stroud: Tempus Publishing Ltd, 2006. 128pp. Illus. £12.99. ISBN 0752441728.

This second collection of photographs on Stockport not only covers the former county borough, but also some of the areas absorbed by Stockport in 1974. The author has not only restricted himself to illustrations from the early twentieth century, but has taken the opportunity to include ones from the post-1945 period, which, as he points out, are 'in historical terms … yesterday'. Several of the sections have short introductions that set the scene for the following photographs. Unlike some of the previous Tempus publications, many of the captions are more substantial and informative whilst there are many others which include people either singly or in groups that adds to the interest of the publication.

Margaret Jane Cryer *Memories of Colne* Blackpool: Landy Publishing, 2006. 82pp. Illus. £10. ISBN 1872895700.

Between March and August 1910, the readers of the *Colne and Nelson Times* were entertained and enlightened by a series of articles by Mrs Cryer, née Margaret Jane Ward, recalling life in this small north-east Lancashire town in the middle of the nineteenth century. So popular were her articles that they were reprinted as a book, still in demand today. The original edition has been long out of print, but now it is possible to buy a copy as a result of this new edition, which has been enlarged by the addition of extra photographs of Colne. The articles were not merely descriptions of the town and its buildings, but include references to everyday things that went on which would pass unnoticed by many people as they took them for granted. This book is an enjoyable read even if you do not know all the places mentioned in the text.

J. Griffiths *The story of our church: St Mary's the Virgin, Disley* Disley: St Mary's Church, new edition, 2008. Illus, diags, bibliog. 45pp.

This new edition of the history of St Mary's church in Disley has been revised to take into account recent research into the early history of the church and has been timed to coincide with the celebrations to mark the 450th anniversary of it becoming a parochial chapelry. The new edition corrects some of the errors found in the earlier editions and has been enhanced by the addition of colour photographs, especially valuable when the author is discussing the stained-glass windows, a diagram showing the ages of various parts of the church and another showing important internal features.

R. L. Hills *Development of power in the textile industry, 1700–1930* Ashbourne: Landmark Publishing, 2008. 256pp. Illus, bibliog. £27.50. ISBN 9781843063506.

Textiles have always been an important part of the economy of this country but until the eighteenth century spinning and weaving was done by hand, often in the domestic situation. During that century, new machines were developed which required new forms of power to drive them, culminating at the end of the century with the adaptation of steam power to drive shafting which in turn drove the machines producing the yarn and the cloth. Dr Hills's latest book traces the development of the power sources used in the textile industry from earliest times to the twentieth century so that the more recent developments can be seen in their proper historical context. An important theme in the book is the way steam engine manufacturers responded to the growing demand for power plants that could provide sufficient power for the increasingly mechanized cotton industry whose main markets were overseas and without which the cotton industry would be in trouble. Whereas many books on the cotton industry concentrate on the financial side of the industry or on the architecture of the mills and associated buildings, this book looks at what must be regarded as a vital element in the development of the industry, namely the source of power to drive the equipment and some of the developments that took place in the machinery used within the mills. This is a book for all those interested in the cotton industry, not forgetting wool and silk, who want to understand the forces that drove it to greatness in the nineteenth century. There is also a useful chronology of developments and a glossary of terms used, valuable if you are not certain of the exact meaning of a word.

Christine Storey *Portrait of Poulton-le-Fylde* Blackpool: Landy Publishing, 2007. 72pp. Illus. £8. ISBN 9781872895734.

This book consists of a collection of around 130 well captioned photographs, with the occasional handbill, showing the Poulton-le-Fylde area over the last century. Not only are there views of streets and buildings, but events and people associated with the district, which now forms part of Wyre Borough Council. The author takes the reader on a sort-of walk through the town before dealing with some of the outlying areas such as Carleton, Singleton and Staining so it is possible to locate and identify many of the places shown in these well reproduced illustrations.

Joan Rimmer *Rufford: its past and its people* Blackpool: Landy Publishing, 2006. 112pp. Illus. £10. ISBN 1872895719.

This book came about, according to the blurb on the back cover, because Joan Rimmer wanted to record the history of the village for future generations. It is not a formal history, but in effect a series of short articles dealing with different aspects of life in Rufford including businesses, buildings, churches, farms, transport and population. The book brings to life this village between Ormskirk and Preston, which people would pass through and give little thought about its history and those who lived and worked there. This is a type of publication that should appeal to many who would not normally pick up and read a more traditional type of village history.

History alive: Tameside Tameside Local History Forum, iss. 2, 2007 and iss. 3, 2008. 64pp each issue. Illus. Free.

This publication seeks to publicize the history of that part of south-east Lancashire and north-east Cheshire that form the metropolitan borough of Tameside. Each issue consists of a number of short articles on a variety of local topics such as the Hollinwood Canal, Ashton Parish church, Park Bridge and the Theatre Royal at Hyde as well as information on local organizations involved in local and family history and reviews of local publications.

T. Hunt and V. Whitfield *Art treasures in Manchester: 150 years on* Manchester: Manchester Art Galleries, 2007. 88pp. Illus, bibliog. ISBN 9780901673725.

This well illustrated book was published to mark the 150th anniversary of the Art Treasures Exhibition held in Manchester during the summer of 1857, an event commemorated by an exhibition at the City Art Gallery. The authors retrace the history of the exhibition and place it in its local historical context, describing it as 'an unprecedented expression of civic pride'. For the first time working people were able to see some of the country's finest art works. This anniversary has enabled historians to look again at this event and to try to evaluate its importance for Manchester and its citizens.

W. K. Jones *Different times: a view of life in inner Manchester during the first decades of the twentieth century* Sandy: Bright Pen, 2006. 393pp. Illus, maps. £14.95. ISBN 0755202104.

This book is an account of life in one of the poorest parts of Manchester, around Angel Meadow, Angel Street and Rochdale Road in the early years of the twentieth century. The author, or narrator as he prefers to be called, has brought together reminiscences of his mother, who died in 1991, together with his own to paint a picture of life for those who were struggling to make ends meet in the decades before the Second World War. All aspects of life are covered, such as the fear of a pauper burial, playing in the streets, moving house and shops, and also how events such as the jubilee of 1935 were regarded by the people of the Rochdale Road. Jones portrays a lost world of the 'bad old days' in his book, but he also draws attention to the sense of community that existed at the time and the fact that people did help not only themselves but one another.

Susan W. Thomson *Manchester's Victorian art scene and its unrecognised artists* Manchester: Manchester Art Press. 245pp. Illus, bibliog. £9.95. ISBN 0955461901.

There has been provision made for those interested in art in Manchester since the 1820s when the Royal Manchester Institution was formed with a view to try and bring some culture into Manchester, a town more renowned for its industrial and commercial pursuits than its artistic ones. Many people know more about the musical and literary life of Victorian Manchester than they do of the artistic life of the town. In this book, Susan Thomson begins the process of redressing the balance by compiling a sort of 'Who's Who' of unrecognized Manchester artists of the nineteenth century, providing biographical information as well as comments by others on their work. In addition, she also outlines the art scene in Manchester during the nineteenth century, including sections on the Royal Manchester Institution, the Manchester Academy of Arts and the City Art Gallery. This is the type of book that contains much useful information and no doubt will be the starting point for further research on some of the artists mentioned and into Manchester's art scene in general.

ARTICLE ABSTRACTS AND KEYWORDS

Hugh Hornby

Bowling for a living: a century on the Panel

'Bowling for a living: a century on the Panel' coincides with the 2008 centenary of the Lancashire Professional Bowling Association. It provides an overview of the Association's history, with a special concentration on the period after World War Two. The unpublished memoirs of Glen Howarth, a Panel player from the late 1940s to the mid 1960s, provide a substantial primary source from which to investigate specific issues such as the viability of a professional career and attitudes to gender in the sport of crown green bowls at this time.

Keywords: *crown green bowling, betting, Red Lion, Westhoughton, professional*

Mike Huggins

Betting capital of the provinces: Manchester, 1800–1900

Throughout the nineteenth century horse-racing laid claim to be England's 'national sport', attracting much higher numbers of spectators than rival sports, and stimulating huge betting interest. This paper traces a long-lost dimension to Manchester's nineteenth-century cultural history – its central role in horse-race betting. It begins by tracing the development of the various racecourses in and around Manchester that met on-course betting needs, from Heaton Park and Kersal Moor to Castle Irwell and New Barns. Manchester also had its own credit-betting 'exchange' at the Post Office Hotel, which from the 1840s until *c*1870s was a serious rival to Tattersall's in London, and acted as a centre for the Manchester 'division' of book-makers travelling the racing circuit. By that time Manchester had become a thriving centre for illegal working-class cash-betting not just on the horses but on other sporting events, and nationally significant Manchester-betting journalism had emerged to cover it.

Keywords: *book-makers, risk, credit, cash*

Alexander Jackson

Sporting cartoons and cartoonists in Edwardian Manchester: Amos Ramsbottom and his imps

The sporting cartoon remains a source infrequently considered by historians. This study considers the production and use of sporting cartoons by the Manchester-based *Athletic News* and the local press more generally, and features a case study of Amos Ramsbottom, a prolific artist active in the Edwardian period. It discusses the problems encountered in researching Ramsbottom's life and career, before assessing his work and suggesting that it, and that of his contemporaries, added a significant humorous dimension to fan culture and played a role in building a body of Edwardian sporting 'stars'.

Keywords: *press, humour, stardom,* Athletic News

Dave Russell

Sporting Manchester, from c1800 to the present: an introduction

Manchester and its hinterland has one of the richest sporting cultures of any English city-region. This study analyses its growth and development from the beginning of the nineteenth century and considers the meaning and significance that sport has held for a number of groups within local and regional society. It suggests that while the Manchester region shares sporting characteristics with many other urban centres, local factors such as the early arrival of industrial society, the nature and structure of the population and patterns of inter-town rivalry have given it a distinctive flavour.

Keywords: *industrialization, amateurism, gender, rivalry*

Steve Tate
Edward Hulton and sports journalism in late-Victorian Manchester
This paper examines the entry of compositor Edward Hulton into the field of sporting journalism in 1870s' Manchester, first as a part-time racing tipster, and then as editor and joint-owner of a turf-news service that grew to embrace weekly and daily specialist sports papers, a Sunday title, and regional morning and evening newspapers. Hulton's success as a newspaper entrepreneur is traced alongside the unprecedented expansion of sports journalism in Manchester in the final three decades of the nineteenth century, a period marked by a growing public appetite for news and comment surrounding organized sport.

Keywords: *horse-racing, Edwin Bleakley, press,* Sporting Chronicle

Joyce Woolridge
'They shall grow not old': mourning, memory and the Munich air disaster of 1958
The mourning and commemoration of the Munich air crash of 1958, which resulted in the death of twenty-three individuals, including eight Manchester United footballers, is examined in the context of academic debates about the shift towards modern attitudes towards death and its remembrance following both the First and the Second World Wars. It is argued that the crash may have provided a space for the expression of grief suppressed after the Second World War, as well as demonstrating the robustness of traditional practices and beliefs.

Keywords: *Manchester United, commemoration, First World War, monuments*